A THEORY OF LEADERSHIP EFFECTIVENESS

McGRAW–HILL SERIES IN MANAGEMENT

Keith Davis, Consulting Editor

A THEORY
OF LEADERSHIP
EFFECTIVENESS

FRED E. FIEDLER

Department of Psychology
University of Illinois, Urbana

McGRAW-HILL BOOK COMPANY

New York · St. Louis · San Francisco
Toronto · London · Sydney

82 6706 1

Library of Congress Catalog Card Number: 67-19147

20675

1234567890   MP   7432106987

1413457

TO J. M. F.

ACKNOWLEDGMENTS

This book summarizes the results of a fifteen-year program of research on leadership and a theory of leadership effectiveness which seeks to integrate these findings. In a sense, this is a progress report of a continuing research enterprise in which a large number of my colleagues and students have been, and still are, actively participating. The editorial "we" is, therefore, more than a polite form. It is an explicit recognition of the fact that research of this nature is of necessity a team effort. None of the major studies could have been performed without the assistance and active collaboration of many others. Nor would the research have been possible without extensive and continued financial support.

I should like to take this opportunity, therefore, to express my gratitude first to the United States government agencies to which the research owes its existence and to our contract monitors who encouraged the work and who provided the extremely important personal link between their agencies and our project. In particular, I wish to express my appreciation to Howard E. Page and Joan S. Criswell, of the Office of Naval Research, who monitored the initial Contract N6-ori-07135, and to Luigi Petrullo, who was and still is monitoring. Contract Nonr 1834 (36); to J. R. Licklider, Lee W. Huff, our previous monitors, and to Cody Wilson, of the Advanced Research Projects Agency, who now monitors our work under ARPA Order No. 454; to David McK. Rioch and William Hausman, of the Walter Reed Institute of Research, Sidney Marvin, Philip Sperling, and James Hodlund of the Research and Development Command of the Office of the Surgeon General, which provided funds under Contract DA-49-193-MD-2060. In addition the National Institute of Mental Health of the U.S. Public Health Service funded work under Grant M-1774; the U.S. International Program for the Exchange of Persons enabled me to work in Holland from 1958 to 1959, under a Fulbright Research Scholarship Grant; and a Ford Foundation Faculty Research Fellowship for the year 1963-1964 permitted me to work at the University of Louvain.

It is with a great deal of pleasure and personal satisfaction that I acknowledge my indebtedness and gratitude to the many coworkers and colleagues associated with the Group Effectiveness Research Laboratory who worked, worried, and puzzled with me over the problems which we encountered each and every year. All of them will see some of their thinking reflected in this volume. In particular, I should like to thank Lynn R. Anderson, Peter Bates, Doyle W. Bishop, Martin M. Chemers, Walter E. Cleven, Eugene Drucker, Elizabeth Ehart, Martin Fishbein, J. Richard Hackman, D. M. Hall, Walter Hartmann, Gerald J. Hunt, Edwin B. Hutchins, James W. Julian, Ping Koo, Irving Lazar, George E.

Leavitt, Duangduen Lekhyananda, Bilha Mannhein, Willem Meuwese, Terrence Mitchell, Charles G. Morris, III, Albert E. Myers, Josephine Naidoo, E. S. K. Nayar, Paul Ninane, Sophie Oonk, Edward Ostrander, George and Eileen Potter, Stanley M. Rudin, Samuel Shiflett, Hubert Touzard, Willard A. Warrington, and Charles C. Wrigley.

I am especially indebted to my colleague, Harry C. Triandis, who has shared with me the direction of the Group Effectiveness Research Laboratory since 1961; S. Alexander, James Alsobrook, Alan R. Bass, Joan S. Dodge, Uriel G. Foa, Eleanor P. Godfrey, Joseph E. McGrath, Stanley M. Nealey, Gordon O'Brian, and Ivan D. Steiner, who directed various phases of the program; to Joseph M. Nuttin, Jr., and his students, with whom it was my privilege to work at the University of Louvain; and to Lee J. Cronbach, who was the principal investigator from 1951 to 1953 and who served as a valued consultant to the project for many years.

I also wish to express my thanks to Joseph McGrath for his critical and careful review of the final manuscript. My secretarial assistance was ably provided by Alfreda Mitchell, Janolee Krueger, and Colleen Cash. Last but not least, I wish to acknowledge my thanks to my wife, Judith M. Fiedler, who shared with me not only some of the substantive work described here, but also the very dubious joys of reading, rereading, and reading again the manuscript in its multitudinous versions to the point of utter, blissless satiation.

FRED E. FIEDLER

CONTENTS

PART I

The topic of leadership has always held a strong fascination for man. The literature abounds with books on how to be a good leader. Advice has ranged from such homilies as being honest, loyal, good, and fair, to the more cynical guidelines laid down by Niccolò Machiavelli.

The control of others for the purpose of accomplishing a common task is both a necessary and a desirable skill, and it is likely to remain so as long as we must cope with tasks which one man cannot accomplish without the assistance of others.

The first part gives a general introduction to our approach. It introduces some basic assumptions and key definitions, as well as the general rationale which has guided the research, and it presents a classification of groups as well as the method for measuring leadership styles with which we will be concerned throughout this book.

1 INTRODUCTION

We take it for granted that groups and organizations will succeed and thrive under good leadership and that they will fail under poor leadership. We look at successful business organizations and ascribe their success to the managerial abilities of their top men. We think of military campaigns which have succeeded or failed and ascribe the outcome to the generalship the country had at its disposal. While we really do not know to what extent the success or failure of an organization is due to the leadership abilities a man brings with him and to what extent to the many other factors which affect the fortunes of an organization or a military campaign, there is little doubt that we hold the leader responsible for success and failure. We admire and respect him, we pay him ten, twenty, and even thirty times the salary of the nonsupervisory employee, and we spend millions of dollars on the recruitment, selection, and training of executives. And yet, even though we believe that the health of our economy, the success of organizations, and the survival of our institutions depend to a considerable extent on the type of leadership we are able to get, we know next to nothing about the factors that make the leader effective or ineffective.

This book attempts to fill some of the gaps in our knowledge. It proposes a theoretical framework for understanding leadership effectiveness. It seeks to spell out the factors which determine how certain of the leader's personality attributes and styles of interacting with others affect the performance of his group or his organization.

Concern with leadership is as old as recorded history. Plato's *Republic*, to give but one early example, speculates about the proper education and training of political leaders, and most political philosophers since that time have attempted to deal with this problem. Leadership has been a particular concern in democracies, which, by definition, cannot rely upon the accident of birth for the recruitment of leaders. Where there is no hereditary aristocracy, every man is potentially a leader, and society has to give thought to the identification and proper training of men who will be able to guide its institutions.

This concern with leadership has become considerably more acute during the last fifty years. An increasingly greater share of creative as well as routine tasks is being carried out by teams, panels, boards, crews, task groups, and corporate bodies of various sorts. Modern production methods and contemporary organizations have become more complex. These complex methods require greater coordination of effort and an increasingly high degree of specialization. One man can no longer master all the skills which may be required for the performance of various tasks. As a result, teams of highly trained specialists must, somehow, be made to work together toward a common goal. This requires competent leadership. Prima donnas, in business, in industry, in government, or in science, no less than in ballet and in opera, are a temperamental crowd whose peculiarities and sensibilities have to be respected. Highly skilled leadership is required to reconcile and utilize constructively different abilities, viewpoints, attitudes, and ideas in the performance of group tasks and organizational missions.

As Stouffer et al. (1949) have noted:

> There are few practical problems facing social science more urgent than that of studying leadership experimentally and developing some tested hypotheses to replace the copybook maxims that now fill most manuals on leadership, whether written for the Army, for industry, or for organizations like the YMCA.

Yet the theoretical status of the field is far from satisfactory. Most reviews of research on small groups and leadership (e.g., Hare, 1962; McGrath, 1962; Steiner, 1964; McGrath and Altman, 1966) have taken pains to point out that we have yet to produce an acceptable theory. As Browne and Cohen (1958) were moved to say quite bluntly:

> Leadership has been recognized to an increasingly greater extent as one of the significant aspects of human activity. As a result, there is now a great mass of "leadership literature" which, if it were to be assembled in one place, would fill many libraries. The great part of this mass, however, would have little organization; it would evidence little in the way of common assumptions and hypotheses; it would vary widely in theoretical and methodological approaches. To a great extent, therefore, leadership literature is a mass of content without any coagulating substances to bring it together or to produce coordination and point out interrelationships.

And McGrath's (1962) summary of small-group literature applies equally to the research on leadership:

> There has been relatively little research which could properly be called systematic, in the sense that it was explicitly designed to explore a wide range

of variables drawn from different aspects of the small group field. . . . In the absence of such systematical programming of research, the rate of progress in understanding small group phenomena is likely to remain relatively slow, even though the rate of production of small group research seems to be increasing without abatement.

● It is quite clear that a systematic body of theory is essential not only for the sake of organizing the research findings in the field. It is also required if behavioral science is to provide practical guidance in the selection, training, placement, and evaluation of leadership in the innumerable situations which require group effort. Leadership research thus far has failed to give us simple answers. Even seemingly straightforward procedures for assembling potentially effective groups, such as making up teams of the technically most qualified men or of the most intelligent men, frequently do not work.

The average of the group members' intelligence scores or measures of their technical qualification correlate only poorly if at all with group performance (Mann, 1959; Fiedler and Meuwese, 1963). And men who are only mediocre in their own field will, under certain conditions, perform outstandingly as members of a group in conjunction with other mediocre men. Differences in performance between the best and the poorest groups may amount in some cases to a few critical percentage points and in other cases to scores in which the best teams perform ten and twenty times more effectively than the poorest teams. While the best groups may produce at a high rate, and with high quality, the poorest teams in the same situation may completely fail to reach their goal or they may fall apart. This is even more important when we consider that even a relatively small difference in performance may spell success or disaster for the entire organization under the highly competitive conditions of business, sport, or military combat.

To be sure, leadership research is plagued by a number of very difficult problems. One of these is that a large sample of comparable cases is difficult to find. How many departments in a store sell exactly the same products or perform exactly the same services? How many crews in a factory make the same parts or tend the same machines?

A second problem is that leadership phenomena turn out to be highly complex social processes, and the data which reflect them entail correspondingly complex statistical interactions. For example, the highly respected leader who gives a man a dressing down may raise the morale of his unit. The disliked and rejected leader who does so may cause resentment or revolt. The leadership behavior may be the same, but we will need twice the number of groups to understand the more complex situations: one sample of groups in which the leader is distrusted and rejected and a comparable sample in which the leader is liked and respected.

Finally, theory of leadership has not kept pace with empirical research in this area. Aside from a few pioneering studies of leadership, such as those by Binet (1900) and Terman (1904) and the landmark studies by Lewin and his associates in the late 1930s, the major thrust in the field dates from the beginning of World War II. However, since that time, re-search on leadership and on small-group behavior has grown at an almost exponential rate. Hare (1962) lists an average of twenty-one studies per year in the period 1930 to 1939, thirty-one studies per year between 1940 and 1944, fifty-five studies per year in the period 1945 to 1949, and 152 studies per year from 1950 to 1953. And McGrath and Altman (1966) re-port an even more rapid increase in small-group studies during the latter part of that decade. The number of published papers in the small-group field is well over 2,500. These papers require systematization to make them meaningful to the theorist and to those concerned with applying social science. The present book represents one attempt at theoretical integration.

DEFINITIONS

A few definitions are required to clarify some of the key terms of this book. Most of these definitions are current in the field and in the lay literature. Some terms, however, call for further elaboration.

The group.   By this term we generally mean a set of individuals who share a common fate, that is, who are *interdependent* in the sense that an event which affects one member is likely to affect all (Campbell, 1958). Typically, the human group shares a common goal, and its members interact in their attempt to achieve this goal. Typically, also, the members are rewarded as a group for achieving their goal; they are punished or they feel that they have failed if their group does not perform as expected.

Task groups, which are our major concern, very rarely are isolated units. It is, therefore, not only unrealistic but often misleading to think of the task group as independent from the larger organization of which it is a part. While we shall return to this problem later on, it is well to emphasize at this point that almost all task groups are creatures of a larger organization and that the organization assigns members to the group, appoints the leader, and specifies the task. The organization, represented by higher management, evaluates task performance and rewards the group or its members for compliance and effective performance, and it penalizes the members or the entire group for noncompliance or poor performance. A group which fails to perform over extended periods of time may be disbanded and its members reassigned or discharged.

It is curious that the concept of group, which is extensively used in social psychology, should have such a wide range of definitions. Andrews (1955) has defined the group as "an association of people who meet face to face frequently; have certain common sentiments, attitudes and values; carry on activities together; have feelings of mutual identification and recognition; and normally, pursue a common goal."

Krech and Crutchfield (1948) have defined the group as follows:

> A group does not merely mean individuals characterized by some similar property. Thus, for example, a collection of Republicans or farmers or Negroes or blind men is not a group. These collections may be called classes of people. The term group, on the other hand, refers to *two or more people who bear an explicit psychological relationship to one another.* This means that for each member of the group the other members must exist in some more or less immediate psychological way so that their behavior and their characteristics influence him.

These are, by no means, the only definitions available. A perusal of the literature will unearth dozens more (see Bonn, 1960a).

For purposes of discussing task groups, it is useful to draw attention to some further distinctions. A classification of groups can be made in terms of the work relations among its members and especially in terms of the leader's role in directing the group's activities. Will the leader need to coordinate the work of his members so that they will not fall over one another? Will he need to motivate his men? Or will he have to spend his time in arbitrating differences among his group members? We shall deal with this problem in the next chapter.

The leader. This term has, if possible, even more definitions than the term "group." Several quoted by Andrews (1955) are here reproduced.

> Leadership is the exercise of authority and the making of decisions (Dubin, 1951).

> Leadership is the initiation of acts which result in a consistent pattern of group interaction directed toward the solution of a mutual problem (Hemphill, 1954).

The leader is the man who comes closest to realizing the norms the group values highest; this conformity gives him his high rank, which attracts people and implies the right to assume control of the group (Homans, 1950).

Leadership is an ability to persuade or direct men without use of the prestige or power of formal office or external circumstance (Reuter, 1941).

The leader is one who succeeds in getting others to follow him (Cowley, in Hemphill, 1954).

The leader is the person who creates the most effective change in group performance (Cattell, 1953).

The leader is one who initiates and facilitates member interaction (Bales and Strodtbeck, 1951).

Leadership, in group discussion, is the assumption of the tasks of initiating, organizing, clarifying, questioning, motivating, summarizing, and formulating conclusions; hence, the leader is the person who spends the most time talking to the group, since he carries out more of these verbal tasks (Bass, 1949).

Leadership is the process of influencing group activities toward goal setting and goal achievement (Stogdill, 1950).

The leader is that person identified and accepted as such by his followers (Sanford, 1949).

Various workers in this area have proposed still other definitions of the term "leader." In particular, there has been a distinction among emergent, elected, and appointed leaders, between leaders and headmen (Gibb, 1954), and between formal and informal leaders. Leadership has also been identified by some in terms of leadership acts, thus defining the leader as the person who behaves most like a leader at a given time (e.g., Hemphill, 1949).

We shall here define the leader as *the individual in the group given the task of directing and coordinating task-relevant group activities or who, in the absence of a designated leader, carries the primary responsibility for performing these functions in the group.* We must take cognizance of the fact that leadership functions are frequently shared among group members and that one person may be most influential at one time and less influential at another (Berkowitz, 1953; Cattell, 1951). However, we shall here designate only one group member as leader, namely, the one who meets one of the following criteria: (1) he is appointed as the leader, supervisor, chairman, etc., by a representative of the larger organization of which the group is a part; (2) he is elected by the group; or (3) if there is neither an elected nor an appointed leader, or if such a leader is clearly only a figurehead, he is the individual who can be identified as most influential by task-revelant questions on a sociometric preference questionnaire.

Leader's effectiveness. This also has been variously defined. Stogdill (1957) has proposed that group effectiveness be defined in terms of (1) the group's output, (2) its morale, and (3) the satisfactions of its members. A similar definition has been advanced by Bass (1960a). Some investigators have also gone on the assumption that any task performance can be utilized as a criterion. On the other hand, it seems at least equally reasonable to take the position that the group typically owes its very existence to the tasks it is supposed to perform and that it will be evaluated primarily on the basis of these task performances rather than on the satisfaction and morale of the members of the group. A group may have low morale or it may give little satisfaction to its members and yet perform well on its mission. However, a group which continually fails to complete its mission will disintegrate or it may be disbanded no matter how high the morale and member satisfactions.

We shall here evaluate leader effectiveness in terms of group performance on the group's primary assigned task, even though the group's output is not entirely the function of the leader's skills. Such events as personality clashes, bad luck, or unfavorable circumstances may affect the group output to a greater or lesser extent. So may member abilities, motivation, and organizational support. However, in terms of the statistical treatment of leadership research such factors manifest themselves as "error variance," which reduces the relationship between leader attributes and group performance. This research strategy errs thus in the conservative direction. Morale and member satisfaction, while certainly affected by the leader's behavior, are here seen as interesting by-products rather than as measures of task-group performance. An exception is, of course, the case where the building of morale, or the increase of member satisfaction, is the primary goal of the leader and is explicitly made the leader's task. (This occasionally occurs when, for example, a military commander or business executive is told to rebuild the morale of a unit.) Usually, however, the major organizational concern is with the effectiveness and performance of a group, be this over a period of hours, days, or weeks, or over a long period of years or decades. Labor turnover, job satisfaction, morale, and personal adjustment are here seen as contributing to group performance, but they are not in themselves criteria of performance.

TWO THEORETICAL PROBLEMS IN LEADERSHIP

While this is no doubt an oversimplification, empirical research on leadership has been primarily concerned with two major questions. These are, first, "How does a person get to be a leader?" or "What determinants are involved in attaining a leadership position?" The second question is "What personality traits, attributes, or behaviors determine the leader's effectiveness?" Both of these are important.

Leadership status. The question of how one attains a leadership position has been extensively investigated. The period preceding World War II and the early 1950s saw well over two hundred studies concerned with the identification of personality traits and attributes that would distinguish leaders from followers. These studies have been reviewed extensively by Stogdill (1948), Gibb (1954), and Mann (1959), as well as in a number of other recent texts. On the whole, the research points to the conclusion that a man becomes a leader not only because of his personality attributes, but also on the basis of various situational factors (what the job requires, who is available, etc.) and the interaction between the leader's personality and the situation. While the leader is frequently chosen from among the group's more intelligent members, intelligence alone will not suffice. Likewise, the tall and the big, the dominant, the aggressive, the masculine, and the visible are more likely to be chosen as leaders. But these and similar traits have turned out to be rather poorly correlated with the attainment of leadership status. Rather, if one is to rise to a position of leadership, it may be more useful to live long in order to have experience and seniority; it may be more useful to have the specific ability and knowledge which are directly related to the job; and for a substantial number of business executives, it has been most useful to own 51 percent of the company stock (Warner and Abegglan, 1955; see also Dill, 1965).

The statement that personality and situational factors interact in determining whether or not a person will rise to leadership status is undoubtedly true. The usefulness of this formulation is, however, limited unless one can also state the conditions under which a specific personality attribute will interact with a specific situational determinant. At this moment, our ability to make such predictions is quite limited.

The degree to which the attainment of leadership status is happenstance is shown by two very interesting and theoretically important studies. R. L. French (1951) conducted one study in a naval training station. He found that, upon their arrival at camp, the men who had been chosen as acting petty officers on the basis of very slight information tended later on to be selected as the preferred leaders by men who served under them. And Bavelas, Hastorf, and others (1965) at Stanford University have shown that an individual can rise to a position of leadership by simply being rewarded for actively participating in the group discussion. These investigators rewarded low-status members by light signals for doing "the right thing" in an unspecified, undefined manner. In other words, they encouraged and rewarded certain low-status group members at random and found that the rewarded group member accepted himself and others accepted him as leader. While we do not know as yet how long the effects of such training would last, these findings are of considerable importance.

The studies of the attainment of a leadership position serve to emphasize that becoming a leader is in large part a matter of such sociological, economic, or political factors as age, financial status, being at the right place at the right time, or being encouraged by happenstance. In other words, the attainment of a leadership position turns out to be a matter of personality to only a limited extent, and certainly to a much lesser degree than the layman believes to be the case and than the psychologist thought likely not too long ago.

Prediction of effective leadership.   The second major theoretical question in the field concerns the prediction of leadership effectiveness. This is the main concern of this book. We are dealing here with individuals who already occupy a position of leadership. The question is whether the individual's psychological attributes, under these circumstances, would appear to be more closely related to his leadership behavior and to the performance of his group. Leadership is, by definition, an interpersonal relation in which power and influence are unevenly distributed so that one person is able to direct and control the actions and behaviors of others to a greater extent than they direct and control his. In such a relationship between the leader and his members, the personality of the leader is likely to determine to a large extent the degree to which he can influence the behavior of his group.

To be sure, we have to recognize here again that leadership of groups does not exist in a vacuum. A multitude of organizational, situational, task-relevant, and social constraints guide and limit the actions of the leader and of his members. The leader has to pay attention to prevailing social conventions. The leader may or may not be able to dominate his men, he may or may not need to show concern for their health and welfare, he may or may not have to make allowances for sickness in a subordinate's family. Certain types of subordinate jobs have high prestige, and the leader cannot ride roughshod over such vested interests. Certain organizations give the leader freedom to hire and fire his subordinates while other organizations limit the leader's authority. These are important differences, which have to be kept in mind if we do not want to develop the kind of theory which in trying to remain simple ends up by saying nothing.

A number of investigators have identified various leader attributes that affect group behavior in important ways. However, the results which have been found in one set of groups, or under one set of conditions, have not always occurred in other conditions, or in other sets of groups. As a result, we have not been able to generalize from one situation to others.

Interest in empirical investigations of leadership style dates back to the classic studies by Lewin and Lippitt (1938) on the effect of demo- cratic, autocratic, and laissez-faire leadership styles on the behavior of boys' clubs. These studies have had a far-reaching impact on the field. They have raised questions about the degree to which the leader should take major responsibility for the direction and administration of the group versus the degree to which the leader should be concerned primarily with personal relations; the degree to which the leader should permit and en- courage participation by members of his group; and the degree to which he should share planning and decision making with his associates.

McGrath (1961) in his summary of the literature has pointed to two clusters of leadership behavior and attitudes which have been the focus of most psychological research in the area. These clusters have been vari- ously labeled as autocratic, authoritarian, task-oriented, and initiating on the one hand versus democratic, equalitarian, permissive, group-oriented, and considerate on the other. The leader can either take the responsibility for making decisions and for directing the group members ("I make the plans and you carry them out") or he can, to a greater or lesser extent, share the decision-making and coordinating functions with the members of his group. He can use the proverbial stick or the equally proverbial carrot for motivating his members. All these methods, and any combina- tion of them, have worked in some situations and not in others (Gibb,

1954; Hare, 1962). The problem of what constitutes the best leadership style has, in fact, been one of the major controversies in the area.

While this black and white categorization is grossly oversimplified, the orthodox viewpoint has been reflected in traditional supervisory and managerial training and practices as well as in military doctrine. It holds that the leader must be decisive, that he must think and plan for the group, and that the responsibility for directing, controlling, coordinating, and evaluating the group members' actions is primarily his and that it cannot be shifted to others.

The opposing viewpoint, represented by the human relations–oriented theorists, holds that the leader will be most effective when he can call out the creativity and willing cooperation of his men and that he can do this most effectively only when he can get his group members to participate in the decision-making processes and in the direction of group action. A number of investigators (e.g., Pelz, 1952) have pointed out that different leadership situations require different leadership styles. Generally, however, there have been few empirical tests to spell out the specific circumstances under which various leadership styles are most appropriate.

The theory presented in this book attempts to do this. In briefest outline and as a way of orienting the reader to the main problem with which we shall be concerned, the theory postulates two major styles of leadership. One of these is a leadership style which is primarily task-oriented, which satisfies the leader's need to gain satisfaction from performing the task. The other is primarily oriented toward attaining a position of prominence and toward achieving good interpersonal relations. In terms of promoting group performance, our data show that the task-oriented type of leadership style is more effective in group situations which are either very favorable for the leader or which are very unfavorable for the leader. The relationship-oriented leadership style is more effective in situations which are intermediate in favorableness. Favorableness of the situation is here defined as the degree to which the situation enables the leader to exert influence over his group. Leadership style is measured by means of interpersonal perception scores which ask the leader to describe his most and least preferred coworkers. The specific scores, the esteem for the Least-preferred Coworker (LPC) scores and the Assumed Similarity between Opposites (ASo) scores, are described in the third chapter.

Figure 1-1 presents a schematic picture of the major hypothesis. As Figure 1-1 indicates, the theory predicts that a task-oriented style will be

Task-oriented style	Relationship-oriented, considerate style	Task-oriented style
Low Assumed Similarity or Least-preferred Coworker scores	High Assumed Similarity or Least-preferred Coworker scores	Low Assumed Similarity or Least-preferred Coworker scores

←		→
Favorable leadership situation	Situation intermediate in favorableness for leader	Unfavorable leadership situation

Figure 1-1   Leadership styles appropriate for various group situations.

maximally effective in favorable leadership situations, a relationship-oriented style will be effective in intermediate situations, and a task-oriented leadership style will again be most effective in unfavorable group situations.

THE ORGANIZATION OF THE BOOK

The main purpose of this book is to present a theory of leadership effectiveness. Because it is a theory which tries to account for complex phenomena, the reader will have to bear with the complexities which the story entails. A pretzel-shaped universe requires pretzel-shaped hypotheses.

The first part of the book presents a classification of groups and group tasks. This classification is the basis for presenting, in roughly chronological order, the major results of the research which we have undertaken during the last fifteen years. This part also deals with the problems of measuring leadership style and with relating our leadership style scores to personality variables and motivational and behavioral phenomena.

The third part presents a theory of leadership effectiveness based mainly on an analysis of the data obtained in our studies up to 1962. The succeeding chapter presents validating evidence, and the third chapter in Part III presents a rationale for viewing group performance as an interaction between leadership style and certain characteristics of the group-task situation. The theory (the so-called "Contingency Model") postulates that the effectiveness of a group is contingent upon the relationship between leadership style and the degree to which the group situation enables the leader to exert influence.

The fourth part deals with leadership problems which are even more poorly understood and require considerable further research, that is, leadership performance under stress, in coacting groups, and in organizations which have multiple levels of leadership.

The final chapter tries to spell out some of the major implications for the recruitment, selection, training, and "organizational engineering" of leadership to upgrade the performance of groups and organizations.

2 GROUPS AND GROUPS

Without a group there can be no leader. An understanding of leadership requires that we know something about the group which the leader directs. Most earlier leadership theories assumed that all groups are basically alike, at least as far as the leader's role is concerned. This point of view is implicit in the "Great Man" theory as well as the layman's belief that it is the individual's personality or charisma which determines whether a man becomes a leader. Hence, the man who has the right personality will emerge as a good leader in most if not all groups and organizations.

Although there have been occasional studies which have provided limited support for this theory (Borgatta et al., 1954; Bell and French, 1955), these investigations turn out to be rather special cases. The investigators have very often controlled for everything but the leader's attributes. Not surprisingly, where the tasks and other relevant aspects of the group situation are controlled, only the leader attributes could be related to performance. The bulk of research, especially under real-life conditions, has shown quite conclusively, however, that the leader's personality is only one factor in determining the group's performance. The leader who performs well in one group, or under one set of conditions, may or may not perform well in other groups, in other tasks, or under other conditions (Knoell and Forgays, 1952; Cleven and Fiedler, 1955; Fiedler, 1966a). But what, then, determines whether the leader will perform well or poorly? In part, as we shall see later, this depends on the particular type of group he heads. This means that we must have a theory of groups before we can hope to predict how a particular leader will perform in directing them.

First of all, we are here concerned with task groups rather than social groups, that is, with groups which exist for the purpose of performing a task, and which generally exist only as long as they do so effectively. This contrasts with social groups or therapy groups which exist to promote the psychological well-being, enjoyment, or adjustment of the individuals who are members of the group.

Beyond this, however, it is also necessary that we identify various types of task groups. This chapter presents one such classification system. The purpose of the classification is limited to assisting us in the prediction of leadership performance. Whether or not this taxonomy will serve additional purposes remains a question for later inquiries.

The organizational context. McGrath and Altman (1966) recently pointed out that about 55 percent of their sample of 250 small-group studies were laboratory experiments, about 30 percent were field experiments, and less than 5 percent of the investigations dealt with natural groups in a field setting (about 10 percent were unclassified). This means that most data about small groups, and the theories which are based on them, are derived from a highly selected and unrepresentative sample of the teams which are found in the real world.

As a result, much of the literature on groups tends to gloss over the fact that task groups in real life are practically always subunits of a larger organization. Most groups in real life exist for the purpose of furthering the goals and the convenience of the organization which brought them into being. If the group performs poorly, the leader may be dismissed or the group may be disbanded. The leader and the group members will, therefore, look to the organization for direction and approval. The organization is, in other words, a very significant aspect of the environment within which the group operates.

While this point about organizations may be perfectly obvious in business, industry, or the military services, it is frequently forgotten in laboratory studies where the organization may be symbolically represented by a university department, a group of researchers, or a single student working on his thesis. Whether or not this type of organization is a realistic model for groups in real life is a pressing question, as is the extent to which groups tested in the laboratory are representative of groups which are constituted for the purpose of a particular experiment. The general validity of results from a small-group study, whether it be conducted in the laboratory or under field conditions, will depend in large part on the degree to which the relationship between the group and the organizational context is an adequate mapping of real life. Of particular importance, in this respect, as we shall see, is the power which the organization (or the experimenter) places at the leader's disposal and certain characteristics of the task which affect the influence of the leader.

A TAXONOMY OF TASK GROUPS

Our taxonomy involves three successive steps. The first of these has already been spelled out. It involves the differentiation between task groups and social or therapy groups. The second step divides the groups into interacting, coacting, and counteracting groups on the basis of the relations among group members which are a consequence of the tasks which the groups are required to perform. The third step involves the further categorization of interacting groups in terms of the influence which the situation provides for the leader.

Interacting, coacting, and counteracting groups. The first classification which appears important is of the internal work relations among the members. A small group is generally defined as a set of individuals in face-to-face interaction who perceive each other as interrelated, or as reciprocally affecting each other, and who pursue a shared goal.

These groups vary, however, in the intensity and degree to which the members interact. Roby and Lanzetta (1958) have suggested one classification of group tasks which differentiates between groups whose members work "in series" and those whose members work "in parallel." In the former, the work of one member is directly dependent upon the completion of work by another. Thus, the riveter cannot perform his job until his coworker has supplied him with the properly heated rivet. In the parallel task, two men perform their jobs at the same time. The work of one salesman in a store does not directly depend upon the performance of another.

The present classification presents a very similar schema, which focuses on the group rather than on the task alone and extends the Roby and Lanzetta scheme. We are here classifying groups first in terms of the work relations among members, namely into *interacting, coacting,* or *counteracting* groups.

Interacting groups   These groups, as already indicated, require the close coordination of several team members in the performance of the primary task. The ability of one man to perform his job may depend upon the fact that another has first completed his share of the task. This is illustrated by a basketball team which requires men to get and pass the ball to others who are in a position to shoot a basket. Many tasks also require the close and simultaneous coordination of two or more men. One man, by himself, cannot move a piano or play a quartet. One man, by himself, cannot run a destroyer. A tank crew requires a series of interrelated activities, such as maneuvering the tank, loading, aiming, and firing the gun, as well as maintaining the equipment. Most of these functions are interdependent to the point where failure on the part of one crew member spells failure for the entire team. Similarly, in the management of a business organization, departments concerned with purchasing, production, advertising, and sales must closely coordinate their work if the enterprise is to succeed.

One major task of the leader in interacting groups consists of coordinating the various task functions or the group's activities so that the work flows smoothly and without interruption, or so that men working together can do so harmoniously and without getting into each other's way. The leader's job is one of directing, channeling, guiding, refereeing, timing, and coordinating the group members' work.

The hallmark of the interacting group is the interdependence of group members. It is generally difficult in these groups to assign credit for good team performance to any one member of the group. It may be possible to identify a team member who failed to perform his assigned job and therefore prevented his group from completing the task successfully. However, it is not easily possible in such teams to identify the degree to which a particular group member directly contributed to success. Each man must do his part if the team is to be successful, and the group is generally rewarded as a group or else the leader alone is rewarded.

Coacting groups   These groups also work together on a common task. However, each of the group members does his job relatively independently of other team members. The characteristic pattern in such groups is that each group member is on his own, and his performance depends on his own ability, skill, and motivation. His reward, not infrequently, is computed on a piecework basis in a production job or on a commission basis in sales work. The group product is typically the sum of the individual performance scores. Thus, the effectiveness of a department in a store is computed as the sum of the sales made by each clerk, and the score of a bowling team or a rifle marksmanship team is the sum of each member's scores. While it is true that each individual member will be affected by the moral and logistic support which he receives from his group, his own performance is relatively independent of that of others within his group. Not infrequently such a team situation leads to rivalry and competition among group members, which serves as a motivating force for better individual performance.

The leader's function in groups of this nature is clearly different from that required of the interacting group's leader. He has little need to coordinate group action or to develop team training and motivation for cooperative team activities. His major purposes are the development of individual group-member motivation and the individual training which will enable each member to perform up to his ability, and the prevention of destructive rivalries and competition. We may here subdivide the leader's functions into a number of separate major categories: (1) the leader as the coach and trainer of the group members or as the adviser and consultant; (2) the leader as the quasi-therapeutic, anxiety-reducing agent who gives emotional support and tension relief to his members; and finally, (3) the leader as the supervisor, evaluator, or spokesman of the group. All these functions may, of course, be performed by the same leader, and certain combinations may be essential if the group is to survive and perform its work.

Counteracting groups   The third category of groups consists of individuals who are working together for the purpose of negotiating and reconciling conflicting opinions and purposes. These groups are typically engaged in negotiation and bargaining processes, with some members representing one point of view and others an opposing or, at least, divergent point of view. Each individual member, to a greater or lesser extent, works toward achieving his own or his party's ends at the expense of the other.

In some respects it may seem a contradiction in terms to speak here of a group. The goal is, in one sense, not shared by all members of the team since each subgroup typically seeks to "win" over the other side. There are, thus, at least two goals within such groups, and the specific aims are not shared by all members. Nevertheless, it is also true that all members share the task of reaching a common decision or a common goal, namely, that of reaching an acceptable accommodation if not a mutually satisfactory solution. Moreover, the members of the group are usually quite aware of the importance of interacting, communicating, and cooperating if a creative solution is to emerge from the the interaction. The criterion of performance here is not the productivity of the individual, nor necessarily the satisfaction of the participants. Rather, it is the degree to which the constituents of the group members will find the solution acceptable and satisfactory. As McGrath's (1963) excellent analysis has pointed out, the primary loyalty of the group member may be to his outside constituency, to the reference group which he represents. He is, at the same time, bound to work closely and effectively with other members in the negotiation group because a solution can be satisfactory to his own group only when it is also satisfactory to the other party of the bargaining or negotiating process. Frequently the issues are further complicated by the necessity to satisfy still a third impartial group such as the public interest, the legislature, or a court of law.

The leader of the counteracting group, that is, the moderator or negotiator, has a task which again differs from that of the interacting or coacting group's leader. It is the leader's job to maintain the group, to facilitate communication and mutual understanding, and to establish a climate conducive to the development of creative solutions to the conflict, namely, to influence the group toward effective performance.

Figure 2-1 schematically indicates the approximate places on several continua which interacting, coacting, and counteracting groups occupy. This figure shows that the relations among group members, and between group members and leaders, differ in these three types of groups and that the demands on the leader will likewise differ in these three situations. Most groups are a mixture of all three types, although one feature generally predominates. Most leaders of interacting or coacting task groups must at times reconcile differences among group members, and most groups perform some interacting and some coacting tasks. Except for

Figure 2-1   Schematic comparison of interacting, coacting, and counteracting groups in three dimensions.

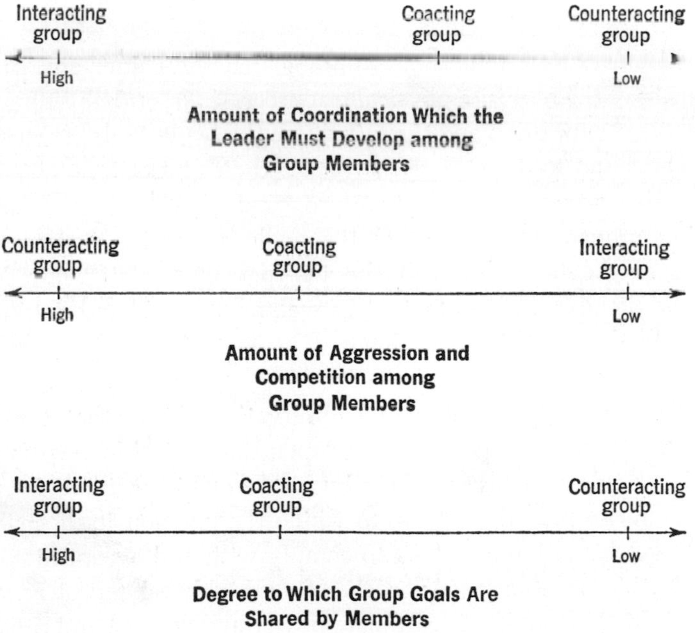

Chapter 13, the major concern of this book is with interacting groups. However, understanding the differences and similarities between these classes of groups may enable us to generalize from one set of groups to others.

A CLASSIFICATION OF INTERACTING TASK GROUPS

Since most of our research has been concerned with interacting groups, our understanding of these groups is relatively more advanced than that of coacting or counteracting groups. We shall here propose a more detailed classification of the interacting group in terms of the group-situational factors which are most likely to affect the degree of influence which the leader will enjoy over group behavior. The empirical studies conducted by myself and my associates will then be described in Part II of this book. It is, of course, obvious that the studies came well before we had a classification system or a reasonably coherent theory. The presentation of the theory and of the empirical research will be more understandable, however, if some of the theoretical exposition, and especially the taxonomy of interacting groups, is described at this time.

The classification system which emerged in the course of the research program is primarily guided by the notion that the leader's style of interacting with his members will be affected by the degree to which the leader can wield power and influence. Assuming that the leader and the group members have the requisite physical resources, skills, and abilities, we may ask how the organization and the task affect the leader's ability to motivate his members and to direct and coordinate their efforts. The classification of interacting groups, which is here proposed, postulates three factors of major importance. These are (1) the leader's position power, (2) the structure of the task, and (3) the interpersonal relationship between leader and members. These factors, as well as other related determinants will here be discussed in some detail.

Position power. The most casual observation shows that the leader's relationship to members of his group depends to a sizable extent upon the power he wields over his members by virtue of his position. By *position power* we mean here the degree to which the position itself enables the leader to get his group members to comply with and accept his direction and leadership. Position power is, therefore, highly related to French and Raven's (1956) concepts of legitimate power and reward-and-punishment power. It is thus the potential power which the organization provides for the leader's use.

Position power can be readily measured or scaled in most situations. It is usually quite clear whether the leader has the authority to hire and fire, whether he can give raises in rank and pay, whether he has an official title indicating his position, and whether he can readily be recognized by some signs or insignia of rank. These external signs may be as formal and traditional as the mace and chain of the lord mayor's office or the gold braid and brass indicating military rank, or they may be as informal as a micrometer and calipers carried only by foremen in a particular plant or workshop. Other symbols may be the number of square feet of office space, the number of secretaries and telephones, the size of the desk, or the name on the door and the rug on the floor.

Our concern here is with the effect which position power has on group performance. It must clearly affect the role relationship between leader and members. It also will affect the compliance which the leader can demand from his group members.

An operational measure of position power is not difficult to obtain. We have developed a simple 18 item checklist which contains various indices of position power (Table 2-1). The sum of the checked items provides a highly reliable scale for measuring leader position power. The average correlation indicating the interrater agreement among four judges rating thirty five tasks was .95.[1] This amount of agreement is not too surprising in view of the highly palpable and manifest nature of the phenomena which we are here measuring.

Although one would think that the leader with high position power will be able to get better performance from his group, this assumption is not at all confirmed by the empirical findings. There is, in fact, very little in the published literature which deals with this problem directly. A number of studies have been conducted by us which address themselves, at least in part, to this question. One of these was a study of Dutch college students. Half of the groups in that study had appointed leaders who had at least a modicum of legitimate power, while the other half of the groups was given no instructions regarding the necessity or the desirability of selecting a leader. The leaders in this second half of the groups were identified *post hoc* on the basis of sociometric preference questions. The groups having

[1] Readers who may have need for a refresher about the meaning of correlation coefficients may find it helpful to read the short note on correlations in Appendix B.

TABLE 2-1   Measure of Position Power *

1. Compliments from the leader are appreciated more than compliments from other group members.
2. Compliments are highly valued, criticisms are considered damaging.
3. Leader can recommend punishments and rewards.
4. Leader can punish or reward members on his own accord.
5. Leader can effect (or can recommend) promotion or demotion.
6. Leader chairs or coordinates group but may or may not have other advantages, i.e., is appointed or acknowledged chairman or leader.
7. Leader's opinion is accorded considerable respect and attention.
8. Leader's special knowledge or information (and members' lack of it) permits leader to decide how task is to be done or how group is to proceed.
9. Leader cues members or instructs them on what to do.
10. Leader tells or directs members what to do or what to say.
11. Leader is expected to motivate group.
12. Leader is expected to suggest and evaluate the members' work.
13. Leader has superior or special knowledge about the job, or has special instructions but requires members to do job.
14. Leader can supervise each member's job and evaluate it or correct it.
15. Leader knows his own as well as members' job and could finish the work himself if necessary, e.g., writing a report for which all information is available.
16. Leader enjoys special or official rank and status in real life which sets him apart from or above group members, e.g., military rank or elected office in a company or organization. (+5 points)
17. Leader is given special or official rank by experimenter to simulate for role-playing purposes, e.g., "You are a general" or "the manager." This simulated rank must be clearly superior to members' rank and must not be just that of "chairman" or "group leader" of the group during its work period. (+3 points)
18. Leader's position is dependent on members; members can replace or depose leader. (−5 points)

* The dimension of leader position power is defined by the above checklist in which all "true" items are given 1 point, except for items 16, 17, and 18, which are weighted +5, +3, and −5 points respectively.

formally appointed leaders did not perform significantly better than did groups having emergent leaders.

A second study, by Anderson and Fiedler (1964), compared participatory and supervisory leaders. It seemed likely in that case that the supervisory leaders had more position power. The results again did not indicate a clear superiority of one type of leadership over the other, even though the participatory leadership condition led to better performance on quantity while supervisory leadership led to better quality of performance on various creative tasks.

Finally, a large study was conducted in cooperation with the Belgian Navy. It compared forty-eight groups under the leadership of petty officers with forty-eight groups under the leadership of navy recruits. Groups having leaders with high position power performed no better than did those with leaders who had low position power.

One conclusion to be drawn from the presently available literature seems to be that the effects of position power on group performance are not monotonic. If position power does affect group performance, it must do so in a more indirect manner, and probably by virtue of its effect on the interpersonal relationship between leader and group members.

What, then, does position power mean to the leader? It means, first of all, that high position power makes his job easier. The leader who has rank and power can get his group members to perform their tasks more readily than would a leader who has little power (as in a volunteer group, for example). The leader with high position power can interact with his members in terms of the roles and mutual expectancies which exist in the group. The leader with low position power must first convince his group members that they should follow him, and he must be continually aware of the fact that his hold on his group members is tenuous and dependent upon his personal relations with the individuals in his group. In many groups he can be readily deposed or ignored. The fact that this disadvantageous situation does not necessarily lead to poor performance is perhaps one of the more intriguing questions in the study of small groups.

Task structure.   Another important dimension of the situation is the task itself. As we shall see later on, the task of a policy- and decision-making group requires different leadership attitudes than does the task of managing the affairs of the company. This was also apparent in a study of bomber crews when we compared the task involving radar and visual bombing with that of minimizing the navigational control-time error score (Fiedler, 1955; see also Voiers, 1956).

While we have recognized for some time that task requirements have considerable importance in leader-member interaction, it is only in relatively recent years that we have begun to inquire more closely into the task dimensions and characteristics which classify and describe the task of a group. Recent research by Shaw (1963) and by Hackman (1966) has dealt specifically with group tasks, and a previous paper by Roby and Lanzetta (1958) has dealt with this problem in a very thought-provoking manner.

In terms of the present analysis, the task is one important element in the situation which faces the leader. It seems hardly necessary to repeat here that the task constitutes in almost all cases the reason for establishing a task group in the first place, and the group's existence depends, therefore, on the satisfactory performance of the task.

Equally important is the point that the task of groups which are subunits of a larger organization constitutes an order from "above." The task is an assignment which the group undertakes on behalf of the organization. And the organization has an obvious stake in seeing that the task is accomplished according to specifications. It holds the leader responsible for seeing that this is done.

In return, of course, the organization gives the leader as much support as it can. It gives the leader at least some power to reward and punish and it gives him prestige and rank and it will back the leader insofar as this is possible. And it is on the important point of backing the leader that tasks differ in a quite fundamental way. Let us for the moment consider two quite different tasks, such as chairing a committee meeting and supervising an assembly job. Both may be of equal concern to the organization, and the organization thus may be equally willing to give the leader moral and tangible support. Let us now ask what support the organization is, in fact, able to offer the leader in each of these cases.

The organization would have relatively little problem in backing a leader whose group performs an assembly-line job. The organization can provide quite specific instructions and standard operating procedures on how a certain piece of equipment is to be assembled. If the leader knows these instructions which tell step by step and "by the numbers" how the group is to proceed, he will be able to detect and correct the worker who misses one step. Moreover, if the leader sees to it that the group follows the instructions step by step the organization can be fairly certain that the piece of equipment will be assembled to specifications. The organization can see to it that the supervisor and his group have the necessary equipment and raw materials, that the personnel is technically qualified, and that the leader's instructions are explicitly obeyed. If the worker does not follow the supervisor's instructions, he can be appropriately disciplined. In the case of military units, the man who refuses to follow instructions can be court-martialed and punished.

The situation is quite different when the task consists of chairing a committee. Here the organization can provide only a very vague, unstructured procedure, and it cannot give the leader much actual influence over his members. After all, bona fide committee work requires that each group member think about and discuss a problem and that the group, as a result of member interaction, arrive at a creative solution. Other than providing the leader with a general task, the organization cannot give him much direct support. Since there is no step-by-step procedure which can be programmed in advance, the leader cannot demand that the group members follow it. Since the leader generally has no more expert knowledge than his members, he cannot influence his group's success by ordering them to vote in certain ways or to come up with a specific solution. And even though the leader may have higher rank or more experience, prudence as well as institutional wisdom require that he does not ram his own solution down his committee members' throats. Above all neither he nor the organization can force an individual to be creative. It is up to the leader to motivate his men to do their utmost, and the power conferred upon him by the organization, or the organization's direct intervention, will not markedly assist him in his job of developing creative solutions to his task. This is clearly recognized—at least in theory—even in such rank-conscious organizations as an army. Thus, a court-martial gives one vote to each member of the board, regardless of his rank, and the junior member is asked to vote first so as to be less influenced by the votes of senior officers on the board. Likewise, in a staff conference, it is customary to assure that all members have had the opportunity to express their opinion, irrespective of their rank in the organization.

When viewed in this light, the nature of the task determines leader influence to a considerable extent. The structured task is, in effect, one way of influencing member behavior by means of the organizational sanctions which can be imposed, and it reinforces position power. Alternatively, we may say that a group which is engaged in a highly structured task does not need a leader with as much position power because the leader's influence is implied by the instructions inherent in the task. The leader of a group which engages in a highly unstructured task cannot use his own position power or the power of his organization because the task dilutes his influence. He has, thus, a much more difficult job in leading his group than does the leader who supervises a highly structured operation. In oversimplified terms, the structured task is enforceable while the unstructured, ambiguous task is difficult or impossible to enforce.

In operationally measuring task structure, we have relied on Shaw's (1963) research, which suggested ten dimensions for the classification of tasks. The dimensions which appear most useful for our particular purposes are, of course, those which indicate the extent to which the leader is able to control and supervise his group members by virtue of the fact that the task is structured or capable of being programmed.

Four scales or dimensions in Shaw's system have been used in our research:

1. *Decision verifiability*   The degree to which the correctness of the solution or decision can be demonstrated either by appeal to authority (e.g., the census of 1960), by logical procedures (e.g., mathematical proof), or by feedback (e.g., examination of consequences of decision, as in action tasks).
2. *Goal clarity*   The degree to which the requirements of the task are clearly stated or known to the group members.
3. *Goal path multiplicity*   The degree to which the task can be solved by a variety of procedures (number of different methods to reach the goal, number of alternative solutions, number of different ways the task can be completed) (reversed scoring).
4. *Solution specificity*   The degree to which there is more than one correct solution. (Some tasks, such as arithmetic problems, have only one correct solution; others have two or more, e.g., a sorting task where items could be sorted in several different ways; still others have an almost infinite number of possible solutions, e.g., human relations problems or matters of opinion.) [2]

[2] Interrater agreement over thirty-five different tasks used in our studies was fairly high (viz., .80 and .88) when the raters were asked to score each of the dimensions on an eight-point scale. The four scale values were then summed for each task. This procedure can undoubtedly be further improved by adding or modifying the subscales. Hunt (1966) has developed a more sensitive scale, which is reported in Chapter 10.

The personal relationship between leader and group members. The task structure and the position power of the leader are group attributes which are determined by the organization. The interpersonal relationship which the leader establishes with his men is at least in part dependent upon the leader's personality. His affective relations with group members, the acceptance which he can obtain, and the loyalty which he can engender are, however, related to the type of person he is and the way in which he handles himself in critical turning points of his group's career.

To be sure, even here the nature of the organization is important, as is the specific history of the group. Some groups have had a long history of poor leader-member relations which have somehow become traditions. It would require an unusually attractive and skillful leader to disrupt such a tradition. More generally, the leader comes into the group with an aura of expert knowledge or competence and the blessings of the organization. In the majority of cases, the appointed leader, by virtue of his legitimate position, is accepted by his group members to a greater or lesser degree, and it will require considerable ineptness on his part to be rejected by those who are supposed to follow him. Thus, in one study of air crews, more than half (52 percent) of the aircraft commanders were the most-chosen members of the crew. A similar result was obtained in a study of tank crews where seventeen of the twenty-five (i.e., 74 percent) accepted their crew commander. Likewise, in a study of consumer owned companies, in twenty-three out of thirty-two, or 72 percent, of the companies the staff members accepted their general manager as leader. And R. L. French (1956) has shown that the appointed leader tends to become sociometrically most chosen even though he may have few if any special skills or personality attributes which would normally have propelled him into a leadership position.

While the attainment of a leadership position may well be highly fortuitous, and while the acceptance of the appointed leader may be overwhelmingly favored by the institutional machinery at work in any organization, the leader-member relationship seems nonetheless to be the most important single element in determining the leader's influence in a small group.[3] The leader who is wholeheartedly accepted or who inspires complete and unquestioning loyalty in his followers needs no signs of rank and no organizationally granted powers to get his men to do his bidding. His men may, in fact, work with him even against the interests of the

[3] M. Fishbein, unpublished manuscript, 1966.

organization. The relationship between the leader and his men may become a very strong tie which indeed does resemble the father-son relationship which Freud (1922) described in his psychoanalytic theory of the group process. This is especially true in groups in which the men are highly dependent upon the leader's skill and wisdom. We see this in combat crews where the crew members in many cases cannot admit the faults and weaknesses of their leaders. As long as the men must entrust their lives and personal safety to the leader, it is just as well that the men idealize the leader as peculiarly worthy of this trust as a means of reducing their anxieties.

The most important aspect of the good leader-member relationship is of course that the leader, because he is liked and trusted, is able to obtain his men's compliance with a minimum of effort. If an individual fails to comply, the leader might withdraw his friendship, his favor, or his protection. Since in many organizations a man's career depends to a considerable extent on his leader's esteem of him, this is no idle threat. Very few men are promoted unless they have the wholehearted endorsement of their superiors. And the negative rating which a man is given by his leader may travel with him for much, if not all, of his professional life.

Where the leader and his members do not get along especially well, where there is some friction in the group, the leader may still obtain compliance, but this compliance will now be given with some reservations, with a certain reserve, and perhaps only at a price which the leader must learn to pay. This price may consist of special favors for the group, it may consist of buying compliance in some tasks by relaxing demands in others, or it may have to be obtained by letting the group members participate more fully in the decision-making processes, that is, by sharing the leadership to a greater or lesser extent.

In groups which completely reject the leader, which are close to open mutiny, or which can no longer strike implicit bargains with the leader (perhaps because the leader cannot or will not bargain in this manner), the leader's position is clearly a very difficult one. Figuratively speaking, his basic problem is to keep himself from getting knifed or having his task sabotaged. Only by maintaining tight control over the group processes can he hope to maintain any reasonable productivity. The slave-driving leader is essentially one who cannot get his men to perform in any other way. We need hardly point out that it is much easier to lead a group which is loyal and devoted than one which is at best tolerant of its leader and that the life of the leader who is rejected and disliked is very difficult indeed.

Hemphill (1961) has provided a very useful analysis of leader behavior by classifying it into (1) *attempted* leadership acts, (2) *successful* leadership acts, and (3) *effective* leadership acts. The attempted leadership act is simply a suggestion that the group do something; it is a recommendation or an order to the group. It is, of course, clear that such suggestions and recommendations, and even orders, may frequently be ignored or evaded by accident or by design. This is especially true in informal groups in which the leader may be safely ignored and in which any member may attempt to lead at least in some situations.

A successful leadership act is defined as one which results in group action or some appropriate change in group behavior. The effective leadership act results in the desired effect. Thus, the suggestion to go for coffee becomes a successful leadership act if the group does go for coffee, and it becomes an effective leadership act if the group finally obtains its coffee. A good leader-member relationship will lead to a greater proportion of accepted or successful leadership acts, while a poor leader-member relationship will lead to a relatively small proportion of successful leadership acts. However, the *effectiveness* of the leadership act is not dependent upon the leader-member relations. Rather, it depends upon the appropriateness and wisdom of the suggestion or the order which the leader has given. There is no reason to believe that the well-liked leader will give better or wiser orders and directions than will the less-liked leader. It is clear that the liked leader's directions, poor or good, are more likely to be followed than those of the disliked leader.

The data at our disposal tend to bear this out. We can compare groups in which the leader is well accepted with those in which the leader is relatively less well accepted. The relationship between leader ability and group performance tends to be highly positive in groups in which the leader is accepted, while it tends to be zero or slightly negative in groups not accepting their leader (Fiedler and Meuwese, 1963).

The degree to which the leader-member relationship is good or poor can be assessed by a number of methods. The most readily available method in many real-life groups is the sociometric preference rating which is filled out by group members. It indicates the degree to which the leader would be chosen under various conditions. Questions are asked such as, "If your group were asked to perform a similar task again, who in your group (or in your organization) would you want to have as your supervisor or leader?" or "Who in your organization would you most like to work with?" or "Who in your group had the most influence on the outcome of your deliberations?"

Another method which we have found especially useful is the leader's rating of the group atmosphere. This rating is obtained on a scale practically identical to the scale for obtaining the Least-preferred Coworker score to be described later. The leader is asked to rate the group on items such as friendly-unfriendly, cooperative-uncooperative, tense-relaxed, etc.[4] A summation of the item scores yields a quite reliable and meaningful Group Atmosphere score, which indicates the degree to which the leader feels accepted by the group and relaxed and at ease in his role (Fiedler, 1962). It should be recognized that the leader's assessment of the group atmosphere is quite often at variance with the group members' assessment. This is not too surprising when we consider that the leader's task is basically quite different from that of his group members. The leader may well become very tense and anxious because his group is too relaxed and playful, and the leader may be quite pleased and at ease when his group members are anxious and tense while trying to do a good job.

The sociometric method seems to provide a valid estimate in real-life groups which live and work together over an extended time. It will not be very sensitive in *ad hoc* groups which exist for a few hours and in which the leader will have little, if any, opportunity to obtain an accurate picture of his standing in the group. Here the Group Atmosphere score is more likely to give the relevant measure of the leader's feeling about himself in relation to the group. Leader behavior will, therefore, depend on how the leader thinks his subordinates feel about him rather than how the subordinates really feel about him.

A THREE-DIMENSIONAL CLASSIFICATION OF TASK GROUPS

We have described three major dimensions which appear critical in determining the degree to which the leader will have influence in his group, and we have spelled out the methods for reliably measuring each of these dimensions. The underlying assumption has been that different types of

[4] Other items used in recent studies are: accepting-rejecting, satisfying-frustrating, enthusiastic-unenthusiastic, productive-nonproductive, warm-cold, supportive-hostile, interesting-boring, successful-unsuccessful. (See Appendix A.)

groups require different types of leadership. A leader with one type of leadership style may perform very well in a group in which he enjoys high position power and very good leader-member relations, but he may fail in a group in which his position power is weak and his leader-member relations are poor.

A classification system which is based on three dimensions can be visualized as a three-dimensional space in which each of the types of groups can be located. As a first approximation we can roughly divide task groups into those which fall into the upper half of each dimension and those which fall into the lower half of groups in each dimension. This procedure yields an eight-celled cube, with each of the cells or "octants" containing groups which have been judged or rated as high or as low in each of the three dimensions. As Figure 2-2 shows, groups in Octant I would be high in all three dimensions, that is, they would be rated as having good leader-

Figure 2-2   A model for the classification of group task situations.
SOURCE: The *Harvard Business Review*, September–October, 1965, p. 117. Reproduced by permission.

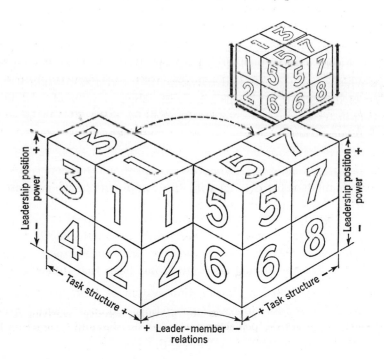

TABLE 2-2   Classification of Group Task Situations on the Basis of Three Factors

Octant	Leader-Member Relations	Task Structure	Position Power
I	Good	High	Strong
II	Good	High	Weak
III	Good	Weak	Strong
IV	Good	Weak	Weak
V	Moderately poor	High	Strong
VI	Moderately poor	High	Weak
VII	Moderately poor	Weak	Strong
VIII	Moderately poor	Weak	Weak
VIII-A *	Very poor	High	Strong

* This cell was subsequently added and is discussed in later chapters.

member relations, high task structure, and high position power. Octant II would contain groups which are high in leader-member relations, high in task structure, but low in position power, and so on. The characteristics of groups in each octant are listed in Table 2-2. Also shown in this table is an additional cell, labeled VIII-A, which we had to include later to accommodate groups with high position power, high task structure, but very poor leader-member relations. Groups of this nature tend to occur only in real-life situations and pointed to the need for a more generalized classification of group situations, which will be discussed in subsequent chapters.

This particular classification system was developed on the basis of groups which had been studied between 1951 and 1963. While it has a number of limitations, which became quite obvious as our hindsight improved (illustrated, for example, by the need for cell VIII-A), the system provides a very convenient starting point for presenting the empirical results which we have obtained in our research on interacting task groups. Therefore, the system of classifying task groups should be seen at this time as a convenient tool for dealing with the complex data which were obtained in the course of our research that led to the development of the Contingency Model.

SUMMARY

We have here presented a classification system of task groups. Groups were first categorized into interacting, coacting, and counteracting groups, based on the degree to which the group members have to interact and coordinate their work in order to complete the common task.

A further classification was made of interacting groups. This classification is based on the degree to which the leader-member relations are good, the degree to which the task is structured or unstructured, and the degree to which the organization endows the leadership position with high or low power.

1413457

A tentative categorization of interacting task groups therefore leads to a three-dimensional system which classifies groups as falling into the upper or lower half of the distribution in each of the three dimensions, hence in one of eight cells or octants in the system. This eight-cell system will be utilized in this book as a framework for presenting empirical studies conducted as part of the research program.

3 MEASURING LEADERSHIP STYLE

As this book hopes to show, the performance of a group depends on both the leader's style of interacting with his group members and on the nature of the group situation in which he and his group find themselves. This chapter describes the particular measure of leadership style which we have used in our work, and it presents the empirical data for interpreting the measure. The chapter is divided into two parts. The first part presents a general discussion of the measure. The second part is a more technical presentation of the theoretical issues and research background which will not be of primary interest to all readers.

It is important, first of all, that we clearly distinguish between leadership style and leadership behavior. By *leadership behavior* we generally mean the particular acts in which a leader engages in the course of directing and coordinating the work of his group members. This may involve such acts as structuring the work relations, praising or criticizing group members, and showing consideration for their welfare and feelings. *Leadership style* will be defined here as the underlying need-structure of the individual which motivates his behavior in various leadership situations. Leadership style thus refers to the consistency of goals or needs over different situations. This definition is akin to Alfred Adler's definition of the life-style as an integrating goal or dominant purpose which determines the individual's behavior (Way, 1962). This contrasts with the use of such terms as response style, cognitive style, or perceptual style which are defined as a mode of behaving that is consistent over different situations. (See Jackson and Messick, 1958.) The distinction between leadership style and leadership behavior is critical for understanding the theory which this book presents; as we shall show, important leadership behaviors of the same individual differ from situation to situation, while the need-structure which motivates these behaviors may be seen as constant.

There has been a great profusion of definitions of leadership and an even greater profusion of operational measures of concepts in this area. This is almost inevitable and probably healthy in a young and vigorous field. It does create difficulties, however, when we try to compare the findings of one investigator with those of another. Research in leadership is especially subject to a proliferation of tests and measures since the area is complex to begin with and since its relevance to so many interpersonal situations invites fishing expeditions that include a variety of *ad hoc* measures.

However, most leadership research has pointed to two or three main modes of interpersonal behavior by which leaders attempt to exert influence and control. In grossly oversimplified terms, the leader can take primary responsibility for the group, he can be autocratic, controlling, managing, directive, and task-oriented in his interactions with his members. Alternatively, he can share decision making and leadership with his group: he can be democratic, permissive, nondirective, considerate of his group members' feelings, and therapeutic in his leadership. Many workers in this area have, therefore, found it expedient to develop or work with tests and measures which tap these two types of leader attitudes and behaviors (see McGrath, 1966).[1]

The present research program, built around a relatively simple method for measuring interpersonal perceptions, deals with the corresponding two styles of leadership. The method involves asking an individual to describe the person in his working life with whom he has been able to cooperate *least* well, that is, his least-preferred coworker. This measure was developed over a period of several years and is based on a rationale which evolved and was modified as new data became available.

DEVELOPMENT OF THE LEADERSHIP–STYLE MEASURE

The author's original interest was in the operational measurement of interpersonal relations. The research, which was particularly concerned with investigating the therapeutic relationship, explored a large number of devices by means of which it could be measured. One of these happened to be a method which required the therapist to predict the self-concept of the patient in psychotherapy. The patient described himself by sorting a set of seventy-six statements on cards, using Q-technique methodology (Stephenson, 1953). He ordered the statements into eight categories ranging from the one most descriptive of himself to the statement which was next most descriptive, and so on until he came to the statement which he considered least descriptive of himself. This description presumably was one measure of the patient's revealed self-concept. The therapist then pre-

---

[1] Some researchers have worked with three or more types of behavior or leadership styles. These include, among others, Bales (1950), Carter (1953), Schutz (1958), and Bass (1960a).

dicted how the patient would describe himself under these given circumstances, using the same sorting method and statements. The idea was that
a clinician who really understood his patient would also be able to tell
how the patient would describe himself. It seemed necessary to control
for the fact that some patients and therapists might in reality be similar
and others might be quite different and that it might be easier to describe
people who are actually similar than those who are different from oneself.
The therapist was, therefore, also asked to describe himself on these same
seventy-six statements. We thus have the patient's self-description, the
therapist's self-description, and the therapist's prediction of his patient.
The similarity between the various descriptions was then determined by
correlating the descriptions.

As it turned out, the typical therapist's predictions of his patient were
neither reliable nor accurate. However, reputedly good therapists tended
to describe their patients as more similar to themselves, while reputedly
poor therapists tended to describe their patients as quite dissimilar. In
fact, the correlation between reputed therapeutic competence and the
similarity which the therapist assumed between himself and his patient
turned out to be .59 for twenty-two therapist-patient pairs (Fiedler, 1951).
In other words, the more competent therapists described their patients as
more similar to themselves than did their less competent colleagues.

The measure, called Assumed Similarity (AS), was at first interpreted
as indicating psychological warmth, acceptance, and permissiveness. This
interpretation was supported by a second study which asked members of
a fraternity house to describe (1) themselves, (2) their best-, and (3) their
least-liked fellow members. As hypothesized, the best-liked person was
perceived as more similar to the rater than was the least-liked member in
the house (Fiedler, Warrington, and Blaisdell, 1952).[2]

These findings naturally raised questions about the effect of these perceptions on the performance of small task groups, and most of our subsequent studies have dealt with this problem. We hypothesized that team
effectiveness would be in large part determined by the interpersonal relations between members of the group, especially between leader and
followers, and that we could measure relevant aspects of these interpersonal relations by means of Assumed Similarity scores or related indices.

Interpersonal perception scores are based on the assumption that the
way in which one person perceives another will affect his relations with
him. Thus, whether or not the other is in fact intelligent, friendly, coopera-

[2] See also Fiedler, Hutchins, and Dodge, 1959.

tive, and helpful may be relatively unimportant to the relationship as long as he is perceived in this manner. This perception may, of course, change in the course of time, but so, presumably, would the relationship.

The underlying assumption, especially in lay circles and in some training programs, has been that accuracy in perception is a prerequisite, or at least a highly desirable attribute, of the good interpersonal relationship. However, there is little evidence to support this view. In fact, accurate, objective but unfavorable perceptions may be less desirable for many good relationships than inaccurate but favorable perceptions. Most people want to be accepted for what they would like to be, not for what they really are. Consider, for the moment, a mother's view of her offspring who might, in fact, be noisy, ill-behaved, and rather dull and repulsive. If she looks at her children through fond maternal eyes, she might see (albeit inaccurately) a group of charming, delightful, well-behaved, intelligent youngsters. It is hardly necessary to ask which of these two ways of perceiving her children will be more likely to engender good interpersonal relations within the family. The husband whose wife may be, in fact, uninteresting, unattractive, and unintelligent, will have a better relationship with her if he perceives her (inaccurately) as fascinating, beautiful, and brilliant than if he sees her objectively and accurately.

Interpersonal situations are highly ambiguous. How many people actually know whether they are liked or disliked by certain other members of their group? How many can really tell whether they are esteemed or merely tolerated? Such judgments, whether based on psychological tests or an extended acquaintanceship, are notoriously inaccurate (Kelly and Fiske, 1951; Soskin, 1953). Bezembinder (1961) conducted a recent study of interpersonal perception among members of a religious order in a monastery. He showed that not even the members of such a closely knit group of men, who live and work together twenty-four hours per day, can accurately predict the thoughts and feelings of others. Most of our interpersonal judgments are colored by misperceptions and wishful thinking, and it is our wishful thinking rather than the accuracy of our perception which is highly reliable and stable over time (Cronbach, 1955).

ASo and LPC scores. The first studies of task groups were conducted on high school basketball teams. We were concerned with the leader's perceptions of particular coworkers as well as perceptions which group members had of one another. This included asking the sociometrically chosen leader and each of the members to describe the most- and least-preferred coworkers within his group. Subsequent studies showed that the best

Figure 3-1

NAME_____

People differ in the ways they think about those with whom they work. This may be important in working with others. Please give your immediate, first reaction to the items on the following two pages.

Below are pairs of words which are opposite in meaning, such as "Very neat" and "Not neat." You are asked to describe someone with whom you have worked by placing an "X" in one of the eight spaces on the line between the two words.

Each space represents how well the adjective fits the person you are describing, as if it were written:

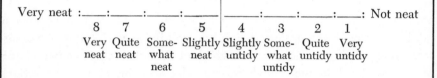

Very neat :___:___:___:___|___:___:___:___: Not neat
        8   7   6   5   4   3   2   1
    Very Quite Some- Slightly Slightly Some- Quite Very
    neat neat what neat untidy what untidy untidy
           neat   untidy

FOR EXAMPLE: If you were to describe the person with whom you are able to work least well, and you ordinarily think of him as being *quite neat,* you would put an "X" in the second space from the words Very Neat, like this:

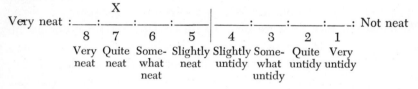

            X
Very neat :___:___:___:___|___:___:___:___: Not neat
        8   7   6   5   4   3   2   1
    Very Quite Some- Slightly Slightly Some- Quite Very
    neat neat what neat untidy what untidy untidy
           neat   untidy

If you ordinarily think of the person with whom you can work least well as being only *slightly neat,* you would put your "X" as follows:

                 X
Very neat :___:___:___:___|___:___:___:___: Not neat
        8   7   6   5   4   3   2   1
    Very Quite Some- Slightly Slightly Some- Quite Very
    neat neat what neat untidy what untidy untidy
           neat   untidy

If you would think of him as being *very untidy,* you would use the space nearest the words Not Neat.

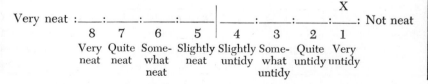

                                 X
Very neat :___:___:___:___|___:___:___:___: Not neat
        8   7   6   5   4   3   2   1
    Very Quite Some- Slightly Slightly Some- Quite Very
    neat neat what neat untidy what untidy untidy
           neat   untidy

Look at the words at both ends of the line before you put in your "X". Please remember that there are *no right or wrong answers*. Work rapidly; your first answer is likely to be the best. Please do not omit any items, and mark each item only once.

LPC

Think of the person *with whom you can work least well*. He may be someone you work with now, or he may be someone you knew in the past.

He does not have to be the person you like least well, but should be the person with whom you had the most difficulty in getting a job done. Describe this person as he appears to you.

Pleasant	:___:___:___:___	___:___:___:___:	Unpleasant
	8 7 6 5	4 3 2 1	
Friendly	:___:___:___:___	___:___:___:___:	Unfriendly
	8 7 6 5	4 3 2 1	
Rejecting	:___:___:___:___	___:___:___:___:	Accepting
	1 2 3 4	5 6 7 8	
Helpful	:___:___:___:___	___:___:___:___:	Frustrating
	8 7 6 5	4 3 2 1	
Unenthusiastic	:___:___:___:___	___:___:___:___:	Enthusiastic
	1 2 3 4	5 6 7 8	
Tense	:___:___:___:___	___:___:___: ___:	Relaxed
	1 2 3 4	5 6 7 8	
Distant	:___:___:___:___	___:___: ___:___:	Close
	1 2 3 4	5 6 7 8	
Cold	:___:___:___:___	___:___:___:___:	Warm
	1 2 3 4	5 6 7 8	
Cooperative	:___:___:___:___	:___:___:___:	Uncooperative
	8 7 6 5	4 3 2 1	
Supportive	:___:___:___:___	___:___:___: :	Hostile
	8 7 6 5	4 3 2 1	
Boring	:___:___:___:___	___:___:___:___:	Interesting
	1 2 3 4	5 6 7 8	
Quarrelsome	:___:___:___:___	___:___:___:___:	Harmonious
	1 2 3 4	5 6 7 8	
Self-assured	:___:___:___:___	___:___:___:___:	Hesitant
	8 7 6 5	4 3 2 1	
Efficient	:___:___:___:___	___:___:___:___:	Inefficient
	8 7 6 5	4 3 2 1	
Gloomy	:___:___:___:___	___:___:___:___:	Cheerful
	1 2 3 4	5 6 7 8	
Open	:___:___:___:___	___:___:___:___:	Guarded
	8 7 6 5	4 3 2 1	

measure for predicting group performance was the similarity the leader perceived between the most- and the least-preferred coworkers he had ever had. This score was called the "Assumed Similarity between Opposites" (i.e., between the *most*- and the *least*-preferred coworkers). As mentioned, these scores were originally obtained by means of Q technique (Stephenson, 1953) and variations of this method (Warrington, 1952). A high Assumed Similarity between Opposites, or ASo, score showed that the individual perceived his most- and least-preferred coworkers as similar. A low ASo score showed that he perceived them as relatively dissimilar. It

Figure 3-2

The computation of ASo and LPC scores is quite simple. A brief numerical example is here presented to illustrate the method of computing these scores. Let us consider two descriptions, both by subject A. The first is the description of his most-preferred coworker (MPC), the second is the description of his least-preferred coworker (LPC). We have scored each scale from the most favorable point of 8 to the least favorable of 1, thus:

$$\text{friendly} :\underline{\hspace{0.5em}}:\underline{\hspace{0.5em}}\overset{X}{:}\underline{\hspace{0.5em}}:\underline{\hspace{0.5em}}:\underline{\hspace{0.5em}}:\underline{\hspace{0.5em}}:\underline{\hspace{0.5em}}:\underline{\hspace{0.5em}}: \text{unfriendly}$$
$$\phantom{\text{friendly} :}8\quad 7\quad 6\quad 5\quad 4\quad 3\quad 2\quad 1$$

An individual who checks his most-preferred coworker as above would be assigned a score of 7 on this particular item of the MPC scale. Let us now compare, say, four items which subject A has marked to describe his most- and his least-preferred coworkers:

Scores of A Describing His

Scale Item	Most-Preferred Coworker	Least-Preferred Coworker	Difference between MPC and LPC	Squared Difference
1 Pleasant-Unpleasant	7	3	4	16
2 Friendly-Unfriendly	4	4	0	0
3 Accepting-Rejecting	8	2	6	36
4 Helpful-Frustrating	6	5	1	1
		LPC $= \overline{14}$		$\overline{D^2 = 53}$

$$D = \sqrt{D^2} = 7.28$$

NOTE: A high difference score, D, indicates a low Assumed Similarity between Opposites (ASo)

SOURCE: Adapted from Fiedler, 1958, p. 16.

should be emphasized that ASo scores were obtained in most studies by asking the individual to think of *all* people with whom he had ever worked, not merely those with whom he worked at the time of rating. These scores can, therefore, serve as predictors since they can be—and frequently are—obtained before an individual joins a particular group.

More recent work has been based on a score derived from only one of these coworker descriptions, namely that of the Least-preferred Coworker (LPC). ASo and LPC scores are based on identical scale sheets. LPC is, in fact, a component of ASo (Cronbach, 1956). The current form follows Osgood's Semantic Differential (1952), with scale sheets containing from sixteen to twenty-four or thirty bipolar adjective items, depending upon the study. One version of the entire scale is here reproduced in Figure 3-1.

Each of the items is scored by a range of numbers from eight at the most favorable pole (e.g., friendly, cooperative) down to one at the least favorable pole. To obtain ASo it is necessary to compute the differences between

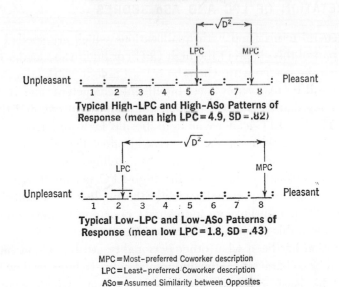

Figure 3-3   Schematic representation of typical scoring pattern, which results in high or low LPC scores. Means and standard deviations of high and low LPC scores (upper third and lower third of the distribution) are indicated, as are standard deviations of high and low LPC scores. Mean of all LPC scores for 320 Ss was 3.32, standard deviation was 1.39.

Typical High–LPC and High–ASo Patterns of Response (mean high LPC = 4.9, SD = .82)

Typical Low–LPC and Low–ASo Patterns of Response (mean low LPC = 1.8, SD = .43)

MPC = Most-preferred Coworker description
LPC = Least-preferred Coworker description
ASo = Assumed Similarity between Opposites
(that is, opposite types of coworkers)

corresponding items on the descriptions of the Most- and of the Least-preferred Coworker scales. The differences in item scores are then squared and summed to yield a D^2. The square root of this score is defined as D. The comparison between the most- and the least-preferred coworkers on these two scale sheets defines ASo. A high D score indicates a low Assumed Similarity (Figure 3-2).

The LPC score is obtained by simply summing the item scores on the scale sheet describing the individual's least-preferred coworker. In terms of average item scores, the means for various samples, expressed as mean item scores, range from 3.19 to 4.13. (This would be 63.8 to 82.6 on a twenty-item scale.) Low LPC scores run from about 1.2 to 2.2; high LPC scores range from about 4.1 to 5.7. The schematic drawing shown as Figure 3-3 shows where these average scores fall on the scale.

Although ASo and especially LPC scores can be obtained in five to ten minutes, a score based on twenty items yields split-half reliability co-efficients about .90. The stability of these scores, depending upon the intervening experience and duration of elapsed time, has ranged from .35 to .70. ASo and LPC scores are highly correlated, i.e., .80 to .90, which is about as high as the reliability of the two scores will permit. We have, therefore, interpreted ASo and LPC scores interchangeably, even though there seem to be some minor differences between these two scores.

INTERPRETATION OF LPC AND ASo SCORES

In very general terms (and with qualifications which are spelled out in the latter part of this chapter) the high-LPC (or high-ASo) leader tells us in effect that the person with whom he is least able to work on a common task might still be reasonably nice, intelligent, competent, etc. It is as if he were saying that he is distinguishing between the *person* and the way he works. The low-LPC leader who describes his least-preferred coworker in a very negative, rejecting manner says in effect that the person with whom he cannot work is uncooperative, unintelligent, incompetent, etc. The implicit personality theory of the high-LPC person thus separates work performance and personality, while the implicit personality theory of the low-LPC person links an individual's poor performance on a joint task with undesirable personality characteristics.

The question has been what other personality attributes and interpersonal behaviors characterize the individual who is high or low in his esteem for his least-preferred coworker. For reasons which seem quite obvious in retrospect, it has been extremely difficult to develop an adequate and readily supportable interpretation of ASo and LPC scores. These scores do not measure attributes which correlate with the usual personality and ability tests or with attitude scales. Nor is there a one-to-one relationship between these scales and behaviors.

A few general trends have been apparent all along. *High*-LPC leaders tend to be more concerned with establishing good interpersonal relations. They are generally described as somewhat more considerate (as defined by the Ohio State Leader Behavior Scale: Stogdill and Coons, 1957) than low LPC leaders, the members of their groups tend to be lower in anxiety, they get along better with one another, and they are more satisfied to be in the group (Meuwese, 1964). The *low*-LPC leaders tend to be more concerned with the task. They are "more task- than relationship-oriented" and more punitive toward poor coworkers (Hawkins, 1962). They are seen as more efficient and goal-oriented in their leadership behavior (Meuwese, 1964). However, even more important are the repeated findings that relaxed, pleasant group climates call out quite different types of behaviors in high- and low-LPC leaders than do group climates which are tense, stressful, or which present difficult leadership situations (Fiedler, Meuwese, and Oonk, 1960; Fiedler, 1962). Rather than visualizing the personality attributes reflected by LPC (or ASo) scores as correlates of particular leadership behaviors, we must interpret LPC quite differently to account for all the data which have been employed.

In brief, we visualize the high LPC individual (who perceives his least-preferred coworker in a relatively *favorable* manner) as a person who derives his major satisfaction from successful interpersonal relationships, while the low-LPC person (who describes his LPC in very *unfavorable* terms) derives his major satisfaction from task performance (Bishop, 1964). This was also seen in a study of rifle teams (McGrath, 1962) which showed that low-LPC men felt more accepted by their groups when they were successful, while success made no difference for high-LPC members. Low-LPC members experienced the group as more pleasant when they were successful than when they had failed on the task. High-LPC persons were uninfluenced by the task success.

Thus, high-LPC leaders are concerned with having good interpersonal relations and with gaining prominence and self-esteem through these interpersonal relations. Low-LPC leaders are concerned with achieving success on assigned tasks, even at the risk of having poor interpersonal relations with fellow workers. The behaviors of high- and low-LPC leaders will thus be quite different if the situation is such that the satisfaction of their respective needs is threatened. Under these conditions the high-LPC leader will increase his interpersonal interaction in order to cement his relations with other group members while the low-LPC leader will interact in order to complete the task successfully. The high-LPC person is concerned with gaining self-esteem through recognition by others, the low-LPC person is concerned with gaining self-esteem through successful performance of the task. Both types of leaders may thus be concerned with the task and both will use interpersonal relationships, although the high-LPC leader will concern himself with the task in order to have successful interpersonal relations, while the low-LPC leader will concern himself with the interpersonal relations in order to achieve task success.

The reader who is not especially interested in a technical review of the methodological studies which have been conducted in order to understand and interpret these scores is advised to turn, at this point, to the next chapter.

TECHNICAL REVIEW OF RESEARCH ON ASo AND LPC SCORES

Assumed Similarity and Least-preferred Coworker scores have been the subject of intensive research since 1950. However, these scores have been extremely resistant to meaningful interpretations which relate them to personality traits and to consistent behavior patterns. For many years we were in the peculiar position of having a score which seemed to correlate with nothing but group performance.

The method for obtaining these scores is simple enough. We ask the subject to describe his most- and his least-preferred coworkers. The difference the individual sees between these two real or hypothetical coworkers is indicated by ASo scores; the degree to which he esteems the person with whom he cannot work is indicated by LPC. Almost everyone describes his least-preferred coworker in less favorable terms than he describes either himself or his most-preferred coworker. However, the high-LPC person is somewhat temperate in his negative description of poor coworkers; the low-LPC person describes them as completely worthless and in highly unflattering terms.

On first glance it may appear that we are dealing with a measure of perceptual accuracy or the ability to differentiate good and poor coworkers. This is not so, however. There is no logical reason why someone with whom we cannot work should have only negative personality attributes. It is, in fact, very difficult to visualize anyone who could be completely incompetent, handicapped, and despicable. This all the more so since least-preferred coworkers supposedly come from the ranks of one's current or former peers, that is, fellow university students, fellow executives, fellow army officers, or fellow workers. The low-LPC person thus seems to overreact to those with whom he finds it difficult to work.

That we are dealing with an emotional overreaction can be seen from the fact that we obtain similarly disparaging descriptions of least-preferred coworkers even when we ask the individual to *predict the self-description* of his least-preferred coworker. That is, we ask the subject to place himself in the shoes of his least-preferred coworker and to mark the scales *as his least-preferred coworker would mark them.* Practically no one in his right mind would describe himself as stupid, incompetent, disloyal, uncooperative, and unstable to the degree to which low-LPC persons tend to predict. The score obviously involves little accuracy of perception, but is, rather, an emotional reaction to people with whom one cannot work.

Internal consistency. We have usually determined the internal consistency of ASo and LPC scores by means of split-half correlations or variants of the method. These coefficients have been uniformly high, ranging from .85 to .95. The content of the scale items, generally speaking, has played a very minor part, and we have used a number of different scale items for these descriptions. The items obviously have to deal with personality attributes (stable-unstable, friendly-unfriendly) rather than personal characteristics (blond-dark-haired, tall-short). However, a variety of different forms of scales have been used without much loss of construct validity. A number of studies have utilized Likert scale items, and early studies were based on Q-technique or modifications of Q-technique scales.

One study by Cronbach et al. (1953) investigated a set of personality items which had been factor analyzed, yielding five different clusters of self-description items. An analysis of these same items, used for obtaining ASo scores, showed that the intercorrelations of items from different clusters were as high as were items coming from within the same cluster. In other words, the content played little part in determining ASo scores. Content may be somewhat more important in determining LPC scores, as was shown by Stafford and Becker (1966), although even here the effect of item content appeared to be relatively slight.

Stability over time. A limited number of studies have been conducted in which estimates of the stability of ASo and LPC scores were provided. One study of B-29 bomber crews enabled us to obtain test-retest correlations over an eight-week period. The subjects were mature air-force officers in a training situation. The test-retest correlation was .68. A similar test-retest correlation was obtained in a study of army tank crews.

A more elaborate study of the stability of these scores was conducted by E. Drucker at Fort Knox, Kentucky. He tested 1,100 men just inducted into the army, that is, prior to basic training, and who were assigned to an eight-week basic training program. Some of the trainees had had previous army experience or experience in the Reserve Officer Training Corps.

It is the custom in basic training units to appoint some of the trainees as acting squad leaders. Drucker studied the effect of this leadership experience on their ASo and LPC scores as compared to those who had not had this leadership experience. These effects were studied separately on men with previous military experience and on men with no previous military experience. The results of Drucker's analyses are presented in Table 3-1.

It is important to note that the stability of ASo and LPC scores depends to a considerable degree on the intervening experience of the men. The most consistent ASo and LPC scores came from acting squad leaders who had had previous military experience. The least consistent scores came from men who had had previous military experience but who had not been given leadership positions in their training units, that is, men whose role relations changed.

These data indicate the extent to which the stability of LPC and ASo scores is a function of changing experience. It should be noted that these men were undergoing very drastic changes in their lives. Most men were eighteen- to nineteen-year-old civilians at the time of the pretest; they

TABLE 3-1   Test-Retest Correlations of ASo and LPC Scores over Eight Weeks

	N	ASo	LPC
Experienced leaders	54	.74	.57
Inexperienced leaders	32	.52	.47
Experienced nonleaders	62	.33	.31
Inexperienced nonleaders	133	.50	.41

were soldiers who had completed two months of basic training at the time of the posttest. These stability coefficients are, in all likelihood, very conservative estimates. We would expect the more typical test-retest reliability of ASo and LPC scores of more mature subjects in stable situations to be around .6 to .7, as was true of the air-force crews.

CORRELATIONAL STUDIES

A large number of studies have attempted to interpret ASo and LPC scores by correlating them with various standard personality and attitude tests and biographical questionnaires. There were, in fact, very few promising measures which we did not try to relate to ASo and LPC at one time or another. Our attempts to find systematic and consistent relations with ASo and LPC scores seemed to be consistent and reliable only in leading to repeated frustration. While occasional results were statistically significant, the findings did not stand up under cross validation. Many interesting relations reported in some studies (e.g., Burke, 1961; Golb and Fiedler, 1955; Steiner, 1959) were not found in replication attempts.

A very large and elaborate study was conducted by A. R. Bass et al. (1964). It involved eighty-one measures which were administered to 163 male college students. Included in the test battery were biographical data, various personality questions and tests, as well as various test-response measures and interpersonal perception indices. This battery is presented in Appendix C.

None of the independent measures correlated above .30 with LPC, and most of the correlations were not statistically significant. A factor analysis of all measures over all subjects showed that ASo and LPC were factorially unique. In other words, just as in previous studies, ASo and LPC scores seemed to measure psychological attributes which were unrelated and presumably different from other psychological traits and attributes represented in the test battery.

It was considered possible, however, that the pattern of psychological attributes or the personality structure of high- and of low-LPC persons might differ. The total sample of 163 subjects was, therefore, split and the test responses of the two subsamples were refactored (using varimax rotation). While there was considerable similarity between the first factors, there was somewhat less correspondence between subsequent factors. These other factors provided some clues about the differences between high- and low-LPC persons.

Three factors were unique for each group. These suggested major differences in factor structure between the high- and the low-LPC samples. For the *low*-LPC group, one factor was primarily defined by perceptions of most- and least-preferred coworkers, as well as of ideal self. This factor seems to indicate a tendency to differentiate between stereotyped social objects, viz., most- and least-preferred coworkers and ideal self.

The next factor was defined by items concerning work situations and task activities, and had a loading on LPC and task orientation. The factor suggests that the low-LPC individual is task-oriented and critical of others in a work situation, and that he has a relatively complex cognitive structuring of his social environment. This factor is also defined by an item indicative of a good team player, "Sticking with my friends in a difficult situation is more important than going my own way," and by the large number of hours spent in outside activities. We have interpreted this factor as related to task leadership. The third factor, unique to the low-LPC sample, appears to be related to individuals who come from a large family and who prefer to be with others in their task and social activities.

Three factors were unique in the sample consisting of *high*-LPC persons. The first is a conservatism factor, primarily defined by high F-scale scores, low category width, and low independence of judgment scores. The second is an interpersonal orientation factor, defined by interests which are in social and physical activities and by low task orientation. It consists of items indicating avoidance of disagreements and arguments, and the desire to be a member rather than a leader of a group. The third unique factor also is concerned with maintaining pleasant interpersonal relations, but in task situations. It is defined by high LPC and ASo scores, by items indicating a preference for being considerate of coworkers and for becoming personally involved with them. This factor has been labeled "coworker orientation."

These results indicate that interpersonal and interaction orientation are highly relevant dimensions for high-LPC persons. Task leadership and task orientation appear more important for the low-LPC individual. The separate factor analyses also indicate, however, that the high- and low-LPC groups may well differ from middle groups. Extensive research on these middle LPC groups still needs to be conducted.

A second study in this series by Bass et al. shows that the high-LPC person tends to make fewer positive statements about himself or his best friend and fewer negative statements about his least-preferred coworker. He appears more noncommittal and more cautious in these evaluations.

The low-LPC person, on the other hand, tends to evaluate himself and his most-preferred coworker in a very positive manner and his least-preferred coworker in a very negative manner. The individual with intermediate LPC scores again seems to differ from high- and low-LPC persons. He appears to be cognitively more complex, less authoritarian or acquiescent, less concerned with socially desirable responses, and more critical and task-oriented than either the high- or low-LPC person. He seems also to be somewhat more concerned with personal competence and somewhat less concerned with personal warmth and industriousness in the selection of his work partners, hence less interested in team work. A third type of interpersonal style might thus be measured by medium positions on the LPC scales.

RELATION TO MEMBER ADJUSTMENT

A number of studies have indicated that the high-LPC leader tends to provide a quasi-therapeutic environment for his group members. This is in line with his concern for establishing and maintaining good interpersonal relations (Chemers et al., 1966). His group tends to be more cohesive (Fiedler, 1954) and his group members tend to be more satisfied with themselves and with the task (Fiedler, 1954; Fiedler et al., 1961). His members tend to be less anxious and tense (Meuwese, 1964) than is the case of groups with low-LPC leaders. While the correlations are generally small, they are fairly consistent in the expected direction.

DESCRIPTION OF LEAST-PREFERRED COWORKERS AS ATTITUDE INDICATORS

Fishbein et al. (1965) have shown that the high-LPC persons tend to think of different individuals than do low-LPC persons when they describe their least preferred coworker. Fishbein asked his subjects to give a written description of the type of person with whom they could work together least well. These descriptions were then categorized and compared. The results showed that the high-LPC persons seemed to experience most difficulty in working with a bull-headed, dogmatic individual who would tend to disturb smooth interpersonal relations in a group. The low-LPC persons, on the other hand, designated as their least-preferred coworkers individuals whom they described as "poor team members," "unintelligent," and "lazy." In other words, low-LPC persons were primarily concerned with the effect which such people would have on the performance of the team.

Fishbein interprets the previous lack of correlations between LPC and personality test responses as indicating that LPC is an attitude measure which is fairly specific to the team situation, and which, therefore, cannot correlate highly with personality-trait measures.

PHYSIOLOGICAL CORRELATES

We have some evidence from a study by Rudin (1964) that ASo scores of the leader affect physiological responses of the members of his group. A comparison of two groups was made in the course of a simulation experiment of crew behavior on a space craft. The crews were assigned to alternating four-hour shifts for a period of twelve days. According to Rudin,

> The leader of the Baker crew (low ASo leader) was active, was quick to reward and to punish, acted authoritatively, but also initiated considerable horseplay, and seemed not concerned with, or sensitive to, the feelings of his crew. The leader of the Able crew (high ASo leader) was more passive, acted more like "one of the boys," took part in horseplay but did not initiate it, showed sensitivity to the feelings of others, related like a peer and did not reward and punish as frequently.

Rudin reported further that analysis of the task data showed the Baker crew under the low-ASo leader to be better in arithmetic and reaction-time tasks. The Able crew, under the high-ASo leader, was significantly better in perceptual tasks requiring organization and discrimination of new stimuli. Perhaps the most interesting finding was that the Able and Baker crews differed in physiological responses. The low-ASo leader's Baker crew showed significantly higher pulse rates and body temperatures than did the Able crew, and "two members of the Baker crew showed definite neurotic symptoms not present previously."

It should be stressed that the observations and ratings of the leaders and crew members were made during the experimental period. ASo scores were obtained *after* the experiment. There was, therefore, no possibility of contamination of the raters, since they did not know the leaders' scores while rating them. The findings, although based on only two crews of five men each, are consistent with our previous interpretations of the ASo scores. This sample is, of course, too small to serve as an adequate test. However, the results provide interesting suggestions for further study of physiological correlates of ASo and LPC scores.

BEHAVIORAL CORRELATES

A substantial number of investigations were devoted to identifying behaviors which would differentiate high- and low-LPC leaders. These studies were carried out throughout the period of the program, and we shall here discuss only those which provided significant insights into the meaning of the scores.

The most important clue to the interpretation of LPC scores comes from studies which show that the behavior associated with high and with low LPC or ASo scores systematically changes as the situation becomes more difficult for the leader.

One investigation (Fiedler, Meuwese, and Oonk, 1961), described in greater detail later, involved four-man teams which were given group creativity tasks. The study was conducted in Holland. Half of the teams consisted of either four Calvinist or four Catholic students, while the other half consisted of teams of two Calvinist and two Catholic students. Half of the religiously homogeneous and half of the heterogeneous groups had assigned leaders, while the other half operated under an emergent leadership situation.

All discussions were tape-recorded and content-analyzed. Leader statements were classified into six categories: (1) procedural remarks concerned with the way in which the group should go about its task; (2) the introduction of new ideas which suggested problem solutions, (3) the elaboration of new ideas, that is, taking up suggestions made by others and carrying them further; (4) remarks criticizing ideas or behaviors of other group members; (5) comments irrelevant to the task, that is, comments concerned with group maintenance, jokes or other tension-relieving remarks. Also, (6) total activity, that is, the total number of comments, was obtained for each of the sessions.

The ten groups which were rated as relatively tense—in terms of the number of critical remarks and sociometric ratings describing one or more of the members as destructively critical in behavior and attitudes—were compared with the ten groups which were most relaxed and free of tension. Results of this analysis are presented in Table 3-2. The two categories most directly related to maintaining good relations in groups, viz., procedural remarks and non-task-relevant comments, were somewhat more

TABLE 3-2   Correlations of Content Categories with Leader LPC and Group Creativity Scores in the Dutch Creativity Study ($N = 10$) *

Category	Leader's LPC Scores	
	Relaxed Groups	Strained Groups
1. New ideas	−.11	−.14
2. Elaboration	−.28	−.59
3. Critical remarks	−.15	.08
4. Procedural remarks	.54	.40
5. Irrelevant comments	.27	.61
6. Total activity	.05	−.52

* $p < .10$ at .56; $p < .05$ at .64.

characteristic of high-LPC leaders, irrespective of the pleasantness of the situation. Task-relevant behavior, that is, elaboration of ideas and, to a minor extent, new ideas, was more characteristic of low-LPC leaders. The low-LPC leaders showed higher rates of activity in strained groups as compared to high-LPC leaders. In other words, in the socially strained situation, the low-LPC leader manifested a higher rate of task-relevant behaviors while the high-LPC leader manifested a higher rate of relationship oriented and task-irrelevant comments.

A more detailed content analysis was made in a study by Fiedler, London, and Nemo (1961) which utilized the Bales system of interaction process analysis (Bales, 1950). Groups consisting of three women were given the task of devising three stories for one TAT card. The twenty-four groups were divided into three divisions of eight groups, each of which was ranked on the basis of the group atmosphere as experienced by the group leader. Table 3-3 presents the results of this analysis.

While most correlations were not significant, they indicate the difference in behavior which high- and low-LPC leaders show under group conditions they perceive as pleasant and as unpleasant. This is especially evident in the so-called "social-emotional" categories 1, 2, 3, and 10, 11, 12. The high-LPC leader generally behaves in a positive, relaxed, tension relieving, and supportive manner in the pleasant group condition; the low-LPC leader tends to behave in a more supportive, more active, and less rejecting, withdrawing, and antagonistic manner in the unpleasant situation. Thus, the situation which is less personally satisfying causes the high-LPC leader to interact on an emotional and personal level while the

TABLE 3-3   Correlations of Leader's Interactions * (Bales Categories) with LPC
Scores ($N = 8$) †

		LPC	
	Category	Pleasant	Unpleasant
1.	Shows solidarity, encourages, praises	.17	−.31
2.	Shows tension release, jokes, laughs	.53	−.05
3.	Agrees, concurs, complies	.14	.33
4.	Gives suggestion, direction	−.45	−.58
5.	Gives opinion, evaluation	.26	.47
6.	Gives orientation, information	−.26	−.14
7.	Asks for orientation, information	.64	−.24
8.	Asks for opinion, evaluation	−.28	.04
9.	Asks for suggestion, direction	−.72	−.35
10.	Disagrees, shows rejection	−.50	.61
11.	Shows tension, withdraws	−.64	.41
12.	Shows antagonism, defends self	.00	.34
	Total Interaction	.02	−.53

* Proportion of comments.
† $p < .10$ at .63; $p < .05$ at .73.

low-LPC leader interacts in a more task-related manner by giving more suggestions and directions, asking for information and orientation, as well as asking for suggestions and direction.

Tension-arousing conditions thus seem to trigger different kinds of behaviors in persons with high than with low LPC scores. The results suggest further that individuals with high and with low LPC scores look for different need satisfactions in the group situation. When the individual's quest for need satisfaction is threatened—as indicated by situations in which he feels uncomfortable, anxious, or tense—the high- and the low-LPC persons concentrate on different goals.

The clue to what this goal might be comes from a study by Bishop (1964) using data from a group-creativity study by Meuwese and Fiedler (1960). Bishop divided the subjects of this study into those who experienced interpersonal success (who felt accepted and comfortable in the group) and those who experienced success in the task. In other words, he identified the men who felt accepted by the group and satisfied with their interpersonal relations and who said they liked their fellow group members. The other subjects were selected from among those who felt they had performed well and that their group had done a good job. The dependent, or criterion, variables consisted of measures of adjustment, such as self-esteem, esteem for others, and change in anxiety.

Bishop found that the high-LPC subjects tended to improve in adjustment if they had experienced interpersonal success regardless of whether they felt they had succeeded in the task. The low-LPC subjects tended to improve in adjustment scores if they had experienced task success regardless of their perceived interpersonal success. Presumably, the needs of the high-LPC persons were satisfied by good interpersonal relations, while those of the low-LPC persons were satisfied by success in the task.

A similar finding emerged from a study by Myers (1962). His experiment compared 30 three-man rifle teams under competitive conditions with 30 rifle teams under conditions which deemphasized competition between teams. Bishop reanalyzed the Myers study and found that the low-LPC group members (seeking self-esteem through task success) felt less accepted by their group and had lower self-esteem when their team failed than when it succeeded in the task under the competitive condition. The self-esteem of high-LPC persons was unaffected by perceived task success or failure in the competitive condition. The opposite was the case in the noncompetitive condition in which task success vis-à-vis another team was deemphasized and each team member felt more on his own. Here the task-oriented, low-LPC person was unaffected by task success or failure. The relationship-oriented, high-LPC person's self-esteem decreased (although not significantly) if he felt that he had failed and that he would, presumably, be less esteemed by his team members (Table 3-4).

This is shown even more clearly by scores indicating the changes in adjustment associated with competitive and noncompetitive conditions. The competitive condition, which stressed teamwork, was more beneficial

TABLE 3-4   Perceived Acceptance of High- and Low-LPC Subjects in the Rifle Team Study under Competitive and Noncompetitive Conditions

LPC	Competitive			Noncompetitive		
	High Success	Low Success	Difference	High Success	Low Success	Difference
High	65.43	58.62	6.81	57.86	53.00	4.86
Low	66.71	54.50	12.21*	56.00	55.20	.80

$*p < .01$

TABLE 3-5   Change over a Three-week Period in Self-esteem of High- and Low-LPC Subjects in the Rifle Team Study under Competitive and Noncompetitive Conditions

	Week 2	Week 5	Change
		Competitive Condition	
High LPC	102.9	107.5	5.6
Low LPC	102.3	114.6	12.3
		Noncompetitive Condition	
High LPC	104.5	104.9	.4
Low LPC	108.7	112.6	3.9

to the self-esteem of persons with low LPC than high LPC scores. The self-esteem scores of high-LPC persons remained almost unaffected, regardless of condition. Thus, the low-LPC person seems more concerned with the task, and he obtains more satisfaction and self-esteem under conditions which permit him to experience team success in a common task (Table 3-5, Figure 3-4).

Figure 3-4   Changes in mean self-esteem scores of high- and low-LPC persons under competitive and noncompetitive conditions in the rifle team study.

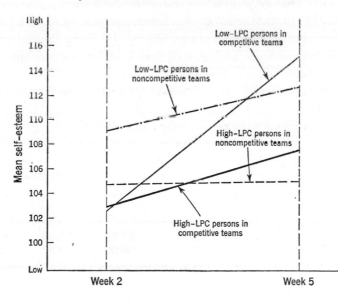

TABLE 3-6 Comparison of Group Atmosphere Scores of High- and Low-LPC Majority Group Members of Successful and Unsuccessful Negotiation Teams

LPC Score	Successful	Unsuccessful	d
High LPC	97.40	98.12	−.72
Low LPC	108.33	93.89	14.44*

* $p < .01$

The same inferences can be drawn from a study of negotiation processes conducted by McGrath and Julian (1962). Low-LPC majority group members experienced negotiation groups as considerably and significantly more pleasant when they felt that their side had been successful than when they felt their side had failed. In contrast, perceived success did not correlate with perceived pleasantness of the group for high-LPC persons. In other words, the low-LPC person evaluated his experiences in terms of task success while the high-LPC person did not, supporting the interpretation that the low-LPC person will seek task success while the high-LPC person will seek success in his interpersonal relations (Table 3-6).

This does not mean, however, that the high-LPC leader will be unaffected by success. On the contrary, since he is motivated to achieve a prominent position and good interpersonal relationships, he will react very strongly to the extrinsic rewards which success may bring. The low-LPC leader, on the other hand, will obtain his rewards from the intrinsic satisfactions of doing the job, and he will, therefore, be less concerned about others' evaluations of his performance.

This is seen very clearly in data from a study by Paul Ninane (unpublished) which compared the leaders' reactions to being told either that their groups had succeeded or that they had failed.

The groups were given a road map and various directions on how to plan a cross-country road race so that the route would be traversed in the shortest possible time. After completing two tasks, half the groups, selected at random, were told that they had performed very well while the other half of the groups were told that they had performed quite poorly. The leaders were then asked (*after* being told of their supposed success or failure) to fill out a series of questionnaires describing themselves, their coworkers, and the group atmosphere indicating their satisfaction with the task.

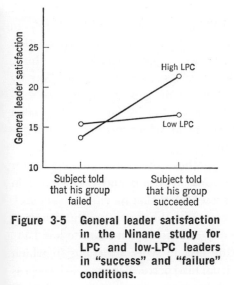

Figure 3-5   General leader satisfaction
in the Ninane study for
LPC and low-LPC leaders
in "success" and "failure"
conditions.

Ninane found no significant differences in the Group Atmosphere scores
of low-LPC persons who were told afterwards that their groups had been
successful or that they had failed. However, the Group-Atmosphere scores
of high-LPC persons were quite different depending upon whether they
were told that their group had succeeded or failed. In other words, the
high-LPC person reacted strongly *to what the experimenter said about his
group* (and presumably thought about him), while the low-LPC leader's
satisfaction with self and with his group was not dependent upon the
evaluations of others. This is well illustrated in Figure 3-5, which shows
that the high-LPC leader's retrospective satisfaction with the task was
markedly affected when he was told that he had been successful, while
the low-LPC leader's satisfaction was essentially unaffected by this information.

LPC AND ASo AS MOTIVATIONAL INDICES

The studies of LPC and ASo lead to the inference that LPC and ASo
scores reflect the individual's motivational structure, an interpretation supported by a recent study (Burke, 1964) which reported a significant correlation between ASo and need-achievement scores of .34. The data
emerging from the studies by Bishop, by McGrath and Julian and others
suggest that the high-LPC person gains self-esteem, satisfaction, and a

lessening of anxiety through gaining prominence and good relations with others (Higgs, 1964), while the low-LPC person increases his self-esteem and lessens his anxiety by performing a task to his own satisfaction (Ninane, unpublished study; Bishop, 1964). It is reasonable to conclude, therefore, that the high-LPC individual will seek need gratification by trying to create situations in which he will gain good interpersonal relations and prominence. In contrast, the low-LPC leader will seek need gratification by trying to create situations in which he will experience success in the task he is asked to perform.

This line of reasoning leads to the hypothesis that the high-LPC leader will passively enjoy his good interpersonal relations and prominence in situations in which these are already present, but that he will actively seek them in situations in which his attainment of these need gratifications is potentially threatened. In like manner, we would expect that the low-LPC leader will actively concentrate on the task in work situations in which his potential for intrinsic satisfaction from task performance or task success is threatened.

SUMMARY

This chapter reviewed studies which have led to better understanding and interpretation of Assumed Similarity between Opposites (ASo) and Least-preferred Coworker (LPC) scores. These studies show that LPC and ASo scores are highly correlated with each other and that they can, therefore, be interpreted interchangeably. The internal consistency of the scores was quite high (.85 to .95). The stability of the scores over time was lower, ranging in one study from .31 to .74 and being .65 in a study of mature air-force officers.

Taken as a whole, these scores appear to be motivational measures. High LPC or ASo scores seem to indicate relationship orientation and motivation to achieve personal recognition and prominence. Low LPC or ASo scores appear to indicate task orientation. The self-esteem and adjustment of the high-LPC or ASo person tend to come from relationships with others in his social environment, while the self-esteem and adjustment of the low-LPC or ASo person tend to be derived from the intrinsic satisfaction of working on a task.

II

The preceding chapters provided an introduction to the problem of leadership performance and to the organizational context within which leadership should be seen. We proposed a taxonomy of groups based on four major factors that presumably determine the favorableness of the situation for the leader, that is, the degree to which the situation enables the leader to exert influence. Finally, we have presented a method for measuring leadership style and the empirical evidence which has accumulated in the attempt to make an adequate interpretation of Assumed Similarity between Opposites (ASo) and Least-preferred Coworker (LPC) scores.

This second part presents the empirical studies of interacting groups which led to our present theory of leadership. The studies cover seven of the eight octants or cells in our classification system. Not all cells or octants are represented with equal thoroughness, not all provide equally clear results, although, as a group, these studies will show that our classification system provides a meaningful way to classify situations on the basis of the leadership style they require.

4 INFORMAL GROUPS WITH STRUCTURED TASKS
(Octants II and VI)

The group-classification system presented in Chapter 2 assumes that different types of groups require different leadership styles. This taxonomy, based on the three major dimensions of leader-member relations, task structure, and position power, provides one convenient frame of reference for discussing the specific leadership requirements of the types of groups on which the theory was based. Most studies in this area deal with a particular set of groups which have the same tasks and the same leadership structure. This is essential if we want to compare the performance of groups. Only the leader-group relations varied. Whether the leader-member relations were good or poor had to be established on the basis of *post hoc* sociometric questionnaires or the leader's Group Atmosphere scales. It will, therefore, be most convenient to combine the discussion of groups falling into cells or octants which are complementary on leader-member relations, that is, Octants I, V, and II, (Octant VI is empty), Octants III and VII, and Octants IV and VIII, since these usually contain groups from the same study.

The first set of studies which we conducted on team performance was based on groups which fall into Octant II, that is, groups having a reasonably structured task but relatively weak leader position power. Since the outcomes of these studies guided further research, the presentation will be more understandable if we begin our discussion with these relatively simple teams which are also commonly called "informal groups." (To follow the chronological order of the research program we will consider groups in Octants IV and VIII before discussing the groups in Octants III and VII.)

The distinguishing mark of teams in Octant II is, first, a leadership which is either emergent or informal or else quite weak and, second, the relative absence of a formally structured role distribution. Leadership is assumed by the person to whom the group members look for guidance and decisions. Typically, the leader is neither appointed nor elected, and he maintains his leadership position only as long as his relations with his members remain good. These groups, by definition, do not have a rigid role specialization. Any member of the group can assume the leadership task if he is able to gain the respect and confidence of the other group members. When the leader loses the respect of the group, and when his relations with his group members deteriorate beyond a certain point, he ceases to be its informal leader, and someone else assumes leadership. This is also the main reason why we cannot expect to find many informal groups in which leader-member relations are poor for any length of time. As a result, informal groups in Octant VI are unlikely to occur in real life.

What, then, are the problems we have to consider in trying to understand the factors and processes which determine the effectiveness of these teams? It may be useful to digress briefly to compare informal task and social groups. First of all, while there are relatively many informal *social* groups, there are relatively few informal *task* groups. Bridge teams, social clubs, street-corner gangs, "cousins clubs," or family associations fall into the former category. The basic need which these groups serve is to provide companionship for like-minded, congenial people in a relaxed, tension-free atmosphere. Such a group demands informality, and it is predicated on the idea that no one is going to make many demands on anyone else or on the group as a whole. Some leadership behaviors are still necessary to coordinate interrelated member activities. Everybody cannot be allowed to talk at the same time. When something needs to be done, such as deciding to go to a ball game or to meet at someone's house, somebody must make the suggestion, take the initiative of obtaining consensus, and arrange the affair. These leadership acts tend to be minimal and uncomplicated. They can be performed by anyone in most of these groups, and the pressure exerted by the leader on his members is generally very light if it is felt at all.

Groups of this nature are possible only if the membership remains small; rarely can more than ten or twelve persons maintain an informal face-to-face relationship for very long. Once the number grows, some administrative action becomes inevitable. A president is elected, a corresponding secretary is appointed, a schedule of meetings is established, and the informal group becomes increasingly formalized. It now must follow an order of procedure. It requires officers who must—or feel they ought to—be given some authority; and the members' actions become motivated less by their own impulse of the moment and more by the wishes of others in the group. Eventually each member must decide whether to conform in order to stay in the group or to drop out. The informal group has become a formal group.

The informal social group is almost always a voluntary association. People may not be able to join at will, but they may certainly leave at will. What keeps the group together is the personal satisfaction which each member derives from his association. The basic criterion for the effectiveness of such social groups is the degree to which they satisfy the personal needs of the individual member. One important test is the degree to which the group maintains itself as a cohesive unit.

The informal task group presents, by contrast, a quite different picture. The main problem of an informal task group is the accomplishment of some group goal. Because the member may voluntarily withdraw, it is essential to provide him with some need satisfaction. But the group's stated aim is the accomplishment of some purpose, the completion of some task. The personal satisfaction of the individual member must, therefore, be closely identified with the accomplishment of the group task. The small social group, in psychoanalytic terms, exists on the pleasure principle—the instant satisfaction of the members' pleasure and comfort. This satisfaction of members should commence as soon as the group congregates. A poker session is a good example.

In contrast, the small, informal task group has to live on the reality principle. Satisfaction of the members' needs must be delayed. Occasionally, in fact, it must be deferred for several years. The member must be willing to subordinate his immediate need satisfaction to the long-range goals of the group. This satisfaction may not even derive from enjoyable interpersonal contacts with other group members.

This is exemplified by the typical athletic team in which members may have to train and work together for years without getting much immediate satisfaction. It may take quite a while before a tennis team or an amateur rifle team gets good enough to walk off with any prizes. In some of these teams, the members may not particularly like one another; under these conditions the personal contact is not much of an inducement to keep the team together. Aside from the intrinsic pleasure of the task, the bonds which sustain the group are the expected satisfactions which may or may not fall to the members at some future time. These expected satisfactions will often come from outside the team, as exemplified by prizes and championship awards, rather than from the relationship within the team.

It takes a great deal of motivation and maturity to remain a member in such groups, especially when the rewards are far in the future and at best uncertain. It is quite clear that the problem of leadership is highly complex under these conditions.

As stated before, the leader may not even be formally recognized, and he can, therefore, be informally deposed by the simple decision of individual members not to pay attention to him. The leadership will then shift to someone else who is perceived as better able to further the group's goals.

This raises an interesting problem for the individual who wants to remain the leader. On the one hand he has to keep the group oriented toward achieving the task. Unless the group members are motivated to pursue the task they will not want to join the group. Unless they see the group as making some progress toward the goal they will not want to stay. But if the leader pushes his members too hard, if he makes the pursuit of the group goal too painful and anxiety-arousing, the members may decide that the price is too high. They may then leave the group or look for a new leader.

One consequence of this potential dilemma is the strong motivation which members of informal task groups require. Once the group is highly committed to its goal, once the members are strongly motivated, the task of being a leader is an easy one since the members, under these conditions, are eager to get the task accomplished, even at the cost of delaying immediate satisfaction.

Basketball teams. The above points are illustrated by studies which we conducted some time ago on high school basketball teams and student surveying parties. These basketball teams are not "pure" informal groups. They are supervised by a highly motivated coach who plays a crucial role in the administration of the team and who provides guidance and direction. However, the typical high school team itself, consisting of eight to sixteen boys, has no formal leader, and the team organization is loose and unstructured. A player may elect to leave the team. Team members are not highly specialized: while each player is assigned to a position, each is expected to guard, pass, and shoot baskets. While most basketball teams elect a captain at the end of the prior season, the position is honorary and usually carries no real authority.

The team's dilemma can be roughly stated in terms of the conflict which the boys have between either wanting to have fun and good interpersonal relations with other boys on the team or wanting to work hard to win games. They can get immediate satisfaction from horsing around and from having a good time. This type of satisfaction comes from within the team. The satisfaction that can be gained from being on a winning team requires hard work and devotion to the team, extended training, and not much social life—perhaps even rather strained relations with one's teammates. The potential extrinsic satisfactions are derived primarily during and toward the end of the successful season, and they come not from within the team but from outsiders. They consist of the admiration of friends and townspeople, being a source of pride to one's parents, and being a local hero to the girls as well as other boys in the school.

The study of the basketball teams was conducted by Fiedler, Hartmann, and Rudin in 1951. We were able to obtain the cooperation of fourteen high school teams in the central Illinois area. Twelve of the squads were tested before they had played their first game. The other two teams were tested shortly after the first game of the season. Each of the schools belonged to a league which consisted of other regional schools of about equal size and resources. A team's performance could, therefore, be assessed on the basis of the percent of games it had won. This turned out to be a very stable performance standard since teams fairly consistently tended to win or lose their games throughout their seasonal league play (reliability, based on a comparison of alternate games won during the season, was .88).

After obtaining permission from the principal and the coach, we presented ourselves at the high school and gave a short explanation of the study to the team members with emphasis on the importance such research might have on group assembly.

Each boy on the squad was then handed a short questionnaire which asked him to name three boys with whom he could work best on his team and three boys with whom he could work least well. He was also asked to name the three fellow squad members he liked best and the three he liked least as a personal friend. Each boy was then given a short Interpersonal Perception scale with which he was asked to describe the one team member he considered his best coworker and the one he considered his poorest coworker.

On the basis of the sociometric responses we could identify the informal leader of the squad, i.e., the boy who in this case received the most votes from his fellow squad members.

We could then determine each boy's interpersonal perception or judgment by comparing his self-description with the descriptions of his most-preferred coworker (ASp) and with his descriptions of his least-preferred coworker (ASn),[1] and by comparing the descriptions of the most- and least-preferred coworkers. These comparisons indicated the perceived or

[1] Assumed similarity to positive (ASp) and to negative (ASn) choices.

assumed similarity (AS) between any of these pairs of descriptions. As will be recalled, a high AS score indicated high perceived similarity between oneself and other people, an attitude which seemed to indicate a warm, accepting feeling toward the person the individual described as similar to himself.

In line with the then prevailing thinking about groups, we had expected that a psychologically close, warm feeling among fellow group members would increase each man's satisfaction and his feeling of security. This, in turn, was expected to lead to less anxiety about one's status in the group and subsequently greater concern with team performance. In fact, however, the correlations between group cohesiveness and performance tended to be negative. At least in this set of groups, the teams in which squad members chose their friends as coworkers performed more poorly than did those in which the team members' best friend and best coworker were not necessarily the same person.

This was by no means the only hypothesis which misfired. We also thought that groups in which the leaders perceived their most- and their least-preferred coworker in an accepting, positive manner would be most effective. Quite the contrary results occurred. When we correlated the percent of games won by midseason with the leader's AS scores, we found substantial negative relations ($-.63$ with ASp, $-.41$ with ASn, and $-.69$ with ASo). This suggested that the leader's warm, accepting interpersonal relationship at the beginning of the season tended to interfere with team performance later on.

These results suggest very strongly that the good basketball team is one which, in a manner of speaking, relegates the satisfactions of good interpersonal relationships to second place in the hierarchy of values. The ineffective team seems concerned to a larger degree with good interpersonal relations, the effective team is concerned first with performance. This finding fits well with the earlier discussion. It is also supported by statements of several coaches that the team with overly close interpersonal ties among teammates tends to set up shots for team members on the basis of friendship rather than ability or advantage to the team, i.e., the particular boys who are "set up" might not be the best players on the team or they might not be in the best position to make a basket. In close games this will, of course, be decisive.

A validation study was conducted toward the end of the season. We selected seven teams from the upper third and five from the lower third of the basketball teams in the state on the basis of their end of season record. Identical tests and procedures were used. As before, the leaders with low ASo scores ($r_{.bis.}$ − .51, p < .023) (though not low ASp scores) had the best teams. A further check of the end of season performance of the fourteen original teams showed that the relationships, while in the same direction, had become weaker. Some attenuation is, of course, to be expected over time since attitudes change. Similarly, informal comments suggested that leadership of a number of teams had shifted, especially if the team had experienced a losing season.

Surveying teams.   A second study of informal teams dealt with surveying parties (Fiedler, 1953). These were twenty-two teams each composed of three to four civil-engineering students who were taking a required course in land surveying. The field work for this course was conducted at the University of Illinois surveying camp in Northern Minnesota. The teams were assigned to six sections; each section consisting of three or four surveying parties was supervised by one instructor. The parties performed fairly standardized and structured tasks of measuring and mapping land, and the students then computed the various measurements. Grades in this course were assigned to students on the basis of individual performance and not on the basis of teamwork. These teams differed, therefore, in this important respect from basketball teams, which not only competed fiercely with other teams but in which each member competed with others on the squad for starting positions.

The major criterion was the team's accuracy of surveying. Each surveying party was ranked by the instructor who based his judgments on the students' calculations and maps as well as on the fairly intensive knowledge he had obtained in the course of supervising the team over a period of six weeks. The instructor was also asked to judge the speed or efficiency with which each team went about its task and the smoothness of the work relationships. The student members of each team were similarly asked to rank the teams in their section from best to poorest.

As in the study of basketball teams, each group member described himself as well as his most-preferred and his least-preferred coworkers. In contrast to the manner of rating in the basketball study, these students (and subjects in all subsequent studies) were asked to think of *all the persons* with whom they had ever worked. They were then instructed to describe the one they could work with best and the one they could work with least well. Thus, the most- and least-preferred coworkers were chosen from among all the people the individual had ever known and not just from

among those with whom he happened to work at the time. These judgments turned out to be more stable than ratings based on actual coworkers
in the team, and the ratings were made on a revised scale which used a
more reliable unforced-item form.

As before, we collected sociometric preference scores. These were
obtained by asking each member to name the individuals in his section
(that is, about twelve to fifteen students assigned to teams under the same
instructor although not necessarily his own work group) whom he liked
best as a work companion, as a friend, as a potential study partner, etc.

The major hypothesis of this study was derived from the basketball team
results. As we can see from Table 4-1, the ASo scores of the team leaders
again correlated negatively with team performance. In other words,
leaders of good teams saw big differences between the most- and least-
preferred coworkers. Leaders of poor teams saw these two opposites on
the coworker dimension as relatively similar. The results of this study thus
confirmed the previous findings.

The study also permitted us to check again whether the members of
good teams in effect tend to renounce the immediate pleasure of good
interpersonal relations for the long-term goals of effective but personally
less pleasant teamwork.

While the results are certainly not as compelling as one might wish,
they are consistent with this formulation. We find, for instance, that the
groups in which the members had the highest liking for one another, in

TABLE 4-1   Correlation of Informal Leader's ASo Score with Team Effectiveness in Basketball and Surveying Teams

Sample	Criterion	Statistic	Corre-lation	N	P
Basketball teams I	Percent games won at midseason	Rho	−.69	14	(.01)*
Basketball teams II	Percent games won at midseason	r_{pb}	−.58	12	.05
Surveying parties	Instructor's rating of team accuracy	r	−.51	22	.025

* This probability estimate must be interpreted with caution since the first study was
exploratory.
SOURCE: Adapted from Fiedler, 1958, by permission of the University of Illinois Press.

which the same fellow team members tended to be chosen as best co-workers and best friends, tended to be poorer than less cohesive or congenial teams. Likewise, teams which the students considered to be best, presumably because team members got along well, turned out to be somewhat less accurate (rank order correlation of .23). Finally, the men did not especially like teams with task-oriented, psychologically distant, low-ASo leaders, as shown by a low but negative correlation of −.34, although these teams tended to be more effective.

The picture of the effective informal task team as it emerges from our studies thus seems to be a rather tense, psychologically somewhat distant group which fares best under a directive, managing leader.

Validation: Scoring the "How Supervise" test.   An independent study conducted by C. H. Hawkins (1962), then at the University of Minnesota, supports the results obtained in our research. Hawkins' investigation involved sixty-seven pairs of students who were given the task of jointly answering items on the "How Supervise" test. This test measures knowledge of good supervisory practices. Items are answered by indicating whether a statement is true, false, or questionable. The criterion score was based on the number of items the pair of subjects could complete in the allotted time. A chairman was designated by the experimenter, although he was given no special functions except to report the results. We are thus dealing here with a leader who has weak position power and a highly structured test situation.

The performance of groups with high-ASo leaders and groups with low-ASo leaders were compared by means of analysis of variance. As hypothesized, the teams under low-ASo leaders were significantly more productive than those under leaders with high ASo scores. Hawkins' data therefore support the results obtained in our earlier work.

SUMMARY

We have here presented the first set of studies we conducted on leadership and group effectiveness. These groups had fairly structured tasks and relatively weak leader position power. They fall, therefore, into Octant II.

The study of two separate samples of high school basketball teams provided the opportunity to obtain highly face-valid performance criteria (which also turned out to be quite reliable) as well as a large pool of groups from which we could choose our sample.

The basketball studies showed that the successful teams tended to choose highly task-oriented persons as informal leaders while the less successful teams chose the more relationship-oriented group members as informal leaders.

A validation study was conducted, using twenty-two surveying parties. These teams, consisting of three to four students in civil engineering, were required to measure and map land. Ratings of accuracy in surveying were obtained from the instructors of the various sections and correlated with the ASo scores of the teams' informal leaders. We again found that the informal leaders of successful teams tended to be low-ASo persons while the informal leaders of less successful, but more pleasant, teams tended to have high-ASo leaders. A study conducted by Hawkins (1960) further supported the findings of our early studies.

These findings raised the question whether ASo might be a leadership trait and whether the choice of an ASo person as informal leader indicated the team's motivation to succeed on the task, or whether the team was successful because it happened to have chosen a low-ASo person as its leader. This question was partly answered by studies reported in the next chapter.

5 GROUPS WITH STRUCTURED TASKS AND POWERFUL LEADER POSITIONS (Octants I and V)

Groups in these octants are defined by (1) a structured task and (2) an explicit role structure in which the leader's position is relatively powerful. In addition to the role differentiation between leader and members, many such groups also have specialist positions. The members of these groups are, therefore, not interchangeable. This is the case, for example, in bomber crews where one man is trained as pilot, one as radio operator, and another as flight engineer or navigator.

Some writers define any group with a recognized division of labor as an organization (see Gibb, 1954). While one cannot object to this definition on logical grounds, we prefer to reserve the label "organization" for interrelated systems of groups which work together in accomplishing a common goal. Teams in which members are assigned to specific, non-interchangeable jobs are here called formal groups.

We had obtained highly promising results in our studies of informal groups, which showed that teams under a task-oriented, task-controlling leader performed better than did teams under relationship-oriented leaders. The obvious next step was to determine whether similar relations would occur in formally organized groups as well. As mentioned before, most task groups in our society are, in fact, formally organized; it is very rare that a task group consisting of more than a few men can operate for any length of time without the guidance of a formally recognized leader.

The first studies, conducted with military crews, were expected to answer two main questions. The first of these was, of course, whether effective teams would again have task-oriented, managing (low-ASo) leaders. The second, more theoretically oriented, question concerned the causality of the relationship.

We had found a correlation between the leader's ASo and group performance in formal task groups. This might mean that the low ASo leader caused the group to perform more effectively. In other words, the person with low ASo scores might have better leadership ability. It is equally possible, however, that low-ASo persons, being task-oriented, express or symbolize the group's feeling about the task. Group members who are highly motivated might express their motivation by preferring task-oriented leaders to relationship-oriented leaders. The group members' choice might then reflect group morale and motivation and it may be the group morale rather than the leader's style which results in good team performance.

If the results support the first alternative, we would have to conclude that low-ASo people behave in some way which enhances group effective-ness. Such a finding would be quite contrary, however, to the many studies reviewed by Stogdill (1948), Gibb (1954), and later by Mann (1959) which showed no evidence that a leadership trait existed, i.e., that having certain personality traits or attributes would make one a good leader.

The question of whether ASo might be a leadership-effectiveness trait nevertheless deserved to be answered. One method for testing it was to work with groups which had an appointed leader. Since the leader in these formal teams was not selected by his group, his having a high or low ASo score could not, in this case, be an indication of the group's morale.

One minor study was conducted with Naval ROTC cadets in which ASo scores of reputedly good leaders were compared with scores of reputedly poor leaders. This study identified good and poor leaders on the basis of sociometric peer nominations by fellow ROTC students and by ratings of tactical officers. Men rated as good leaders did not differ in ASo scores from those rated as poor leaders, and a simple trait hypothesis did not seem to be the answer. Ratings of leadership are, however, notoriously un-trustworthy. Therefore, further work was undertaken on real-life groups.

The bomber-crew study. The first empirical investigation in this series was conducted in 1953 on seventy B-29 bomber crews (Fiedler, 1955). These crews came from four successive training classes at Randolph Air Force Base, where they were undergoing crew training preparatory for action in the Korean conflict. Many of the men were "recallees," that is, reservists who had served in World War II and who were less than enthu-siastic about having to return to duty. They were well aware of the fact, however, that the training they received was essential not only for the accomplishment of their future mission but also for their personal safety and their chance of survival.

Each B-29 bomber normally carried a complement of five officers and six enlisted men. The aircraft commander, irrespective of rank, occupied the formal leadership position in the crew. His position power was quite high. (In several of these crews the navigator, radar observer, or even the copilot held higher military rank than the aircraft commander.)

The primary mission of these crews was radar bombing, which was carried out according to fairly detailed standard operating instructions. The tasks were, therefore, structured. Simulated radar bombing runs were made at considerable altitudes, frequently in cloudy weather or at night when the crew had to rely on navigational aids and radar readings for locating and hitting the target. Only the radar observer and navigator had radar equipment. These two officers were, therefore, considered to be keymen on the crew in radar bombing missions in the sense that they performed the critical task-relevant functions.

Radar bombing was simulated by means of complex airborne radio equipment and ground-based computers, which indicated the average estimated accuracy of Radar Bomb scores (RBS) measured in Circular Error scores over ten missions. These Radar Bomb scores, corrected for equipment errors and weather conditions, served as the major criterion during training on simulated radar bombing missions. Reliability was estimated to be .45 (Forgays and Knoell, 1952).

Visual bombing—again a highly structured task—was conducted under conditions requiring low-altitude flying, generally in the daytime. In these tasks, the bombardier, manning the bomb sight, performs the key functions on which the success of the mission depends. The criterion for this task was the Percent of Satisfactory Visual Bomb Runs (%SVB) as indicated by the circular error of bomb drops over various ranges. This criterion was somewhat unsatisfactory, however, since nearly half the crews obtained a perfect score of 100 percent accuracy.

ASo scores were obtained from all available crew members. We also obtained sociometric preference scores. As in the study of surveying parties, the test instructions asked each man to describe the responses of the coworker with whom he had worked best and the responses of the coworker with whom he had worked least well in the past. (Note again that this did *not* have to be a fellow crew member.) The test was given in two sessions, four weeks apart. Reliability of ASo scores based on this eighty-item test was .86 for 178 men.

We originally hypothesized that the Assumed Similarity between Opposites score (ASo) of the aircraft commander would correlate negatively with his crew's performance, i.e., that the task-oriented, psychologically distant leaders would obtain better results than the relationship-oriented, considerate leaders. This hypothesis turned out to be unsupported by the results. While the aircraft commander's ASo score did correlate −.24 with Radar Bomb scores in the fifty-five crews for which we had adequate data, it did not correlate significantly or even in the predicted direction with other criteria. In fact, the intercorrelation among criteria was essentially zero, which, in itself, indicates that no single leader attribute could correlate with all group performance criteria.

On the other hand, it will be recalled that the leaders of basketball and surveying teams had been identified on the basis of sociometric preference questions. It seemed worthwhile, therefore, to check the analogous case for bomber crews. We asked whether the relationship between leader ASc and the criteria might only hold for formal leaders who were, in addition sociometrically accepted as leaders by the members of their crews, that is, leaders who enjoyed good relations with their crews and who were therefore, very influential. Again we found no simple relations.

After running a large number of different analyses, some meaningful sociometric patterns finally did emerge. These analyses suggested something we should have known all along. We had to pay special attention to the fact that all members of the crew were not equally important in performing the specific tasks which contributed to a particular crew performance. For example, in working with the Radar Bomb score criterion only two of the crew members aside from the leader had any direct influence on the crew performance criterion. These were the radar observer and the navigator, whose stations were equipped with radarscopes and bomb-release buttons. The aircraft commander's relationship with these two keymen was, therefore, especially important as compared, for instance, with his relationship with the tail gunner, whose function had no effect on radar bombing. For this reason, we divided the crews which accepted their aircraft commander into those in which the aircraft commander sociometrically endorsed these two officers, those in which he endorsed them only mildly, and those in which he ignored them in his rating and, by implication, rejected them.

The analyses based on this subsampling procedure showed that the task-oriented, low-Aso leaders seemed most effective in crews in which they had good relations with the crew, that is, in which (1) they were sociometrically accepted and (2) expressed strong endorsement of the keymen. The relationship-oriented, considerate (high-ASo) leaders were most effective in crews which also accepted them, but in which they rejected these key crew members (Table 5-1). These were only moderately good leader-member relations. A negative correlation between the aircraft

TABLE 5-1   Correlation of the Aircraft Commander's ASo Score with Radar Bombing Criterion under Selected Sociometric Relations between the Aircraft Commander and the Keymen

Sociometric Condition *	Rho	N	p	Octant
AC = MPC → VO/N	−.81	10	(.01)†	I
− VO/N	−.14	6	−	−
↛ VO/N	.43	6	−	V
AC = MPC → VO/N	−.03	18	−	−
− VO/N	−.80	5	−	VIII–A‡
↛ VO/N	−.67	7	−	VIII–A

AC = Aircraft commander	→ High sociometric choice
VO = Radar observer	− Neutral sociometric choice
N = Navigator	↛ Low sociometric choice
MPC = Most-preferred coworker	

* The high sociometric choice symbol (→) indicates that either the VO and N, or both, were given ranks 1 to 2 by the AC. The low sociometric choice (↛) indicates that both the VO and N were given ranks 3.5 to 10. All other cases are in the neutral (−) category. These cutoff points are in part based on the desire to divide the groups into three equal subsamples; however, the second rank is considered indicative of high preference, even though this makes the highly liked group somewhat larger than the other two subgroups.

† As this study explored many hypotheses, tests of significance are not interpretable.

‡ These results do not fall into any octant in the original classification scheme. There was no octant which incorporated groups with *very poor* leader-member relations. Such octants, in groups with structured tasks and high leader position power will be designated as VIII–A.

SOURCE: Adapted from Fiedler, 1955, by permission of the American Psychological Association.

commander's ASo and team performance was obtained in crews in which the aircraft commander and his keymen had strong mutual choices. A zero correlation was obtained in crews in which these choices indicated poorer relations (Table 5-2).

The findings obtained in this study are quite complex and difficult to interpret. They suggested that leadership style influences crew performance, but that the influence of the leader is strongly modified by his interpersonal relations within the crew. Task-oriented leaders could perform well in crews in which they had a very good relationship with other crew members; considerate, relationship-oriented leaders performed

TABLE 5-2   Correlation of the Aircraft Commander's ASo Score with the Radar Bombing Criterion in Crews in Which the AC Reciprocates his Keymen's Choices *

Sociometric Condition	Rho	N	p
AC ↔ VO and/or N	−.48	22	(.05)
AC ↮ VO and/or N	.05	27	

* See footnotes to Table 5-1.

better in crews in which their relationship with their keymen was poor even though they were accepted by the other members of the crew.

Table 5-1 also shows that the correlation between the aircraft commander's Leadership Style score, ASo, and the performance of his crew was again negative in sets of crews in which his relationship with group members was relatively poor. These latter were crews which did not accept their aircraft commander and in which the aircraft commander had a relatively poor relationship with his keymen. The overall relationship between leadership style and group performance thus appeared to be curvilinear, with managing, controlling, psychologically distant leadership styles most appropriate in crews in which the leader-member relations were very good or very poor. Relations intermediate in this respect seemed to call for a considerate, psychologically close leadership style. Since the samples were very small, we had to set the results aside until the findings could be validated in further studies. In view of the complexity of these relations, it was nearly ten years before these findings began to make sense.

Results which supported the findings for crews with very good and with moderately good leader-group relations were also obtained with the second crew-performance criterion, namely with the Percent of Satisfactory Visual Bomb Runs. This score correlates only .08 with Radar Bomb score and probably is, therefore, independent of the other criterion (Table 5-3). The biserial correlations obtained for these data, while not significant, were in the expected direction and again suggested that groups with strong position power and high task structure require different leadership when the leader's relationship with his group is good than when it is less satisfactory.

These complex results were tentatively interpreted as indicating that effective team performance requires an optimal psychological distance

TABLE 5-3   Correlations between Aircraft Commanders' ASo Scores and Percent Visual Bomb Run Criterion

Sociometric Pattern	Rho	N	Octant
Aircraft commander is sociometrically most-chosen crew member and strongly endorses bombardier	−.52	7	I
Aircraft commander is neutral to bombardier	.47	9	V
Aircraft commander does not endorse bombardier	.30	5	VIII–A

between leader and key crew members. A naturally distant leader would need to have good relations with his men to mitigate his distant leadership style. A naturally close, considerate leader would be better off if he did not get along too well with is keymen, since his personal warmth and permissiveness would tend to make him too lenient with liked crew members and perhaps too dependent upon their goodwill for the maintenance of good and harmonious relations within the team. While these interpretations had to be modified to some extent to take account of new findings, in our later work they served well as working hypotheses in a number of studies which were conducted to validate these relations.

The tank-crew study. This investigation was conducted for the purpose of validating the findings which emerged from the bomber-crew study. It tested the hypothesis that the leader's ASo score would be (1) negatively correlated in crews in which the leader is most-preferred crew member and sociometrically endorses his keyman, but (2) positively correlated in crews in which the sociometrically accepted leader rejects (or fails to endorse) his keyman. The findings on crews which did not sociometrically accept their leaders could not be tested in this study: seventeen of the twenty-five crews accepted their leaders, leaving only eight tank-crew leaders who could be considered as having been rejected by their crews. These were not included in these analyses.

The data came from an experiment known as "Project STALK," which was conducted in 1953 by the Ballistics Research Laboratory of the United States Army. This experiment was designed to compare the performance of five models of army tanks as well as certain items of tank equipment.

The basic experimental design involved twenty-five crews from a fairly typical tank battalion. The Army General Classification Test scores of these men ranged from 58 to 139, with a mean of 90.6. About 30 percent of the 142 men in the group had completed no more than eight years of school.

Each crew consisted of five men, viz., a tank commander (TC) in charge of four men, namely, a gunner, a driver, a loader, and a bow gunner. The experiment was designed as a modified Greco-Latin square: each platoon, consisting of five crews, worked with a different tank model in each of five phases of the experiment. Criterion scores for our purposes could thus be obtained by comparing crews within a platoon during one particular phase or by comparing all platoons during all phases.

The leaders' ASo scores were obtained from a test similar to that used in the B-29 study, but containing only sixty items, with a split-half reliability of .91. Leader-group relations were measured by means of sociometric questionnaires. These asked each crew member to name the men of his platoon whom he preferred as fellow crew members, who would be likely to get battlefield commissions, whom he would like to have as friends, etc. Crew members were also asked to list those whom they least preferred.

Each crew competed with other crews of the same platoon in all phases. The two main criteria for assessing the performance of these crews were (1) the average number of seconds required to hit various targets (T/H) and (2) the average number of seconds required to travel from target to target (T/T). These again seemed to be independent performance criteria. The correlation between these two scores was −.07.

The results of the analyses clearly supported the findings obtained in the bomber-crew study. The task-oriented leader with low ASo score obtained better performance in situations in which the leader-group relations were good; considerate (high-ASo) leaders had better performance from crews when the leader-keyman relations were moderately poor (Table 5-4).

The results of the tank- and the bomber-crew studies indicated that good relationship between leader and group members requires one type of leader attitude for effective performance while a poor relationship requires a different leader attitude. These studies also showed that the leader's attitude as measured by ASo affects the performance of the group rather than representing merely the group's expression of its own preference. In other words, while the correlation between ASo and performance

TABLE 5-4   Correlations between Tank Commanders' ASo Score and Crew Performance in Crews Which Accepted Their Leaders

| | | Leader's Preference for Keyman | | | | | |
| | | High | | Neutral | | Negative | |
Criterion	Keyman	Rho	N	Rho	N	Rho	N
Average time to hit target	Gunner	−.60	6	.11	6	.60	5
Average time to travel to target	Driver	−.33	5	.39	6	.43	6

in informal groups could have been interpreted as a reflection of the group's morale by choosing a task-related, controlling leader, this interpretation would not apply in cases where the leader was appointed. Rather, the leadership style and the leader-member relations interacted in influencing the group performance.

While it may be of historical interest to present the theory to which these complex findings gave rise, we will try to spare the reader and assume that these earlier interpretations (Fiedler, 1958), by grace of some kind fate or a much-needed invention, have simply been "depublished." We will, therefore, defer the presentation of a theory until later.

A number of additional studies, with groups falling into Octants I and V, have been conducted by the author and his associates, as well as by several independent investigators. These are here discussed in brief outline.

Antiaircraft artillery crews.   One study by Hutchins and Fiedler (1960) investigated team performance as well as quasi-therapeutic relations in fifty-three antiaircraft crews of an air defense command. These units, which are commanded by a senior noncommissioned officer, varied in size from six to seventeen men. The crew commander sets up work schedules, supervises the crew's task and housekeeping functions, and administers disciplinary action for minor infractions. The leader's position power in these groups is clearly high.

The primary mission of these groups is the defense against aerial attack of their geographical region. Although crews vary in specific tasks, the gun crews are required to (1) detect and "lock" their guns onto unidentified targets with their electronic equipment, and all crews must (2) maintain their radar sets or guns and (3) man the equipment as quickly as possible when called to battle stations. Adequate performance scores which would be comparable for all groups could not be developed since equipment varied from station to station and for different types of crews. The criterion of group effectiveness was therefore based on ratings by officers in charge of various crews under their command. Where these ratings could be correlated with objective performance criteria, they showed quite satisfactory agreement with these measures. The task of each of these groups, which is spelled out in detailed standard operating instructions, is, of course, highly structured.

The results of this study supported previous findings. Correlations between leaders' ASo scores and group performance ratings were $-.19$ for all groups, but $-.36$ (significant at $p < .05$ one-tailed) for the twenty-six groups which sociometrically accepted their crew leader.

As will be recalled, we had subdivided the sample in the bomber-crew study into subgroups on the basis of the aircraft commander's relationship with his group insofar as this could be inferred from the pattern of sociometric preference scores. The sample of antiaircraft units lent itself to a similar analysis. The crews were subdivided into the ten crews which most strongly endorsed their crew commander (Octant I), the ten which most strongly rejected their commander (Octant VIII-A), and the ten crews intermediate in the sociometric preference ratings (Octant V).

The results of this analysis closely paralleled those obtained in the B-29 bomber-crew study (Table 5-5). We again found that the directive, managing leaders performed best in very favorable or in very unfavorable group situations, while the considerate, nondirective, high-ASo leaders performed best in situations intermediate in favorableness for the leader.

Two points should be noted, however. First, the analysis presented in Table 5-5 was made long after the original data had been collected. Second, the particular analysis summarized in Table 5-5 was in part a validation of the hypothesis which will be presented in a later chapter. This integrative hypothesis did not emerge until quite a few years after the antiaircraft crew study had been completed.

TABLE 5-5   Correlations between Leader-LPC Scores and Antiaircraft Artillery Crew Performance

	Rho	N	Octant
Most highly chosen crew commanders	−.34	10	I
Middle range in sociometric choices	.49	10	V
Lowest chosen crew commanders	−.42	10	VIII–A

Infantry squads. A massive investigation was conducted by Havron et al. (1954), under contract with the United States Army's Personnel Research Board, which involved performance and training tests of infantry rifle squads. ASo scales were among the large number of measures administered to the men of these squads. The criterion of performance consisted of highly standardized and carefully scaled ratings of squad behavior under standard field test conditions which were developed at the Infantry Center, Fort Benning, Georgia.

The correlations between the ASo scores and group performance were low and insignificant when computed for all squads irrespective of the sociometric preference patterns within the squads. However, in squads which sociometrically endorsed their leader, ASo correlated significantly in the expected direction ($-.33$).

Combat engineer squads. A study by Julian et al. (1964) dealt with squads of a combat engineer battalion. This study was conducted to investigate quasi-therapeutic relations of groups, as was the study by Hutchins and Fiedler described above. In addition to adjustment criteria, ratings of squad performance were obtained. These were based in part on standard performance tasks, such as digging machine-gun emplacements, building pontoon bridges, or laying wire fences.

The leaders of these groups were noncommissioned officers who supervise the work teams and form the link between squad members and higher echelons of the organization. This study utilized the more easily obtained and interpretable LPC scores, i.e., the rating of the least-preferred coworker obtained with Semantic Differential scales. Octant I groups, which sociometrically accepted their leader, yielded a correlation between squad leader LPC and performance of $-.39$, which is consistent with other results presented in this section.

OTHER STUDIES

Hawkins conducted a series of studies at the University of Minnesota (1962) which investigated the relationship between Assumed Similarity scores and group performance. He tested sales-display teams and gasoline service station crews. The former set up sales displays in various stores according to detailed company instructions. The latter provided the usual products and services of the gasoline stations, part of a chain of service stations. These were managed in accordance with detailed standard operating instructions. Performance was evaluated by inspections of records and stock rooms and by spot checks to determine the compliance with company instructions.

Hawkins' data showed in both sets of these groups that the team leaders or managers with low ASo scores performed more effectively than did those with high ASo scores.

It is unfortunate for the purposes of our discussion that sociometric preferences scores or other indices of leader-member relations were not reported. It is, therefore, not possible to assign these groups unequivocally to octants in our model.[1]

SUMMARY

This chapter has presented studies of various military combat units as well as work teams in business. The military groups, which have a relatively structured task and high leader position power, fall into Octant I or Octant V depending upon whether they have good or poor leader-member relations. Groups with good leader-member relations performed better under task-oriented low-ASo or -LPC leaders. Groups with relatively poor leader-member relations performed better under relationship-oriented, high-ASo or -LPC leaders. Subsequent reanalyses showed that task-oriented, low-ASo or low-LPC leaders also perform better in groups in which the members reject the leader. These findings have required that we define an additional cell, Octant VIII-A, in the classification schema for interacting groups described in Chapter 2.

TECHNICAL NOTE

The need for classifying groups is, of course, obvious as soon as we attempt to specify the type of leadership style which will be most appropriate in various situations. The hypothesis itself demands a typology. However it also seems worth pointing out that the typing or classification of group

---

[1] One might speculate, of course, that the leader-member relations in these two sets of teams would span the range from very good relations to intermediate to very poor leader-member relations. Since these teams have highly structured tasks and high leader position power, they would then fall into Octants I, V, and VIII-A respectively. We would then expect negative correlations between leader ASo and performance in Octants I and VIII-A and a positive correlation only in Octant V. It is, therefore, not inconsistent with our hypothesis that the overall relationship obtained by Hawkins would be in the negative direction.

s a way of making a sample more homogeneous and thus enhancing the
probability of obtaining statistically significant results.

The situation is somewhat analogous to that involved in refining an
achievement or personality test by making the items homogeneous. We
take a pool of items and we then construct a tentative scale. This scale is
defined by means of statistical techniques which attempt to increase the
test's reliability. We may run correlations between each of the items and
the total score in order to eliminate those items which do not belong,
which are somehow outside the realm of discourse.

In our studies we have approached this problem by subsampling cases
which fall into the same category or classification. For example, we have
frequently obtained a sizable sample of task groups. We have then attempted to correlate the leader's LPC score or his intelligence score with
group performance. These attempts generally have not led to interpretable
results until we subsampled. This may be seen in the following case: Let
us say that we wish to determine the contribution of leader intelligence to
performance. This relationship is likely to be zero, one reason being that
all leaders are not equally powerful in their groups. Unless the leader has
influence in the group, his intelligence score is unlikely to correlate with
group performance. Only after we refine the sample so that it is limited to
those groups in which the leader does have influence do we find a relationship between a leader attribute and group performance which is
higher than that for the total sample.

The rationale for this procedure is fairly obvious. We clearly need
homogeneity not only among test items, but also among the objects of a
study. This rationale underlies the procedures utilized throughout the program which is here described.

6 CONSTITUENT TASK GROUPS IN COMPLEX ORGANIZATIONS

Chapter 5 dealt with small task groups which operate at the first level of the organizational hierarchy. The present chapter discusses groups within organizations in which the leadership is distributed over at least two levels of management. The specific problems of leadership at a higher level in the organization will be discussed further in Chapter 14. We shall here again be concerned with the performance of work groups in which the leader's position power is high and the task is relatively structured (Octants I and V), but in which the leader's functions include the coordination of subgroups in his organization. We shall also discuss policy-making groups which develop guidelines for the executive groups in an organization (Octants IV and VIII).

Military units, which we discussed in Chapter 5, represent a rather special type of task group. The military crew is, as a rule, a relatively short-lived group and it operates under fairly strict discipline. It is typically seen by its members, and especially by draftees, as a transitory work situation which must be endured for a period stretching from a few short months to, at most, one or two years before a man is transferred, promoted or discharged to return to his civilian pursuits. Military units generally have an involuntary membership. The individual group member is rarely given much say in choosing his coworkers or his supervisors. While the member of an industrial work crew is by no means his own man, he has somewhat more latitude since he can leave the group as a last resort. Alternatively, he can, in concert with others, protest his treatment and working conditions or strike. Since it is to the organization's advantage to reduce labor turnover by providing good working conditions, men tend to remain in industrial work units for much longer periods of time than could be expected in military crews.

These and similar differences between military and civilian work groups made it advisable to determine whether the results we had obtained in military units could be generalized to other groups, as for example, industrial and business organizations. Two complex organizations were investigated. The first one was a large steel mill, which permitted us to study four open-hearth shops. The other was a federation of small consumer sales cooperatives, which enabled us to study the boards and management teams of thirty-two different companies.

OPEN–HEARTH STEEL SHOPS

The steel industry in the United States has enjoyed unusually low industrial labor turnover. It is not uncommon that the same men work together for ten or more years. A skilled workman or a man at the lower management level tends to view his association with the company as permanent and as likely to last for the duration of his working life.

Four open-hearth shops were involved in one investigation. The working conditions in these four shops were quite comparable, although the equipment varied somewhat from shop to shop. Open-hearth shops are operated on a twenty-four-hour, seven day week basis, with each shift working eight hours. Each shift (or turn) has a full complement of first- and second-line supervisors and their crews. Since one turn is off duty in any one twenty-four-hour period, each shop requires four turns. A total of sixteen turns constituted our sample.

Shops are organized with two second-level supervisors in charge of each turn: a general foreman and a senior melter. The general foreman and his subordinate stock and pit foremen conduct the supporting operations of raw-material assembly and final steel pouring. The senior melter and his subordinate junior melters are in charge of the manufacturing process and they are thus most directly responsible for the performance of the shift. In three of the four shops the senior melter supervised two junior melters and their five to eight furnace crews. In the fourth shop, the senior melter had one junior melter reporting to him.

The index of group effectiveness was based on the time elapsed from one "tap" (pouring molten metal from the furnace) to the next tap of a particular furnace. Steel company officials regard this "tap-to-tap time" as the most important production index, and this criterion is generally accepted by the men and lower management officials.

The reliability of tap-to-tap time scores, standardized by shops, was computed on over 25,000 batches or "heats" of steel obtained over a seven-month period preceding the testing. We excluded the summer months on the recommendation of company officials in order to avoid the atypical work patterns during vacation schedules. An even- versus odd-month split-half procedure was employed to estimate reliability of these scores. This was .82 for 16 shifts.

TABLE 6-1   Correlations (Rho) between ASo of Various Supervisors and Average Turn Tap-to-tap Time

Supervisor ASo	N^*	Rho	p
Production crews			
Senior melter (2nd level)	15	−.54	<.05
Junior melter (1st level)	28	.10	—
Support crews			
General foreman (2nd level)	15	−.13	—
Stock foreman (1st level)	15	−.42	—
Pit foreman (1st level)	14	−.72	<.01
Supervisor average	16	−.71	<.01

* N varies due to missing data.

As shown in Table 6-1, the correlations between average tap-to-tap time and ASo scores over all shifts in the sample are significant in the case of senior melters and pit foremen. The correlation falls short of an acceptable significance level for stock foremen, and it is negligible for general foremen. The average ASo of the foremen and senior melter on each turn was also significantly related to the performance criterion of the shift. These data thus support the conclusion that groups of this nature require managing, task-oriented leaders.

It is noteworthy that these correlations in the case of open-hearth shifts were obtained without reference to the sociometric preference ratings indicating the degree to which the various leaders of the groups were accepted by their subordinates. It is also noteworthy that the performance of open-hearth crews could be predicted more accurately from the leadership style scores of the production manager at the second level (the senior melter foreman) than from the scores of his first-level supervisors (the junior melters). This point struck us as curious at the time, although we were unable to interpret this difference with any confidence.

It was only after developing the present theory that we further reanalyzed the open-hearth data. We divided the set of shifts into (1) those with good leader-member relations (those in which the senior melter was highly accepted by other foremen on sociometric ratings), (2) those in which the acceptance of the senior melter foreman fell into the intermediate range, and (3) those in which the senior melter foreman obtained very low sociometric acceptance ratings. Correlations between senior melter ASo and tap-to-tap time were then computed for each of these

TABLE 6-2 Correlations between Senior Melter ASo Scores and Production Criterion (Tap-to-tap Time) in Three Octants

Leader-Member Relations Measured by Sociometric Relations	Senior Melters		Junior Melters		Octant
	Rho	N	Rho	N	
Most chosen	−.30	5	−.09	9	I
Intermediate	.30	5	.48	9	V
Least chosen	−.90	5	−.52	8	VIII–A

subsets, each containing five groups. A similar analysis was made for the junior melter foremen. We again found negative correlations in sets of groups in which the foremen were either highly chosen or in which they were relatively rejected. The ASo scores of junior melters correlated positively with performance in groups in which they received intermediately favorable sociometric ratings. The results of this analysis are shown in Table 6-2. As can be seen, these results are highly consistent with those obtained in bomber crews and antiaircraft artillery crews. These and similar results will be discussed more fully later in this chapter.

CONSUMER SALES COOPERATIVES

The second investigation of complex organizations dealt with thirty-two farm-supply companies (Godfrey, Fiedler, and Hall, 1959), a group of cooperative service companies owned by farmer cooperators but essentially run as autonomous business organizations.

The open-hearth study already showed that second-level supervisors have considerable influence over group performance at the employee level. Would we find similar results in the more typical management situation in a business concern in which the general manager directs and coordinates the work of several diverse but interlocking departments? In addition, we were interested to see the effects of the policy- and decision-making group, the board of directors, on the executive group consisting of the general manager and the assistant managers in the company.

The management teams, that is, the general manager and the two to four assistant managers, have a fairly structured task and a leader with high position power. Given good leader-member relations, these teams would fall into Octant I; given relatively poor leader-member relations, they would fall into Octant V. The boards of directors were, however, judged to have low leader position power and an unstructured task. They would, therefore, fall into Octants IV and VIII, depending upon the respective leader-member relations. It seems meaningful, in this particular case, to depart from the organization of this book and to present the data on boards as well as on management teams together so that we can see more clearly what the interrelations among these two sets of groups might be.

The thirty-two farm-supply companies belong to a statewide organization of farmer-owned cooperatives. The companies ranged in size from nine to sixty-five employees. Each of the 101 companies in the system typically serves the area encompassed by one county, although some companies serve two small counties in the state. The thirty-two campanies in our sample came from among the more typical rural and farming counties in the state. Only those companies were included which had had the same general manager for a minimum of three years prior to the study. All of the companies which were selected cooperated in the investigation.

Each of the companies is headed by a board of directors which is elected annually by the company's shareholders. The main difference between these cooperative companies and a regular corporation lies in the fact that each shareholder is limited in the number of shares he may purchase and that each member of the board is entitled to one vote, irrespective of the number of shares or shareholders he represents.

As in other companies, the board elects its own president, vice-president, secretary, and treasurer. The board determines company policies and monitors the overall operations of the company. It hires the company's general manager as well as the several assistant managers who head the various departments within the company. There is usually an office manager, a sales manager, and an operations manager. A few companies have warehouse managers or managers who are in charge of various product lines, for example, a petroleum manager.

The general manager is responsible to the board. He proposes policy changes, prepares plans for operating the business, and implements the board's policies and decisions. Some boards become involved in specific operating decisions, others do not. Some are strongly guided by advice from the statewide federation to which the companies belong, while others tend to ignore it.

Most companies within the system sell the same products, follow the same or very similar personnel, sales, credit, and operating policies, and use the same financial accounting and reporting methods. It was thus possible to compare the performance of various companies in a statistically meaningful way, especially since the state organization maintains very careful records of company sales, overhead expenses, and net income, which are used for evaluating the performance of each company in the state. These records also serve as the basis for incentive pay, that is, for computing the general manager's bonus as well as awarding the prizes and awards which are given to the outstanding assistant managers and managers on a statewide basis.

Company performance is measured by two indices. These are (1) the percent of net income of the company over a three-year period of time, computed as a proportion of gross sales volume, and (2) the percent of operating expenses (salaries, rents, depreciation, etc.), expressed as a proportion of total income, again based on a three-year period. Net income and operating efficiency measures correlated .61 with each other. Intercorrelations over the three-year period for the indices were in the neighborhood of .80, which shows that the measures are stable over time. The index of net income is considered by the state organization to be the most useful overall measure of company performance, while the index of operating efficiency is to a larger extent a measure of efficient intraorganizational management and economy.

Although we had anticipated that the company's net income and operating efficiency would be related to the economic well-being of the county or the growth or decline of the farm population, this did not turn out to be the case. The net income and operating efficiency measures were independent of various economic measures.[1] Companies located in the economically more-advantaged regions apparently have to contend with more competition, which might well equalize the advantage an economically growing area might otherwise provide.

As in previous studies, sociometric questionnaires and interpersonal perception tests (yielding LPC and ASo scores) were administered to all important members of the organization. This included all available members of the board as well as all general and most assistant managers. The questionnaires and tests were generally administered at the beginning of a board meeting. Only three individual board members in all thirty-two companies refused to complete the questionnaires.

These included such measures as the size of the average farm, average farm income, number of tractors in the county, value of livestock, proportion of full- versus part-time agricultural employment, etc., as well as trend indicators.

On the basis of the test and sociometric questionnaire data we identified the most influential member of the board, that is, the board's informal leader. While the president of the board is nominally the head of the company, the board presidency in some companies is rotated or it tends to be awarded to the oldest board member as a sign of honor and respect. In these companies the board president is not always its real leader. The leader, in these cases, might be the vice-president, the secretary-treasurer, a past president, or a board member with no official position. Since the president's position is held at the pleasure of the board, the position power of the board president over his fellow board members is relatively low.

The sociometric questionnaire also enabled us to determine (1) the relationship between the board's informal leader and the general manager of the company, (2) the board members' acceptance of the general manager, and (3) the degree to which the general manager was accepted by his staff of assistant managers. The board of directors are charged with policy- and decision-making functions and are therefore judged to have a relatively unstructured task.

MANAGEMENT TEAMS

The general manager's position carries considerable power in the company. He not only proposes policy for the company, but his recommendations are generally accepted. He can also hire and discharge employees and he has a major voice in the promotion, transfer, or discharge of his assistant managers.

This particular study is especially well suited for showing how the relationship between the general manager and other key members of his company affects the correlation between his ASo score and company performance. The method for inferring the influence of the manager over company performance and the leadership style most appropriate for different leader-group relations was as follows: We obtained a correlation between general managers' ASo scores and company performance for (1) all thirty-two companies, (2) those companies in which the board of directors and/or its accepted leader endorsed the general manager, (3) those companies in which the leader was endorsed by his board as well as by his staff of assistant managers, and finally (4) those companies in which the general manager was accepted by board and staff and in which he also strongly endorsed the assistant manager whom he considered to be his keyman.

These successive correlations are shown in Table 6-3 and clearly indicate the indirect or "moderating" effect which the personal relations in the company have on the correlation between leadership style and performance. We originally interpreted this relationship as indicating that the general manager's ASo score and the personality attribute which this score reflects can affect performance only when the general manager has personal influence over his team. This interpretation is not quite sufficient as we shall see from a more recent reanalysis of the data.

Table 6-4 presents these same data (here based on LPC) for companies which strongly endorse the general manager (i.e., board and staff endorse him), for those in which neither the board nor the staff endorses the general manager, and for companies which are intermediate in their endorsement of the general manager.

These data, as well as comparable analyses of data from the antiaircraft units, open-hearth shops, and the B-29 bomber crews, have led recently to a reinterpretation of the relationships. Rather than holding, as we had done before, that the sociometric pattern indicates whether or not the leader will be able to influence his group, we are now inclined to follow the new analyses suggesting that the disliked leaders can be as effective as well-liked leaders and that different patterns of intragroup relations call for different leadership styles. The liked and accepted leader of groups with high position power and structured tasks (Octant I) is able to per-

TABLE 6-3   Correlations between the General Manager's Assumed Similarity between Opposites (ASo) Score and Company Effectiveness

Sample	N	Net Income	Operating Efficiency
All general managers	32	−.14	−.16
General manager endorsed by staff	19	−.09	−.22
General manager endorsed by board	19	−.07	−.08
General manager endorsed by most influential board member	23	−.39*	−.24
General manager endorsed by staff and most influential board member	13	−.70†	−.59*
General manager endorsed by staff and most influential board member, and manager endorses key assistant manager	8	−.74*	−.73*

* $p < .05$ (one-tailed test).
† $p < .025$ (one-tailed test).

TABLE 6-4   Correlations between General Manager's ASo Score and Company
             Net Income

	Rho	N	Octant
General manager is most chosen by board and staff	−.67	10	I
General manager is chosen by board but rejected by staff	.20	6	V
General manager is rejected by board but chosen by staff	.26	6	V
General manager is rejected by board and staff	−.75	7	VIII–A

form best if he has a managing, task-controlling style. In other words, his group is ready and willing to take his direction, and the managing, task-controlling (low-LPC) leader will satisfy this role expectation by giving structure and direction to the group. Where the leader's status in the eyes of his group is less secure (Octant V), he will be more effective if his high-LPC style leads him to take a nondirective role, calling upon others in the group to share in the decision-making functions and interacting in a relatively permissive, considerate, human relations–oriented manner. This more human relations–oriented, diplomatic course of action is likely to result in a more harmonious work relationship, which will also lead to better performance.

It should be noted that the group which accepts and endorses the leader is already harmonious, at least in accepting his leadership. The situation in which the leader is rejected by his group (or in which, in the case of the consumer company study, he is accepted neither by board nor by staff) makes his position clearly very difficult and uncomfortable. The leader cannot motivate the group by threatening the withdrawal of his personal esteem and approval, since his personal approval does not carry much value for the members to begin with. Likewise, a permissive, nondirective attitude will not be conducive to good performance. A group which is hostile and not motivated to perform will not have any incentive to exert itself under a nondirective leader. Under these conditions the group is likely to remain passive unless the leader gives a good example or specific directions to the group members on how to perform their jobs. Thus, again, a task-oriented, managing leader will perform better under

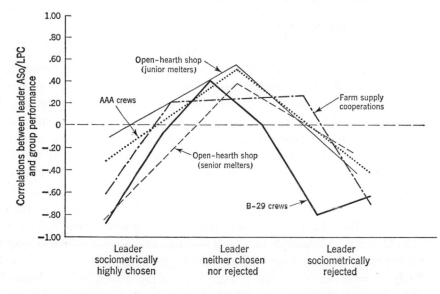

Figure 6-1   **Correlations between leader LPC or ASo scores and group performance under three conditions of leader acceptance by the group in studies of bomber crews, antiaircraft-artillery crews, and consumer cooperatives.**

these very unfavorable conditions. Figure 6-1 presents the performance curves for four sets of real-life groups on which we could obtain sociometric data and in which the groups' reactions to their leaders spanned the entire range from high endorsement to strong rejection.

As was mentioned previously, a strong rejection of leaders is almost impossible to obtain within the context of a laboratory study or an investigation involving *ad hoc* or very short-lived groups. Unfavorable relations of the type here described are to be found primarily in real-life groups. For these, Octant VIII in Figure 2-2 is no longer adequate for describing the highly unfavorable group situation. The tendency in American culture is to accept legitimate leadership. Leaders are, therefore, less likely to be disliked and rejected than to be liked and accepted. It is almost impossible to work up a strong negative affect toward a person with whom one expects to work for only one or two hours and who will be able neither to threaten nor to affect one's future life and career in any conceivable manner. The studies of real-life groups provide data which cannot be adequately duplicated with *ad hoc* groups in a laboratory. These results will be further discussed in Chapter 10.

BOARDS OF DIRECTORS

Teams which have both an unstructured task and leaders with high position power are relatively uncommon in everyday life. An unstructured task seems to call for permissive, nondirective leadership. Most unstructured tasks require a creative effort on the part of the group's members: the group is asked to solve a problem, to develop a new policy, to make a decision which will benefit the larger organization, or to propose a new course of action. These types of tasks require an environment in which the group members can feel at liberty to participate in the deliberation by making suggestions, criticisms, evaluations, and by engaging, as it were, in vicarious trial-and-error learning. This, as Osborne (1962), Parnes (1962) and others have pointed out, requires the freedom provided by a nonthreatening environment in which one can explore ideas which may seem offbeat and even, after further thought, foolish.

Such an environment is easier to establish in a group in which the leader position is weak than in one in which it is strong. It is generally difficult for the group member to determine in advance whether his suggestion or comment related to an unstructured task will sound appropriate or inappropriate, wise or foolish, to the leader. The group member will, therefore, hesitate to voice his opinions if his career and future advancement depend on the leader's opinion of him.

Parenthetically, one of the exceptions to this rule of thumb might be a situation in which the powerful leader calls in consultants or outside advisers. This situation leaves the leader free to make his own decisions, and it makes him responsible for the performance of the group. At the same time, the consultant is not dependent upon the leader's good will in most situations of this type. At most, the leader can ignore him and not invite him back, but the leader's power does not typically extend over the professional life of the adviser. It is, in the final analysis, up to the leader to choose whose advice and which suggestions he will accept.

Because the creative group typically operates under conditions of weak position power, these groups will be dealt with first. Our interest in creative groups of this type was first aroused by the study of the farm-supply companies. As already mentioned, the management teams of these companies were classified as having high position power and high task structure. The corresponding boards of directors, on the other hand, clearly have a highly unstructured task. These groups customarily meet once each month to discuss the operation of the company with the general manager and, in some cases, also with the assistant managers. They listen to such proposals as those concerning the purchase of new equipment, a new sales campaign, or needed changes in company policy. The board then may vote on these actions, approve past actions, and make recommendations on company policy. This is clearly a highly unstructured task.

The leadership of the board is officially vested in the board president, who is elected by the board membership for the term of one year. His job is to preside at board meetings as well as at the company's annual shareholders' meeting and to represent the company in its relations with the state organization and the public, as well as with the management team.

The job of company president is thus itself a very ambiguous, vaguely structured position, and it is carried out in widely differing ways depending upon the tradition within the company and the ambition, ability, and energy of the incumbent. As already mentioned, in some companies it is a ceremonial office and the board presidency is seen as an honor to be awarded to board members with long years of service. It is a very powerful office in other companies in which the board president plays a central part in running the company. In all of these cases, however, the official power of the board president is fairly circumscribed. In analyzing the data, it has seemed most appropriate to work with the informal leader of the board, who was identified on the basis of sociometric questionnaires. This turned out to be the board president in seventeen of the thirty-two companies in our sample. Most of the other strong men on the board were secretary treasurers, vice presidents or past presidents.

As Table 6-3 showed, the correlation between the general manager's ASo score and group performance was negative in companies in which the relations between general manager, staff, and board were good. But under these same conditions, the ASo score of the board's leader correlated positively with company performance (Table 6-5). Thus, while the harmonious company required a managing, task-oriented general manager, the boards of these harmonious companies required a relationship-oriented president or informal leader. These results suggested that the unstructured task requires a different leadership style than does the structured task and that the effectiveness of the leadership depends in part upon the attitude of the leader and in part on the function of his group.

CASE STUDIES OF TWO COMPANIES

We have spoken in terms of correlations and other statistical relations, and we have described interpersonal relations by means of sociometric indices. It is often difficult to visualize what these actually mean in day-to-day

TABLE 6-5   Correlations between the Board Leader's Assumed Similarity between Opposites (ASo) Score and Company Effectiveness

Sample	N	Net Income	Operating Efficiency
All board leaders	31	−.06	.05
Companies in which the general manager is endorsed by his staff	23	−.08	.20
Most influential board member endorses accepted general manager	13	.20	.07
Most influential board member endorses accepted general manager, and manager endorses key assistant manager	8	.62	.64*

* $p < .05$.

behavior. The reader may find it useful, therefore, to get the flavor of organizations managed by high- and by low-ASo leaders.

Since the decisions and policies of boards, panels, committees, and similar groups must nearly always be implemented by an executive or an action group, the relationship between these two organizational components becomes of critical importance in understanding the factors that determine eventual success and failure of the entire company. To illustrate this point we shall present analyses of intensive interviews with board members and managers, comparing a successful and an unsuccessful company. The former had a low-ASo person as general manager, the latter had a high-ASo manager. The case studies were developed by Eleanor Godfrey and are quoted verbatim from a monograph (Godfrey, Fiedler, and Hall, 1959) which described the farm-supply company investigation.

CHOICE OF COMPANIES.   The case analysis was designed to uncover differences in the way managers and directors saw their cooperative, their coworkers, and themselves in relatively successful and unsuccessful companies. We tried to hold external economic variables and critical sociometric conditions constant to highlight the relationship between attitudes and success. To maximize differences in effectiveness, we chose two companies from the top ten in the sample and two companies from the bottom ten, in terms of effectiveness, but we describe here only one of each. We shall call the more successful cooperative, Company A; the less successful, Company B. We shall call the managers Mr. Allen and Mr. Brown, respectively.

FINANCIAL COMPARISONS.   Company A had realized a net income of 7.5% of its dollar sales while Company B had achieved a net return of 6%. Company A had consistently returned a larger share of profits to its customers in patronage refunds, whereas operating expenses take a larger proportion of gross income for Company B. Economic factors are not sufficient to explain this contrast in financial success. Although Company A has three times the volume of business, serving a county twice the size of Company B, it has four to five times the profits. Both companies operate in fairly prosperous areas. Both handle the three major products of petroleum, plant food, and feed. Both managers would like to expand sales of feed and plant food, and neither has exhausted his potential market for any product.

SOCIOMETRIC COMPARISONS.   Both Mr. Allen and Mr. Brown enjoy the endorsement of their co-workers, being chosen by the strongest board member, the keyman, and the staff and board as a whole. Thus, the companies are similar in the critical sociometric conditions used in the study.

However, there are some interesting sociometric differences between the two cooperatives. While Mr. Brown chooses the strongest board member and key staff assistant as preferred co-workers, Mr. Allen makes more of his choices *outside* his company. Both men have had experience in other cooperatives, so this difference is probably not so much a function of knowledge as it is a matter of preference. Although both managers receive almost equal and high acceptance from their most influential director and the board as a whole, Mr. Brown was given more staff choices, particularly as a desirable hunting and fishing companion.

To summarize the sociometric picture for the two companies under discussion, we find high mutual choices between the general manager and his key associates in the poorer company, and high one-sided chosenness of the manager by the board personnel in the better company. This result is in line with our theory that the low ASo person is more emotionally detached from his working companions.

ASo COMPARISONS.   Mr. Allen has a considerably lower ASo score than Mr. Brown, ranking 18th in a sample of 32; Mr. Brown is 5th. While not extreme, these differences in ASo scores justify a contention that Mr. Allen should have more of the characteristics of the low ASo leader than does Mr. Brown. An analysis of the interview data will illustrate our point.

BOARD MANAGEMENT RELATIONS.   A critical matter in any complex organization is the division of duties among its parts. Each member or group should know where the responsibilities and authorities lie. Yet various leaders may see this division of labor differently. Is there any difference between how responsibility is divided between board and staff in these two companies?

Everyone interviewed at both companies agreed that the directors set the policy and the general manager carries it out. Both managers clear any major expenditure or possible introduction of a new line of products with the board. Administrative details are management's concern. However, when responsibility for specific decisions was discussed, certain important differences in attitudes appear.

DIVISION OF RESPONSIBILITY IN COMPANY A.   Company A gives the manager almost free rein although the directors are fully aware of their ultimate responsibility for policy. The manager handles emergency business between monthly meetings and reports any action taken to the board. He works with no set budget or money allowance and can buy major equipment on his own only in an emergency. Matters such as hiring a clerk or initiating a new bookkeeping procedure are left to the manager. The directors feel that this freedom of operation works fine as long as they have confidence in their executive. If they did not have this confidence they would set rules and "pull in the checkreins." They expect the general manager to provide them with full information on any issue with ample time to reach a decision. Sometimes they said "no" to Mr. Allen's suggestions or withheld a decision for more information.

Mr. Allen respects the strength of his board but feels that good boards are made not born. The directors are wise people, but they are laymen and must be trained. One of his functions is to help in training the directors. He works with the president to orient each new board member to the philosophy, policies, and procedures of the company. Mr. Allen thinks it is a good thing to have a nonmanagement board which makes the cooperative unlike other business directorates. Directors act as a sounding board in the county, but one has to work with and realize their professional limitations. While the directors are responsible for policy, it is the general manager's function as a professional resource person to outline the problems that exist and suggest alternative decisions. But he respects the board's right to originate policy and occasionally they have done so.

DIVISION OF RESPONSIBILITY IN CCMPANY B.   The directors of Company B appear more concerned with all facets of the business, detailed or not. All expenditures come before the board unless they represent a continuation of an already approved and standard operation. If any emergency comes up between board meetings, the president calls an emergency meeting or at least consults with the other directors. Neither he nor the manager handles the matter alone. The board expects to decide whether or not to institute a new office procedure, and a board committee meets with the manager when he hires new personnel.

Mr. Brown feels that he has a lot of freedom and can follow his own time schedule. He thought that he had free rein in hiring a clerk or initiating a new office procedure, although his board felt otherwise. Mr. Brown stressed the importance of proceeding cautiously with a board, and pointed out that some managers get into trouble by moving too fast. He feels he has to consult with the directors, give them a chance to express their opinions, and then he can have a pretty free hand.

Both managers agreed that the board has a right to set company policy. However, Mr. Allen felt that the general manager had a right, almost a duty, to leave if he could not accept a policy decision or the basic principles behind it. Mr. Brown felt that the manager should go along with the board and try again later.

THE GENERAL MANAGER AND THE STRONGEST BOARD MEMBER.   Both companies have strong board leaders who accept and work with the general manager. Mr. Allen looks at his board leader as "his associate on the board" and respects his technical competence and ability to understand issues brought before the board. Mr. Brown considers his board leader as a master of public relations and admires the fact that this director always takes time to speak to employees, shows a personal interest in their affairs, and praises good qualities even when he is criticizing a piece of work.

ROLE EXPECTATIONS.   These two companies differ in how much responsibility is delegated to the manager by the board and in how the general manager describes his relationship to the board. Do they also differ in their expectations of a good manager or a good director, couched in more general terms?

QUALIFICATIONS OF A GOOD MANAGER.   Company A's board considers their manager tops. He is a good man with great integrity and a conscientious worker. If a job is to be done he is there to do it. One of Mr. Allen's strongest points is his ability to see the board turn down one of his proposals and not have it affect his work or relations with the board. Another is his willingness to make quick decisions. "You can always unmake a decision, but some managers never will make a decision in the first place." Still another point in his favor is his ambition. A good manager should not be content just to be successful but he should shoot for the top. Ten of the fifteen qualifications of a good manager, listed by the board on one questionnaire, stressed work competence such as looking for new business or keeping expenses down; only five brought out personal qualities such as being pleasant or cooperative with employees.

Company B's directors are also quite pleased with their own manager, but expect different qualities in him. He should, first of all, be conservative. After that he should be a good public relations man and maintain good staff relationships. Their twenty-four responses on the opinion questionnaire split in half with twelve stressing business efficiency and twelve emphasizing personal qualities—especially harmonious staff relationships.

Mr. Allen and Mr. Brown differ considerably in their views of a good manager. Mr. Allen sees the general manager as a leader and a professional operating within clearly defined lines of authority. He must accept direction from his board and the state staff (his "general managers") and set an example for his assistants. He must constantly delegate authority but accept responsibility for the operation of the company.

Mr. Brown emphasized throughout the interview that the "crux of the whole success of a manager is his ability to work with people" as a general manager constantly is in front of people. He should not be domineering but more like "one of the boys." A company cannot afford a domineering, driving manager. The manager should also represent the company in the community through service in civic, business, or charity organizations.

QUALIFICATIONS OF A GOOD DIRECTOR.   Of course, a director should attend board meetings and support his company by buying its products. Everyone agreed on this. But the companies stressed somewhat different attributes of a good director.

Both the board and manager of Company A agree that a director must be a strong, independent man who is not easily persuaded but will stand up and be counted. He must vote for the greatest good for the greatest number, and not just to benefit a few or for personal glory. Directors should even refuse a request from the Farm Bureau for the good of all their patrons. To operate the company efficiently and to hold the support of other patrons, board members must be completely sold on the company. An ideal board is conservative yet aggressive—always mindful of its responsibilities to the patrons but ready to strike out into new territory at the right time.

Mr. Allen also emphasizes wholehearted company support. Whenever one of his assistant managers goes out to interview for the job of a general manager, Mr. Allen advises him to make sure the board itself supports the company 100 percent. If it does not, the young man should not take the job.

Both Mr. Brown and his board feel that it is very important for directors to get along well with each other and the patrons. They are "good will ambassadors" in the county. Mr. Brown did not expect 100 percent support of the company. It is not democratic to expect patrons to buy only from the service company. In listing the things a young man interviewing for a general manager's job should check, this manager again demonstrated his interest in interpersonal relations. How talkative is the board? Are they good listeners? Do they ask good questions? Could a director admit he was wrong, swallow his pride and not sulk?

GENERAL MANAGER–STAFF RELATIONS.   The most striking difference between the two companies is in the way the two managers work with their assistants. Here Mr. Allen's stress on professional abilities and Mr. Brown's emphasis on personal relations are most clearly apparent.

COMPANY A.   In Company A, the general manager (with the low ASo score) works with an organizational chart and job descriptions for all assistants. Each assistant, then, clearly understands the limits of his own authority. Mr. Allen sets general policy and expects any assistant manager to "take the ball from there." Once policy is agreed upon, it is up to the department head to enforce it, and the general manager should have nothing more to do with it. When there is an opening for new personnel, the assistant manager secures the applications and screens them to a final two or three candidates from which Mr. Allen makes a selection. This procedure enables the younger man to profit by the general manager's experience, but the employee feels loyal and responsible to the assistant manager who "put him in the job." Otherwise the assistant would be just a figurehead. Each staff member is held accountable for the actions of his employees, and he is expected to handle all difficulties within his department in his own way without bringing the general manager into it.

General policy and procedures are discussed at a weekly staff meeting, which is a very important part of the company program. While the general manager sets all policy and is ultimately responsible for it, if one of his assistants can convince him, Mr. Allen will change his mind. The staff is given as much rein as possible because the job of an assistant manager is primarily a learning experience. Mr. Allen knows he has made mistakes; his assistant managers have to learn, too. Any ambitious man, the only kind to have, should want to move up, and should be ready for promotion after an apprenticeship of *a maximum of three years,* even though this rapid turnover means more work for the general manager.

Assistant managers attend board meetings and give their own reports as an important part of their training. The directors may question the staff membe directly in the meeting, but any criticism of the man or his job goes through the general manager.

COMPANY B. Mr. Brown (the high-ASo manager) does not operate with an organizational chart. He does not hold, or believe in, regular staff meetings because they are too formal. Anyone in the office is encouraged to come to him at any time with any sort of problem and get it off his chest. Each situation should be dealt with by the general manager as it arises. He strives for a democracy of organization with free give-and-take among all employees from top to bottom, which is appreciated by his staff.

While each assistant has technical responsibility in his own department, he does not have complete knowledge, and he may make errors. Mr. Brown, therefore, helps by making all final decisions. Besides, two heads are better than one. Because the general manager is ultimately responsible, he should present all reports to the board. Matters may be discussed at board meetings which are of no concern to the assistant managers. Therefore, none of the staff attend board meetings. However, the board members feel that they may come directly to any assistant manager with questions or suggestions about his work without going through the manager.

Mr. Brown felt strongly that smooth company operations would be jeopardized if personnel turned over too rapidly. Assistant managers should stay *a minimum of four years.* Certainly they should get ahead and move to other jobs, but not before they were ready to do so, and they could not be prepared in less time.

Evaluation of Company Success

Both companies are proud of their organizations. Success is important to them, but both the directors and managers judge success in somewhat different terms.

BOARD EVALUATIONS. The directors of Company A judge a company mainly by the strength and honesty of its personnel. Are there good relations with the patrons and is business run efficiently on the up-and-up? Does it have a strong independent manager and directors who can stand up and be counted? The directors of Company B's first criterion of success is "how much money you have in the bank at the end of the year." Other important criteria are progress over the previous year and the ability to give a sizable patronage refund.

MANAGER EVALUATIONS.   Mr. Allen leaves the determination of criteria of success up to the state organization. They know what they are doing and he accepts their appraisal of his company's operations. Mr. Brown emphasizes community acceptance of the organization, a "remarkable" increase in sales, the type of employees the company holds, the strength of the board, and the soundness of the company's financial structure.

SUMMARY COMPARISON OF THE TWO COMPANIES

As these two case reports show, the two managers who have different Assumed Similarity scores tend to handle interpersonal relations within their own companies in quite different ways. Major differences between the two companies are summarized in Table 6-6. These support our interpretation of ASo scores.

A number of points are especially noteworthy. It is quite clear that Company A, which has the task-oriented (low-ASo) manager, differs from Company B, which has the relationship-oriented (high-ASo) manager. We do not know in this case which came first. Did the company boards look for, and find, a manager who shared their philosophy and value system, or did the manager, once he was selected, transform the climate of the company in his own image? Both managers had been with their companies for a number of years, and both alternatives are equally probable. It would be most instructive to see whether companies tend to hire managers who have the same leadership style. It seems very likely that a company board will inquire about the views and expectations of men whom the state organization proposes as candidates for the manager's job. The chances are, therefore, that boards will tend to choose the types of managers who will be able to live with the formal and informal work relations established by the board. However, in a company in which the manager has been successful over many years or by which he is ardently wooed, it may well be the manager who determines how he and his board will interact.

The most striking differences between the two companies are, of course, in the work relations between board and manager, and between the manager and his subordinates.

Company A, under the low-ASo manager, stresses formal role relations: staff meetings, communication through channels, training of assistant managers for responsibility, and a firm division of labor between board and management functions.

Company B, which operates under the high-ASo manager, stresses interpersonal relations: good public relations, informal rather than formal communication, informal interpersonal relations rather than role relations. The manager's role is one of arbitrator or conciliator. The board member can go directly to the assistant manager or employee and therefore intervene in management functions. Above all, the manager wants personal prominence and control: he wants to present reports to the board, he wants to make decisions for his subordinates just as the board insists on making decisions for him, and he wants to hold his assistant managers for a minimum of four years while his low-ASo counterpart wants them to stay only for a maximum of three years.

Finally, the task-oriented manager felt it to be very important that he be able to count on his board members' backing and that he be able to agree with his board on policy issues. The relationship-oriented manager was less concerned with this aspect than he was with the personal relationship as is shown by the advice these two men would give to assistant managers.

It should be emphasized that the interviewers did not know at the time of their visits which company had the high- and which had the low-ASo manager, nor which was the more successful company of the two. The case studies fit our other findings. We must, nevertheless, recognize that two case studies can at best serve only as an illustration. The case studies do give some of the flavor of the interpersonal relations and the climate which characterized these two organizations.

At the same time, we should point out that not all the conceptions of the task-oriented manager were good, nor were all those of the high ASo leader bad as far as company performance was concerned. For example, the task-oriented, effective manager felt that he could not remain effective in a company in which he and the board disagreed on important policies. L. Sandlow (unpublished Ms) systematically obtained data on important policy issues from all thirty-two companies. He then compared the extent to which board members agreed with one another, with the board president, or with the manager, as well as the extent to which the manager agreed with his board members, the board president, or his assistant managers. The issues, such as introduction of new sales policies, new personnel policies, etc., were considered crucial by members of the organization. Yet, the amount of agreement among key personnel in the company did not correlate with company performance in any systematic fashion.

A second example is the high-ASo manager's implication that he should participate in civic affairs. We compared the effective and less effective companies with respect to the number of civic organizations to which the

TABLE 6-6   Comparison of Organization and Philosophy in Company A and Company B

Company A	Company B
1. One of top ten companies in sample.	1. One of bottom ten companies in sample.
2. General manager endorsed by board, staff, keyman, and strongest board member.	2. General manager endorsed by board, staff, keyman, and strongest board member.
3. General manager does not endorse keyman and strongest board member as most preferred coworkers, but makes several sociometric choices *outside* his member company.	3. General manager endorses keyman and strongest board member as most preferred coworkers.
4. General manager has a relatively *low* ASo score.	4. General manager has a relatively *high* ASo score.
5. General manager is given *great freedom* of operation by the board of directors, who nevertheless realize their ultimate power.	5. General manager is given *less freedom* of operation by the board. Directors are more concerned with details of company operations.
6. General manager sees his relationship to the board as that of a *professional* working with and training lay directors.	6. General manager sees his relationship to the board in more personal terms and stresses the need for making directors feel important.
7. General manager respects the board's right to set company policy and appreciates the value of a strong board.	7. General manager respects the board's right to set company policy and appreciates the value of a strong board.
8. General manager sees his strongest board member as his "assistant on the board."	8. General manager sees his strongest board members as especially adept at working with people.
9. Board of directors respects general manager's ability to make quick decisions and accept board authority.	9. Board of directors expects a manager to be conservative and handle public and staff relationships harmoniously.
10. Mr. Allen sees the general manager as a *professional leader* operating within a clearly defined hierarchy of authority.	10. Mr. Brown sees the general manager as primarily a *public relations man* maintaining good relations with board, staff, and community
11. Directors should be faithful in attendance and support the company.	11. Directors should be faithful in attendance and support the company.
12. Mr. Allen expects 100 percent company support from directors.	12. Mr. Brown does not expect 100 percent company support from directors.

TABLE 6-6   Comparison of Organization and Philosophy in Company A and Company B

Company A	Company B
3. General manager has an organizational chart and staff job descriptions.	13. General manager does not have an organizational chart or job descriptions.
4. General manager holds weekly staff meetings.	14. General manager does not hold regular staff meetings.
5. General manager delegates authority and responsibility.	15. General manager works directly with all staff members.
6. Assistant manager should be ready for promotion in a *maximum of three years.*	16. Assistant manager should stay a *minimum* of four years.
7. Assistant managers report at board meeting.	17. Assistant managers do not report at board meetings.

manager belonged, as well as the number of offices he held. No significant differences or even trend effects could be detected. Whether or not these are major issues will need to be resolved in other studies. Quite clearly, however, the leadership style of the general manager played a very interesting, and apparently important, part in the operation of the company.

SUMMARY

This chapter reviewed studies of two complex organizations, namely open-hearth steel shops and small farm-supply cooperative companies. The production groups in these organizations have leaders with high position power and structured tasks. The policy- and decision-making groups in the farm-supply companies, the boards of directors, have leaders with low position power and relatively unstructured tasks.

The leadership style scores of the production managers were highly correlated with organizational performance. In the sixteen open-hearth shops, the task-oriented senior melters had better production records than did the more relationship-oriented melters, irrespective of the sociometric preference patterns in these shops. Subsequent analyses showed, however, that the relationship-oriented senior melters performed better than task-oriented senior melters in shops in which they were only moderately accepted or endorsed on sociometric preference ratings, while the task-oriented melters performed better in situations in which they were either

highly endorsed or relatively rejected by other members of their manage
ment team.

We had originally obtained very low correlations between the ASo
scores of junior melter foremen and the performance of their groups. A
reanalysis of these data showed, however, that junior melter foremen with
low ASo scores performed more effectively than did those with high ASo
scores, especially in groups which did not sociometrically endorse them,
while the junior melters with high ASo scores performed better than junior
melters with low ASo scores in groups in which they were moderately
endorsed. The open-hearth findings are thus essentially similar to those
obtained in bomber and tank crews and indicate the type of leadership
style required by leaders with good, medium, or poor affective relations
with others in their organizations.

A second investigation dealt with thirty-two farm-supply companies.
Each of these had a board of directors and a management team consisting
of a general manager and several assistant managers. We again found
that the task-oriented general managers performed more effectively in
situations in which they were highly accepted, as well as in situations in
which they were relatively rejected by important members of their company, that is, by the board and the staff of assistant managers. The relationship-oriented general managers performed better than task-oriented
managers in companies in which they had an intermediately good leader-
member relationship, that is, in which either the board or the staff accepted them. In contrast to the relations obtained between the leadership
style scores of general managers and company performance in harmonious
companies, the leadership style score of the board's informal leader, that
is, its most influential member, correlated positively with company performance, indicating that the relationship-oriented leaders tended to perform better than task-oriented leaders in this context. This finding
suggested the important part played by the nature of the task in determining the appropriate leadership style. Two case studies illustrated the work
relations of companies with high- and low-ASo general managers and provide some insight into the differences in organizational patterns and processes which are associated with high- and low-ASo managers.

7 CREATIVE GROUPS WITH UNSTRUCTURED TASKS AND WEAK LEADER POSITION POWER (Octants IV and VIII)

The study of farm-supply companies showed that the leadership style of effective general managers differed from that of effective board leaders. In companies with good interpersonal relations among major officials, the task-oriented (low-ASo) manager performed more effectively; in these same groups, the relationship-oriented (high-ASo) leaders of the boards of directors were most effective. Differences in task, therefore, seemed to call for different types of leadership styles. In contrast to the structured management functions, the tasks of the boards of directors were highly unstructured. They resembled the "divergent thinking" (Guilford, 1954) required of creative tasks which do not have a single solution. It seemed fruitful, therefore, to conduct more intensive investigations of groups that are engaged in tasks which require creative problem-solving behavior.

Creativity has become a very important topic of psychological and educational research within recent years. The problem is especially relevant in view of the current reliance placed upon groups which are engaged in team research. This can be seen, for example, by the increasing number of publications with multiple authorship and by the increasing number of task forces in government which are established to propose new and creative solutions to social problems. In a wide range of creative human activities the single practitioner was the rule and the team the unusual and exceptional case. Committees, panels, boards, juries, staffs, and a variety of similar groups are now proliferating to an increasing extent, not only in industrial development and in research work, but also in law, in architecture, in medicine, and in the performing arts.

Despite the obvious importance of this problem, only a few research workers have dealt with group creativity in a systematic fashion.[1] By the

---

[1] See for example, Bush and Hattery (1956), Parnes and Meadow (1959), Pepinsky (1959), Taylor (1958), Triandis et al. (1962), and Hoffmann (1959).

term "group creativity" we generally mean a group interaction leading to an original *and* useful solution of an assigned problem; this may also consist of a novel way of recombining given elements into new forms or combinations.

While we often think of originality as being equivalent to creativity, it is important to keep in mind that one can be original without being creative. A solution which is just unusual or original can, after all, be generated by means of a computer which merely combines previously present elements at random into new patterns. Thus, given a set of fifty nonsense syllables, it is easy to recombine these mechanically into two or three syllable "words" which are original and unusual but meaningless. The selection of one or two of these combinations as a new and catchy trade name for a product may well be a creative act, but the random combination of syllables is not. The creative product must have some social utility, or some new meaning. Our research has been concerned with creativity rather than with originality in this sense of the term.

Our definition of group creativity does not imply, of course, that a group, as a group, thinks or creates. It does assume, however, that group members may stimulate one another, reject poor solutions, and propose improvements to solutions which were previously available. The test of group creativity is, in a sense, the difference between the product created by the group members as individuals working alone and the product which emerges after group discussion (see, for example, Triandis et al, 1963).

We frequently find in laboratory studies of group creativity that the product of the group tends to be more banal and trite, less spontaneous and, for all these reasons, less creative than would be expected from individual contributions. This had led to comparisons which show that individuals are more effective than groups (McCurdy and Lambert, 1952). This is not too surprising. It is in the nature of teamwork that inefficiencies arise as a result of slippages in communication, as a result of the additional effort which is required to coordinate the work of team members, and the result of the fact that only one person can talk at the same time (Steiner, 1966). Team efforts are rarely, if ever, justified if the same end can be accomplished by one individual working alone. The question we must ask is not whether these particular tasks could be done better by individuals, but whether and how closely the model which underlies our experiment simulates the conditions of real-life groups. The main question is how groups perform creative tasks and what factors contribute to their creativity. It is to this last question that we have addressed our studies. Since the tasks are highly unstructured and the leader positions weak, these groups fall into Octants IV and VIII in our classification system.

THE DUTCH CREATIVITY STUDY

Although it may appear rather farfetched to draw an analogy between the board of directors of a farm-supply company and group creativity in a laboratory situation, it seemed worthwhile to conduct an experiment on group creativity which was modeled to some extent after the farm-supply company boards. As the reader will recall, we had found that the relationship-oriented board leader performed best, that is, appeared to contribute to company success, when his relationship with his key personnel in the company was good. The task-oriented board leaders performed best when the intracompany relations were strained and unpleasant. A study was conducted at the University of Amsterdam which enabled us to test the relationship between leadership style and group creativity under well-controlled laboratory conditions (Fiedler, Meuwese, and Oonk, 1960).

The experiment explored three different factors which were presumed to influence group creativity. These were (1) the interpersonal relations between the group members, (2) the leadership position in the group, and (3) the leader's interpersonal perceptions as measured by his Least-preferred Coworker score.

Our interest in the first of these variables was aroused by the long-standing social and political conflict between Northern Protestants and Southern Catholics in Holland. This cleavage, which permeates Dutch life, has existed to a greater or lesser extent ever since the eighty-year War of Independence from Spain from 1568 to 1648. Even in cities with a mixed religious population, the social and business contacts between members of these two religious populations tend to be formal and somewhat strained. We expected similarly strained relations in our laboratory groups, which included both Calvinists and Catholics. Since the membership of most political bodies and governmental commissions in Holland is deliberately selected so as to include representatives of these two population sectors, the question concerning the effectiveness of groups heterogeneous in religion is far from academic in Dutch life. The degree to which the members of these heterogeneous groups can fruitfully collaborate in policy- and decision-making functions vitally affects the social and economic well-being of the country.

The second main variable concerned the group's creativity under appointed and emergent leadership. Several previous investigations have failed to find systematic differences in the performance of groups having formal and informal leaders (Borg, 1957; Carter et al., 1951). Yet, it seemed reasonable to believe that these factors might well interact with others in influencing the creativity of groups.

The third factor, the leader's LPC score indicating his leadership style, remained, for obvious reasons, a central aspect of our investigations.

The study utilized Calvinist and Catholic male students from various universities in the Netherlands. Each subject completed a set of Interpersonal Perception scales describing his most- and his least-preferred co-workers, as well as a brief intelligence test modeled after the Miller Analogies scale and containing biographical items regarding the individual's place and date of birth, the school he attended, and his religious background and practice.

On the basis of these tests, thirty-two students from each religious group were selected to participate in the study. These men were assembled into 16 four-man groups. After completing one set of tasks, the men were reassigned to a second set of sixteen groups of completely different composition. Each subject was, thus, a member of two groups. He was once a member of a homogeneous group and once a member of a heterogeneous group. Sixteen of the groups were heterogeneous, consisting of two Catholic and two Calvinist students. Sixteen groups were designed to be homogeneous, containing either four Catholic or four Calvinist students. Because of a clerical error, two of the groups had to be discarded, and we were thus left with seven Catholic and seven Calvinist groups. In half the groups within each category, the experimenters appointed a chairman or formal leader, while the other groups operated under emergent or informal leadership conditions in which leaders were identified after the task session by means of sociometric preference questions.

The main task for each group consisted of devising three stories within twenty minutes. These were to be based on the same TAT card. The stories were to be as original and as different as possible. Each of the stories was rated by two independent judges using a scoring manual. Inter-rater reliabilities were .82 and .89. At the termination of the task, subjects completed sociometric questionnaires indicating the informal leaders of

TABLE 7-1   Correlations between Leader's LPC and Productivity Scores in the Dutch Creativity Study

Group Structure	Homogeneous Groups	Heterogeneous Groups
Formal	No competition for leadership status	No competition for leadership status
	Little social strain; few problems in communication	Much social strain; impeded communication
	$\overline{X}$* 105.28 SD* 37.23 N 7	$\overline{X}$ 116.62 SD 34.37 N 8
	^{rho}LPC Creativity +.75 †	^{rho}LPC Creativity −.72 ‡
Informal	Competition for leadership status	Competition for leadership status
	Little social strain; few problems in communication	Much social strain; impeded communication
	$\overline{X}$ 87.50 SD 16.64 N 7	$\overline{X}$ 105.75 SD 10.30 N 8
	^{rho}LPC Creativity −.67	^{rho}LPC Creativity −.21

* Means and standard deviations refer to creativity scores.
† $p < .10$.
‡ $p < .05$.
SOURCE: Adapted from Fiedler, 1962a, and reproduced by permission.

the group, i.e., group members who "had most influence on the opinions of others," with whom the subject would most like to work again on a similar task, and whom the subject would choose as a leader in a similar task.

The results of this study are shown in Table 7-1. The most obvious finding which this table presents indicates that the homogeneous groups did not perform significantly better than did the heterogeneous groups. Likewise, we found no significant differences between groups in which the leader was appointed, and therefore had at least minimally legitimate position power, and the groups with emergent leadership and hence extremely weak position power. The main question which remained was, therefore, whether different types of groups required different styles of leadership.

To determine the influence of the leader on group creativity his LPC scores were correlated with the group performance. In formally organized groups the chairman's score was utilized, while the sociometrically chosen leader's score was used in the informal teams. The overall rank-order correlations between group performance and the leader's LPC scores were not significant. However, when the groups were subdivided into homogeneous and heterogeneous groups, and by leadership type, the following results were obtained: In homogeneous groups with formal leaders, the formal leader's LPC score correlated positively with group performance. In all heterogeneous groups and in all groups with informal leaders, the correlations were negative.

These results suggested a complex interaction between LPC, group creativity, and the group's organization. In attempting to interpret these findings we assumed that formal homogeneous groups would tend to be more pleasant and relaxed than the others since homogeneous groups, containing men from the same religion and cultural subgroup, would make the members feel more at ease and less defensive. Likewise, groups having an appointed leader would operate under less stress since the appointment of a leader would make it less likely that the men would compete for leadership status. Presumably, then, the formal homogeneous groups would be relatively pleasant and relaxed, i.e., fall into Octant IV, while all other groups would have less pleasant interpersonal relations and should thus be classified as belonging to Octant VIII. This interpretation was supported by the finding that subjects indicated the presence of a "destructively critical group member" in only 14 percent of formal homogeneous groups, but in 50, 67, and 87 percent of the groups in the other three cells.

The findings of the Dutch study led to the hypothesis that the relationship-oriented leaders would obtain the best group performance on unstructured tasks in pleasant, relaxed groups while the task-oriented (low-LPC) leaders would obtain the best performance in groups operating under socially more strained, unpleasant conditions.

These findings are quite reminiscent of the results we had obtained in the study of farm-supply companies. There, too, the relationship-oriented

board leaders performed better in a relaxed, tension-free group climate.
The task-oriented board leaders performed best in companies in which
the relationship between board and management was strained. (For example, when the general manager rejected the board leader, the ASo score
of the latter correlated −.02 and −.46 with net income and operating
efficiency scores, respectively.)

THE HYPNOSIS STUDY

A second experiment on group creativity was conducted shortly after the
results of the Dutch study had been analyzed. This experiment (Fiedler,
London, and Nemo, 1960) was designed to elucidate the meaning of LPC
and ASo scores as well as to validate the findings of the Dutch study. We
hoped to modify the attitudes related to ASo scores by means of post-
hypnotic suggestion, causing the individual's ASo to be high one time,
low another time, and having him interact in a "normal" manner the third
time, that is, in the way he would usually behave.

The procedure was quite complex in order to control for artifacts which
might occur as the result of the hypnotic manipulation.

In brief, we selected twelve highly hypnotizable women and twelve
women who were very resistant to hypnotic suggestion, using the Weitzen-
offer-Hilgard scale (1959). All women were given to understand that
they were excellent subjects and that they had been in a hypnotic trance
while receiving the suggestions. As far as we could tell, all women believed
this to be the case.

Each of the women then participated in a three-person group, the other
two women being confederates. The order of suggesting high, low, or
"norm" ASo attitudes was counterbalanced, and the sequence of subjects
was randomized. The experiment was so arranged that neither the confederates nor the administrator of the experiment would know (or in fact, did
know) whether a subject was hypnotizable and what the order of ASo
instructions had been. The naïve subject was always elected by the confederates to serve as the group's leader. The task, as in the Dutch study,
consisted of telling three different stories about a TAT card. All sessions
were recorded and later analyzed by means of the Bales (1950) interaction process analysis.

Since we had hypothesized that high-LPC leaders would perform more
effectively in group sessions which were pleasant and relaxed while low-

LPC leaders would perform better in tense, unpleasant sessions, we obtained Group Atmosphere (GA) [2] scores for subjects and confederates. These were given to the group leader as well as the two confederates.

The elaborate hypnotic manipulation in this experiment, unfortunately, failed to provide the information we had hoped for, although the data proved very useful in later studies of hypnotizability by London. The study is described here in some detail since we shall return to it in a later chapter.

The hypothesis of the study, based on the results of the Dutch creativity study, could be confirmed with the data obtained in the "norm" sessions in which the subjects were told to act as they normally would in situations of this nature. To test the hypothesis, we divided the twenty-four groups into groups of eight on the basis of high, medium, and low leaders' Group Atmosphere scores. The groups were similarly divided into three groups of eight on the basis of the group members' (that is, the confederates') Group Atmosphere scores.

Table 7-2 presents these results. As can be seen, all correlations are in the expected direction. The relationship-oriented (high-LPC) leaders performed best in groups they described as relaxed and pleasant; the task-oriented leaders performed best in groups they described as unpleasant and tense. While still in the same direction, the correlations based on groups which were divided according to the confederates' Group Atmosphere scores were notably lower.

This finding raised a number of questions. First of all, did this mean that it was primarily the feeling of the leader about the group which made the main difference? Or did we get these particular results perhaps simply because the group members were confederates rather than regular group members? Furthermore, certain questions arose regarding the generalizability of the task. Since we had utilized TAT stories in our Dutch study

[2] The Group Atmosphere (GA) scale was modeled after the LPC scale. It contained ten highly intercorrelated bipolar adjective items, e.g.,

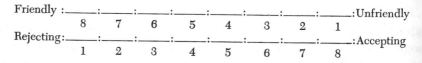

The remaining items were: unenthusiastic-enthusiastic, lots of fun–serious, unhelpful-helpful, nonproductive-productive, distant-close, cold-warm, cooperative-uncooperative, supportive-hostile, boring-interesting, successful-unsuccessful. As with LPC scores the positive end of each scale received a score of 8 while the negative end received a score of 1. (See Appendix A.)

TABLE 7-2   Correlations between Leader's LPC and Group Creativity in the Hypnosis Study ($N = 8$)

	Group Atmosphere Scores		
Groups Divided on Basis of Score of	Top Third	Middle Third	Lower Third
Leaders	.64	−.33	−.72*
Members	.27	−.28	−.62

* $p < .05$, one-tailed.

SOURCE: Adapted from Fiedler, 1962a, and reproduced by permission.

s well as in the hypnosis study, might this particular type of task evoke ertain results which are peculiar to it? It seemed important, therefore, to est whether other types of tasks would yield the same results and whether ve would find similar data in groups in which all members were naïve ubjects in the experiment.

HF LFADFRSHIP TRAINING STUDY

third investigation (Fiedler, Bass, and Fiedler, 1961) was conducted as art of a national leadership training conference which brought together xperienced church administrators and lay leaders of the American Uni- .rian Association.[3] The group consisted of seventy one women and thirty- ven men, most of whom were between thirty-five and fifty years of age. 1any participants held responsible leadership positions in their com- unities, their church organization, and/or in their regular employment. his group was, obviously, quite different from the university students or ilitary personnel with whom we had worked before. It was, therefore, ssible to determine whether our previous findings could be generalized yond the previous groups.

The leadership conference was organized so that four consecutive morn- gs could be devoted to group-creativity problems. In the course of this ogram, subjects were assembled into five-person teams. Each team con- ted of a designated chairman, three members, and an observer who did t participate in the group discussions but administered questionnaires, ned the session, and directed the postsession critique.

ow the Unitarian-Universalist Association, whose cooperation is gratefully acknowl- ged.

New groups were formed each day so that each person served as a leader on one day and as an observer one day, and so that no two group members worked together on more than two days. The group composition on the first and second days was completely different. Moreover, the creativity score of the group of which an individual was a member on one day was uncorrelated with the performance of groups in which he served on succeeding days.

On the first day, before being assigned to any groups, the conference participants completed Interpersonal Perception scales from which LPC scores were derived. Immediately after each session, subjects rated the group's atmosphere on the same scale as used in the hypnosis study.

All groups worked on the same task on the same day, and a different task was presented on each successive day. The tasks were to be completed within a thirty-five-minute period.

On the first day the groups were to write a 250-word statement justifying a decision by the congregation's minister not to divulge the intent of a local physician (not a church member) to commit a mercy killing.

On the second day, the groups had to invent a Sunday school parable for six- to eight-year-olds which would illustrate the desirability of the doctrine of separation of church and state. (This study took place just before the Kennedy election in 1960.)

The groups on the third day were asked to develop an appeal for fund (directed to members of the conference) to send a ministerial student through divinity school.

On the fourth day, the groups planned a three-minute skit for presentation that evening to illustrate the need for better music in the worship service.

These problems were designed to tap different aspects of group creativity, and they also differed from the task of telling stories about TAT cards, which had been used in the preceding studies. The criterion group performance consisted in each case of the judgments and rating of all other conference participants. Subjects did not rate the product their own group.

The reliability of the criterion ratings was assessed by randomly dividing the ratings into two subgroups and computing separate rankings. The rank-order correlations between the two sets of ratings were .91, .76, and .90 for the first, second, and fourth day respectively. The criterion score for the fund-raising problem was based on the amount of play money deposited in the collection boxes which each of the groups set up next

TABLE 7-3   Correlations between Leader's LPC Scores and Group Creativity under High and Low Leader GA Scores in the Leadership Training Study (N's $= 6$–7)

	Leader's Group Atmosphere Scores		
	Top Third	Middle Third	Lower Third
First day (justification)	.28	.10	.03
Second day (parable)	.89*	.67	−.03
Third day (fund appeal)	.14	.19	−.40
Fourth day (skit)	.37	−.08	−.60

* $p < .025$.
SOURCE: Adapted from Fiedler, 1962a, and reproduced by permission.

its appeal. This method of collecting judgments precluded the computation of a reliability estimate.

The hypothesis was tested by dividing the teams on the basis of the leaders' Group Atmosphere scores into a top, middle, and lower third and correlating the leaders' LPC scores with group performance. As we had expected, the relationship-oriented leaders tended to perform better in groups which they described as pleasant and relaxed. The task-oriented leaders tended to perform better in groups which they described as relatively tense and unpleasant. While only one of the sixteen correlations was significant, only one of the eight correlations, namely, .03, was not in the hypothesized direction. (The hypothesis covered only the relations in the groups with the high and the low Group Atmosphere scores, not those with medium scores.) The relationships were again less marked when the groups were subdivided on the basis of the members' Group Atmosphere scores. In other words, it was the leader's perception of the group climate and of the tension in the group which determined whether his style would be appropriate. The group members' descriptions of group climate determined the appropriate leadership style to a much lesser extent (Table 7-3).

SUMMARY

A series of group-creativity studies has been described in which the leader's position power was relatively weak and the task was highly unstructured. These groups, depending upon the leader-member relationship, fell into Octants IV and VIII.

The relationship-oriented leaders performed best in groups which were relatively pleasant and relaxed, either as indicated by objective scores obtained in the Dutch creativity study or by the leader's own descriptions of the group atmosphere. Task-oriented leaders performed best in groups which were relatively tense and unpleasant and in which the leader felt less well-accepted. The findings of these studies are highly consistent, both over different types of tasks and over different types of subjects.

These findings might mean that we are not really dealing with group climate at all, but only with the leader's feeling about it.[4] Yet, we found similar relations in the Dutch study and in the farm-supply study in which we inferred group climate from external evidence. This would suggest that the leader's perception in these other studies was quite accurate or that the leader and members in experimental situations do not experience the relevant aspect of group climate to the same degree. This "relevant" aspect may well be the acceptance which the leader enjoys in the group and the corresponding feeling of relaxation and enjoyment the leader has in being in the group.

While the samples were very small and only one of the correlations shown on Table 7-3 reached an acceptable level of significance, the relations are quite consistent from day to day, suggesting that the findings we had obtained in the Dutch study and in the hypnosis study could be generalized to other creativity tasks.

The major significance of the church-leadership training study was in the cross-validation and extension of the first two experiments reported in this chapter. The findings obviously held not just for college students but also for mature, experienced leaders; they held for mixed sex groups and over four different creative tasks. The fact that these findings are also very similar to those obtained in real-life groups, namely, the boards of directors of farm-supply companies, suggests that we are dealing with psychologically meaningful and important phenomena.

---

[4] To determine whether the correlation between the leader's LPC score and group creativity would be more positive as the leader's Group Atmosphere score increases, the leader's average GA score within each cell in Table 7-3 and the corresponding correlation coefficients between LPC and creativity were correlated. This correlation was .60 ($N = 12$), which is significant in the expected direction at the .025 level of confidence. Hence, the direction and magnitude of the LPC–Group Creativity relationship was related to the leader's perception of group climate. As was the case to some extent in the previous study, the relations between LPC and group creativity were not highly influenced by group members' GA scores. Here the corresponding correlation was −.26.

8 GROUPS WITH UNSTRUCTURED TASKS AND POWERFUL LEADERS (Octants III and VII)

There are relatively few groups in real life which have an unstructured task but a very powerful leadership position. Generally speaking, creative performance cannot be commanded, and creative teams are, therefore, not amenable to direction in the same sense as the more typical work groups with highly structured tasks.

Groups of this type do exist, however. They are occasionally found in research organizations, in military planning staffs, and in business and industrial concerns. The conditions can, of course, be created in laboratory experiments. We have conducted two such studies of groups which could be considered as falling into Octants III and VII. These are described in this chapter.

THE ROTC STUDY

The first study in this set (Meuwese and Fiedler, 1964) investigated group creativity under varying conditions of stress. It dealt with the effects of two variables on group performance, namely, the intelligence of the group leader and members, and the leader's style as measured by LPC. These relations were studied under three different conditions of stress: relatively low stress, stress internal to the group (interpersonal stress), and stress from the external environment. In addition, we compared the performance of these groups on two tasks; one of these was designed to create stress by engendering controversy among group members while the other task was relatively neutral in this respect. The specific effects of stress on group creativity will be discussed in a later chapter. We will here concern ourselves only with the relationship between leader style and group performance. The comparison of group performance under different conditions of stress was, in fact, the major purpose of the study, and it was not until later that we attempted to fit these studies into our general theoretical schema.

The study utilized 162 students enrolled in the Army and Navy Reserve Officer Training Corps (ROTC) programs. All participants were seniors who expected to obtain their regular or reserve commissions at the end of the semester.

These young men were assembled into 54 three-man groups which were assigned to three conditions. In the *internal-stress* condition the eighteen groups consisted of two army cadets and one navy midshipman. The men were asked to appear in uniform to emphasize differences in reference-group affiliation. The army cadet with the *lower* cadet rank was appointed as leader of the group. This gave the leader a very low position-power rating, and hence placed these particular groups into Octants IV and VIII. (For the sake of clearer presentation, these groups are discussed in this section rather than in the preceding chapter.)

A second set of eighteen groups assigned to the *external stress* condition consisted of three army cadets. These men were also in uniform, and the highest-ranking man was appointed as leader. To create realistic tension and anxiety we asked several high-ranking military officers, with rank of full colonel, lieutenant colonel, and major, to assist in the study. These officers were seated right across the table from the group, facing the men. They were given the task of rating the group interaction almost continuously without indicating to the group why they were there and what they were doing. This experimental manipulation was unusually successful in creating realistic stress. The men reported and manifested considerable anxiety, and they were highly relieved when they were later informed that this aspect of the research had been introduced merely as a way of introducing stress.

A third set of eighteen groups was assigned to the control, or *low-stress* condition. These groups also consisted of three army cadets. The men were asked to come in civilian clothes to minimize the relationship of the project to the ROTC and every effort was made to create a relaxed, pleasant atmosphere. The highest-ranking man was appointed as leader, the men were assured that their performance would not affect their military career, and the men were introduced to one another without reference to their ROTC rank. They were aware of the fact, however, that their participation in this study was required by the ROTC.

In each set of eighteen groups, nine groups had high-LPC leaders and nine had leaders with low LPC scores. Three group leaders in each set had high intelligence scores, three had medium, and three had relatively low scores.

Each group worked on two tasks. The first of these was designed to generate task stress in the internal-stress condition by capitalizing on the anticipated difference in attitudes between army and navy cadets. This so-called "Proposal Task" stated:

> A commission recently proposed to Congress that the ROTC program benefits be standardized. Specifically, the present system of financing the Navy ROTC program provides for tuition, books, and $50 monthly allowance for four years while Army and Air Force ROTC cadets do not receive comparable benefits, especially during the first two years. According to the Commission's report, this has attracted many exceptionally capable individuals into the Navy program purely for the financial benefits which it offers, although only 25% of these men remain in the service.[1]
>
> Your committee has been appointed to write a brief proposal to be submitted to the Joint Chiefs of Staff. This proposal should recommend a fair and equitable implementation of this policy, without exceeding the total of currently available funds for ROTC training, and justifying the recommendations as convincingly as possible.
>
> You will have 25 minutes in which to complete your proposal.

The second task was a group-creativity problem which would not normally arouse interpersonal conflict. It was assumed that this task would perhaps generate interpersonal stress in the internal-stress condition because of differences in reference group only. This "Fable Task" read,

> A nation-wide program has been instituted to alert the public to our defense problems. The ROTC has been assigned the task of helping elementary school children understand our current national defense problems. Your committee has been instructed to compose, for children from eight to ten years old, a fable or a story that clearly shows the need for a large army in peacetime. The fable or story must be clear to the young children, and it should be as interesting and original as possible. Your main point should be that a trained land army is the most important element of protection even when a country is not engaged in a major war but still must protect its coastline.
>
> Write down the complete fable or story, including an appropriate title. Remember that the story will be read by elementary school children. You will have 25 minutes in which to complete your story.

After completion of the first task, the groups in the low-stress and internal-stress conditions were informally told in a "by the way" fashion that they had performed quite well. Groups in the external-stress condition were told, as a way of further increasing stress, that their performance had been quite poor and that they would need to improve. Postsession

The statement was written by members of the project and is, of course, fictional.

interviews indicated that these comments were generally accepted at face value.

The Proposal Task was rated by three judges, and the Fable Task by five judges. The ratings yielded a Proposal Quality score and a Fable Quality score which indicated the creativity of the group products on the first and on the second task respectively. The scores were obtained from the combined ratings of independent judges. The estimated interjudge reliability (corrected for the number of raters) for the first task was .88, that for the second task was .87. These were, therefore, quite reliable criterion scores.

After each session, the subjects completed questionnaires designed to measure subjective experiences of the group process. These sessions were tape-recorded and later analyzed (see Morris and Fiedler, 1964). As in previous studies, the leader-member–relations dimension was measured by means of a seventeen-item Group Atmosphere scale administered after each of the task sessions.[2]

The Group Atmosphere scores in the external-stress condition were quite low, as we had hoped they would be. We had also hoped, however, that the control condition would seem fairly pleasant and relaxed. We had assured the group members that their performance scores would not influence their military career and that the results of the experiment would not be communicated to their officers. Nevertheless, a comparison of the Group Atmosphere scores with those obtained in previous experiments clearly showed that the men had felt under noticeable pressure despite these assurances. Even the Group Atmosphere scores which fell into the upper half of the distribution in this experiment—and which were supposedly high—were below the mean of scores of groups with low group atmosphere in other studies conducted with college students or with participants in the leadership-training workshops. The low-stress condition could, therefore, not be considered to have a pleasant, relaxed group atmosphere.

An Analysis of Variance showed that low-LPC leaders performed significantly better than high-LPC leaders in all three conditions on the Fable Quality score ($p < .025$). No difference was found between groups with high- and low-LPC leaders for other performance measures we had obtained.

[2] This scale was identical in form to the LPC scale containing the same items: friendly-unfriendly, rejecting-accepting, helpful-frustrating, unenthusiastic-enthusiastic, lots fun–serious, tense-relaxed, distant-close, cold-warm, cooperative-uncooperative, supportive-hostile, boring-interesting, quarrelsome-harmonious, self-assured-hesitant, efficient-inefficient, gloomy-cheerful, and open-guarded.

To make the results of this study comparable with other studies described here, we have computed rank-order correlations based on the six groups in the upper third and the six groups in the lower third of the leaders' group atmosphere distribution. These are presented in Table 8-1. While none of the correlations is significant (being based on only six cases) it can be seen that the correlations between LPC and performance were negative in groups with high Group Atmosphere scores in the low- and external-stress conditions but positive in groups with low Group Atmosphere scores. The groups in the low-stress condition clearly fall into Octants III and VII. Whether the groups in the external-stress condition should also be classified in this manner is more problematical. This depends on the effect of stress on the leadership situation, as will be discussed more extensively in Chapter 12.

STUDY OF SUPERVISORY AND PARTICIPATORY LEADERSHIP

We conducted one other study of group creativity (Anderson and Fiedler, 1964) which investigated groups with relatively high position power. The main purpose of this experiment was the evaluation of group performance on different group-creativity tasks under supervisory and participatory leadership. The effects of different leadership styles on group creativity are relevant to the present discussion.

TABLE 8-1   Correlations between Leader LPC and Group Creativity under Three Conditions of Stress ($N = 6$) (ROTC Study)

Task	Group Atmosphere	Low Stress Octant	Rho	External Stress Octant	Rho	Internal Stress Octant	Rho
Pay proposal	High	III	−.43	III	−.14	IV	.49
Fable	High	III	−.72	III	−.60	IV	−.03
Pay proposal	Low	VII	.04	VII	.11	VIII	−.04
Fable	Low	VII	.24	VII	.57	VIII	−.47

The men who participated in this experiment were enrolled in the Navy Reserve Officer Training Corps (NROTC) at the University of Illinois. The study utilized 30 four-man groups. The thirty leaders were senior midshipmen enrolled in a required naval leadership course; the group members were NROTC freshmen and sophomores. All men were given to understand that their participation in the exercise constituted part of their regular training and that their performance would be evaluated by their officers and made part of their record.

After assigning men to groups on the basis of pretests of intelligence and individual creativity, the groups were divided at random into two subgroups of fifteen teams each. Leaders of the fifteen teams in the participatory condition were told that they were to act as chairmen of their groups and that it was their responsibility to obtain maximum task performance. They might do this in any way they wished, including, of course, participation in the group discussion.

The leaders in the supervisory condition were instructed to take a role which they would frequently have to assume as navy officers, namely, to oversee the work of others. Supervising leaders were told that they could encourage their group members, that they could make procedural suggestions, and that they could praise or reject ideas which were proposed by their group members, but under no circumstances were they allowed to contribute ideas of their own to the solution of the problems.

Since the group sessions were part of the NROTC course, navy officers in uniform assisted in these testing sessions. The presence of these officers operated to increase the leaders' motivation to have their groups perform well, but it also made the experience somewhat tense and anxiety-arousing. This could be seen from the posttest measures, including Group Atmosphere scales, sociometric ratings, and ratings of leader and member behaviors, which were obtained at the end of the group tasks.

Four different types of task were utilized to determine the generality of previously obtained findings. Each of these tasks was timed, and all groups worked on them in the same order.

1. *Thematic Apperception Test (TAT) stories*   This task consisted of writing two short stories based on TAT Card no. 11 (dragon in ravine). The groups were given fifteen minutes in which to complete this assignment. The stories were to be written out, and handed in at the end of the allotted period of time. The evaluation of performance followed the manual developed in a previous study, which yielded interjudge correlations of .72. The two stories correlated .43 ($p <$ .05) for the thirty groups.
2. *Unusual uses test*   A modification of Guilford's test was given with instructions that the groups were to think of unusual uses for two common objects, viz., a wire clothes hanger and a ruler.

   This task was scored on the basis of how frequently a given "use" or response occurred in any of the thirty groups. Each response was scored from one point (frequent response) to five points (unusual, offbeat, or infrequent response) based on a frequency distribution of the occurrence of all of the responses produced by the thirty groups. A repetition of the same response in the same group was scored zero. The total group score represents the sum of the points given to each of the ten uses which the group listed for each of the two items. The correlation of the two items over the thirty groups was .60 ($p < .01$). The score indicates the degree to which the group was able to produce unusual responses in comparison with the other groups in the experiment.

3. *Argument construction* A third task [3] required the subjects to develop arguments for, as well as against, a controversial issue. The problem involved the use of a military-training program of a very rigorous and dangerous nature which could be expected to result in a relatively high rate of casualties during the training phase, but which would pay off by leading to a relatively low death rate during actual battle conditions.

After a five-minute period in which the group members worked individually on the problem, group members were asked to develop additional arguments jointly, i.e., arguments which differed from those produced by the members individually.

4. *Fame and immortality task* The last task was somewhat similar to the third in that the members first worked alone for five minutes and then as a group for the remaining five minutes. The problem of the task was "how a person of average ability can achieve fame and immortality even though he does not possess any particular talents." This task was developed by Triandis et al. (1963) and was scored by means of Triandis' manual. The qualitative score was the average evaluation by judges of each of the suggested answers, while the quantitative score was a tally of solutions produced. The split-half correlation of the qualitative score for the thirty groups was .89 ($p < .001$). The scores obtained for different tasks were essentially uncorrelated.

The main question of concern to us here is the effect of relationship- and task-oriented leadership styles on the performance of groups with

[3] This task was developed by Lorand Szalay for this study.

TABLE 8-2   Correlation of the Leader's LPC Score and Group Performance under Relatively Low Group Atmosphere ($N = 15$)

Task	Leadership Condition	
	Participatory	Supervisory
TAT stories	−.30	−.56*
Argument construction	−.40	−.44
Fame problem	−.51	.14
Unusual uses	.63*	.31

* $p < .05$.

four different creative tasks. Table 8-2 presents the main results. As can be seen, in both the participatory and the supervisory conditions, the low-LPC leaders tended to produce better TAT stories and Argument Construction scores. The groups under high-LPC leaders tended to perform better on the Unusual Uses test than did the task-oriented leaders.

While *ad hoc* explanations must always be suspect, we offer a tentative interpretation of the curious reversal of the expected results in the case of the Unusual Uses test. The main difference between the Unusual Uses test and the other tests seems to lie in the nature of the group behavior which these tasks require. The first three tasks present problems which the group members must solve in interaction with one another. In each of these problems, there is only one final end product on which the members must agree. The Unusual Uses task, on the other hand, requires that the group members invent as many unusual uses for common objects as possible. The score is basically a sum of unusual uses which are proposed by the several members of the group. Such a task could have been performed equally well by these men working independently.

In retrospect, this may have been a coacting task since the contribution of one member is relatively independent of the contributions of other members. In fact, this result first served to focus attention on the need to classify groups into interacting and coacting categories.

In attempting to interpret this finding we also should take note of the fact that the participants indicated in postsession interviews and question-naires that they had felt under pressure because they feared that the performance data might become part of their grade in military science. The group climate was, therefore, relatively unpleasant for most leaders and members. It seemed likely, therefore, that the less threatening be-

TABLE 8-3   Correlations of the Leader's LPC Score and Group Performance in Groups with High- and with Low-leader Group Atmosphere Scores ($N = 6$)

| Task | Leadership Condition | | | |
| | Participatory | | Supervisory | |
	High GA	Low GA	High GA	Low GA
TAT stories	−.26	−.14	−.39	.47
Argument construction	−.07	.07	−.43	.01
Fame problem	−.44	−.07	.84	−.10
Unusual uses	.50	.54	.13	−.14

haviors and attitudes of high LPC leaders were quasi-therapeutic, thus enabling the groups to produce more off-beat and unusual suggestions than was the case in groups led by the more task-oriented and less permissive low-LPC leaders.

To assign the groups to Octants III and VII, we selected in each of the two leadership conditions the six groups with the highest leaders' Group Atmosphere scores and the six groups with the lowest Group Atmosphere scores. The correlations between leader LPC and group performance scores for these four sets of groups are shown in Table 8-3. None of the correlations, being based on a sample of six cases, was significant, nor were the patterns of correlations sufficiently clear-cut to permit a meaningful interpretation of this table.

SUMMARY

Two studies are here described which contain groups in Octants III and VII, that is, groups in which the task is unstructured but the leader's position power is high. Neither of these studies was especially designed to test the relationship between leadership style and group performance under these specific conditions, and the data obtained in these studies are quite weak. Insofar as we can tell from the available evidence, the groups in both studies tended to be anxiety-arousing and relatively unpleasant for leaders. Groups directed by task-oriented leaders who experienced a relatively pleasant group atmosphere performed better on all tasks except on one which, in retrospect, might be considered to have been coaching rather than interacting.

PART Chapter 9, which introduces this part, presents a theoretical integration of the empirical findings which were
described in Part II. It develops a leadership theory, the
Contingency Model of leadership effectiveness, which
has as its underlying hypothesis that the effectiveness
of a group depends upon the interaction between the
leader's style of relating to his group members and the
degree to which the situation enables the leader to exert
influence over his group. Chapter 10 describes recent
validation research supporting the Contingency Model,
and Chapter 11 deals with group processes which provide an explanation for the results which the Contingency
Model predicts.

A THEORETICAL MODEL OF LEADERSHIP EFFECTIVENESS

Chapters 4 to 8 have described the major studies of interacting groups conducted between 1951 and 1963. These studies investigated a very wide range of different groups and leadership situations. Unfortunately, these studies also yielded an equally wide range of results which were quite difficult to understand. Why, for example, should the sociometrically accepted leader's LPC score correlate positively with group creativity but negatively with performance of antiaircraft units or bomber crews? Why should the leader of the successful board of directors perform better when he is relationship-oriented, while the foreman of the successful open-hearth shift performs better when he is task-oriented?

The major turning point in our understanding of these results came with (1) the classification of groups into those with interacting, coacting, and counteracting tasks, and (2) the further categorization of interacting groups according to the three dimensions of leader-member relations, leader position power, and task structure. This taxonomy led to a three-dimensional coordinate system of eight cells shown in Figure 2-2.

The method of classification, described in Chapter 2, sought to order the studies so that the relations between leader LPC and team effectiveness would be similar in direction and magnitude for leaders falling into the same class. In other words, we tried to develop a taxonomy that would meaningfully cluster group situations on the basis of the leadership style they seemed to require.

The extent to which this attempt was successful can be seen in Tables 9-1 and 9-2. The first table summarizes the results of the various studies that have been described in the five previous chapters. The second table presents the median rank-order correlations obtained in each of the cells. The last column shows the number of studies on which the median correlations have been based. (This table does not include validation studies.) Since the table is based on an inductive ordering of data, a statistical test to determine the significance of this set of data is not legitimate. Inspection of Table 9-2 shows, however, that the median rank-order correlations

TABLE 9-1   Summary Table of Relations Obtained in Research with LPC and ASo Scores

Octants I and V
High Leader Position Power—Highly Structured Task
Good/Moderately Poor Leader-Member Relations

Study			Leader-Member Relations			
			Good Octant I	Moderately Poor Octant V	N_I	N_V
B-29 Bomber Crews. Military commander in Octant I is sociometrically most-preferred crew member and endorses keyman; is sociometrically most-preferred crew member in Octant V, but rejects his keyman on crew.	PP*	18.5				
Criterion 1: Radar bomb score circular error average (radar observer or navigator are keymen).	TS	8.0	−.81	.42	11	7
Criterion 2: Percent satisfactory visual bomb runs (bombardier is keyman).	TS	8.0	−.52	.27	6	7
(Fiedler, 1955)						
Army Tank Crews. Tank Commander in Octant I is sociometrically most-preferred crew member and endorses keyman; in Octant V is sociometrically most-preferred crew member, but does not endorse his keyman.	PP	18.5				
Criterion 1: Time to hit target (gunner is keyman).	TS	8.0	−.60	.60	6	5
Criterion 2: Time to travel to target (driver is keyman).	TS	8.0	−.33	.43		
(Fiedler, 1955)						
Antiaircraft Artillery Crews. Commander in Octant I is sociometrically most-preferred crew member; in Octant V is among ten sociometrically least-preferred crew members.	PP	18.5				
Criterion: Location and acquisition of unidentified aircraft.	TS	7.3	−.34	.49	10	10

Criterion: Umpire ratings of field tests.
(Havron et al., 1951)

TS 7.5   −.36   26

Open-hearth Steel Shops. Foremen accepted by crew.
Criterion: Tap-to-tap time (tonnage per unit of time)
(no rejected foremen were identified).
(Cleven and Fiedler, 1956)

PP 18.5

TS 7.2   −.52   15

Company Management. General manager in Octant I is sociometrically accepted by board and staff; in Octant V is
sociometrically accepted by either board or staff.
Criterion: Percent of company net income over three
years.

PP 18.0   −.67   .23   10

TS 5.6   −.52   .42   10

(Godfrey, Fiedler, and Hall, 1959)
Median Correlation

VALIDATION EVIDENCE

Sales Display Teams. Teams with detailed instructions for
setting up sales displays and preparing merchandise. No
data indicative of the leader-member relations available.

PP 17.0   76

Criterion: Ratings by higher supervisors on conformity
to performance standards. Tested by analysis of variance; low-ASo leaders performed better than high-ASo
leaders.

TS 5.8 $(F < .10)$

(Hawkins, 1962)

Service Station Management. Managers of gas stations in various communities. Company has detailed operating procedure for servicing, stock control, and reporting. No data
indicative of the leader-member relations available

PP 17.0   60

Criterion: Stock control, sales, monthly audit, and checks
by inspectors. Low-ASo man-
agers performed better than high-ASo managers. Tested by chi square.

TS 5.8 $(X^2 < .05)$

(Hawkins, 1962)

TABLE 9-1   Summary Table of Relations Obtained in Research with LPC and ASo Scores (*continued*)

Octants II and VI *
Low Leader Position Power—Highly Structured Task
Good/Moderately Poor Leader-Member Relations

Study			Leader-Member Relations		N_{II}	N_{VI}
			Good Octant II	Moderately Poor Octant VI		
High School Basketball Teams. Leader is sociometrically the most-chosen team member, but is not appointed or elected, although he wields considerable influence.	PP	3.8				
Study I Criterion: Percent of games won by midseason.	TS	7.2	−.69		14	
Study II Criterion: Seven good and five poor teams tested at end of season (Pt. bis. r). (Fiedler, 1954)	TS	7.2	−.58		12	
Student Surveying Parties. Leader is sociometrically most-preferred team member.	PP	3.2				
Criterion: Accuracy of surveying preselected parcels of land as rated by instructors. (Fiedler, 1954)	TS	7.3	−.51		22	
Median Correlation			−.58			

VALIDATION EVIDENCE

Study			Leader-Member Relations		N_{II}	N_{VI}
Team Judgments. Two students were paired to judge which answers are best for "How Supervise" test. A leader was designated by experimenter, but leader had no special function.	PP	2.0				
Criterion: Number of items completed. Tested by analysis of variance, low-ASo leaders were better than high-ASo leaders.	TS	8.0	($F < .05$)		67	

High Leader Position Power—Unstructured Task
Good/Moderately Poor Leader-Member Relations

Study			Leader-Member Relations			
			Good Octant III	Moderately Poor Octant VII	N_{III}	N_{VII}
ROTC Creativity Study. Three-man ROTC groups with leader officially appointed. Study was part of ROTC course. Highest-ranked cadet chosen as leader. Leader-member relations measured by Group Atmosphere scores from upper and lower third of distribution.	PP	9.0				
Criterion 1: Propose new pay scale for all ROTC services which will equalize pay scales (creativity rated by judges).	TS	3.4	-.43	.04	6	6
Criterion 2: Tell fable on need for peacetime army (creativity rated by judges).	TS	2.2	-.72	.24	6	6
ROTC Creativity Study—High-stress Condition. Same as above, but groups worked under close supervision of senior army officers.	PP	9.0				
Criterion 1: Pay scale proposal.	TS	3.4	-.14	.11	6	6
Criterion 2: Fable.	TS	2.2	-.60	.57	6	6
(Meuwese and Fiedler, 1964)						
Navy ROTC Creativity Study. Four-man NROTC groups participated as part of NROTC leadership class problem. Senior midshipmen were appointed leaders, and freshmen and sophomores served as members. Leaders chaired and *participated* in session.	PP	9.0				
Criterion 1: Tell two stories based on "AT card (creativity rated by judges).	TS	2.4	-.26	-.14	6	6

TABLE 9-1   Summary Table of Relations Obtained in Research with LPC and ASo Scores (*continued*)

Octants III and VII
High Leader Position Power—Unstructured Task
Good/Moderately Poor Leader-Member Relations

Study			Leader-Member Relations		N_{III}	N_{VII}
			Good Octant III	Moderately Poor Octant VII		
Criterion 2: Develop arguments pro and con for tough military training (rated by judges).	TS	4.2	-.07	.07	6	6
Criterion 3: Suggest how average person can win fame and immortality (rated in terms of originality and uniqueness of solutions).	TS	4.7	-.44	-.07	6	6
Criterion 4: Suggest unusual uses for two common objects.†	TS	4.7	.50	.54	6	6
Navy ROTC Creativity Study. Same as above but leaders *supervised*—were not permitted to contribute to task solutions, but could suggest procedures and veto ideas.	PP	11.8				
Criterion 1: TAT stories.	TS	2.4	-.39	.47	6	6
Criterion 2: Arguments.	TS	4.2	-.43	.01	6	6
Criterion 3: Fame and immortality.	TS	4.7	.84	-.10	6	6
Criterion 4: Unusual uses.†	TS	4.7	.13	-.14		
(Anderson and Fiedler, 1962) Median Correlation			-.33	.05		

Octants IV and VIII
Low Leader Position Power—Unstructured Task
Good/Moderately Poor Leader-Member Relations

Study		Leader-Member Relations		N_{IV}	N_{VIII}
		Good Octant IV	Moderately Poor Octant VIII		
Dutch Creativity Study. Four-man groups consisting of Dutch university students. Leader-member relations inferred from tension indicators in content analysis and group composition, viz., homogeneity versus heterogeneity and formal or informal leadership.					
Criterion Task: Tell three stories about TAT picture; find alternative uses or invent plot titles (creativity rated by judges).	TS 1.7				
Composition: Homogeneous religious membership and formal leaders, appointed by experimenter.	PP 5.8		−.72		8
Composition: Heterogeneous groups, appointed leaders.	PP 5.5	.75		7	
Composition: Homogeneous, informal leaders.	PP 2.0		−.64		6
Composition: Heterogeneous, informal leaders.	PP 2.0		−.23		8
(Fiedler, Meuwese, and Oonk, 1961)					
Hypnosis Study. Three-person groups, leader selected by experimenter's confederates. Leader-member relations based on Group Atmosphere scores.	PP 5.0				
Criterion: Tell three stories about same TAT card (creativity rated by judges).	TS 1.7	.64	−.72	8	8
(Fiedler, London, and Nemo, 1961)					

TABLE 9-1   Summary Table of Relations Obtained in Research with LPC and ASo Scores (*continued*)

Octants IV and VIII
Low Leader Position Power—Unstructured Task
Good/Moderately Poor Leader-Member Relations

Study			Leader-Member Relations			
			Good Octant IV	Moderately Poor Octant VIII	N_{IV}	N_{VIII}
Church Leadership Study. Four-person groups participating in leadership workshop. Leaders selected by experimenter, groups changed each day. Leader-member relations measured by Group Atmosphere score.						
Criterion 1: Justify minister's position on mercy killing (creativity in this and other tasks rated by all participants).	PP	4.8				
	TS	2.7	.28	.03	6	6
Criterion 2: Tell fable to illustrate need for separation of church and state.	PP	4.5				
	TS	2.2	.89	−.03	6	6
Criterion 3: Devise campaign to raise funds for young student minister.	PP	4.8				
	TS	3.2	.49	−.40	6	6
Criterion 4: Plan and perform skit on music for the worship service.	PP	4.5				
	TS	2.2	.37	−.60	6	6
(Fiedler, Bass, and Fiedler, 1961)						
Mental Health Leadership Study. Three-person groups, with chairman selected by experimenter. Leader-member relations measured by Group Atmosphere score.	PP	4.5				
Criterion Task: Justify use of elementary schools for			44	− 76	7	7

ROTC Creativity Study—Internal Stress Condition. Three-man groups, two army and one navy cadets. Leader was lowest-ranking army man. PP 4.5

Criterion Task 1: Develop new pay schedule for ROTC programs.	TS 3.4	.49	−.04	6	6
Criterion Task 2: Tell fable about peacetime army (creativity rated by judges).	TS 2.2	−.03	−.47	6	6

(Meuwese and Fiedler, 1964)

Chairman, Board of Directors. Boards of directors of small co-operatively owned corporations. Leader-member relations estimated on basis of sociometric ratings. PP 7.0

Criterion: Company net income over three years.	TS 4.1	.21	−.60	10	10

(Godfrey, Fiedler, and Hall, 1959)

Median Correlations	.47	−.43

VALIDATION EVIDENCE

Church Leadership Study II. Three-person groups assembled ad hoc, with leader designated by experimenter. Leader-group member relations assessed by leader's GA scores and postmeeting questionnaires. PP 4.5

Criterion Task: Justify your position to children on reading prayers in school.	TS 2.2	.27	−.04	19	19

* PP = leader's position power; TS = task structure.
† Probably a coacting task.

142   PART III

TABLE 9-2   Median Correlations between Leader LPC and Group Performance in Various Octants

	Leader-Member Relations	Task Structure	Position Power	Median Correlation	Number of Relations Included in Median
Octant I	Good	Structured	Strong	−.52	8
Octant II	Good	Structured	Weak	−.58	3
Octant III	Good	Unstructured	Strong	−.33	12
Octant IV	Good	Unstructured	Weak	.47	10
Octant V	Moderate Poor	Structured	Strong	.42	6
Octant VI	Moderate Poor	Structured	Weak		0
Octant VII	Moderate Poor	Unstructured	Strong	.05	12
Octant VIII	Moderate Poor	Unstructured	Weak	−.43	12

are likely to reflect systematic effects rather than random fluctuations of correlation coefficients.[1]

The classification of group-task situations into eight cells as well as the data in Table 9-2 quickly suggested one further step. We had started with the assumption that leadership is an influence process and that each of the three dimensions measures one aspect of the situation which determines the amount of influence the leader would have at his disposal. In other words, the classification system can tell us approximately how favorable a particular situation would be for anyone who happened to be a leader, i.e., to what extent the situation will make it easy or difficult for the leader to influence his group members. We could now attempt to order the octants in Figure 2-1 (also listed in Table 9-2) still further according to their favorableness for the leader.

An ordering of this type requires several assumptions. It is not difficult to decide that the situations represented by Octant I would be most favorable and that those in Octant VIII would be least favorable for the leader. Under normal conditions, the leader who is liked and accepted by

[1] This is suggested by a X^2 of 15.928 ($p < .05$) testing the deviation of the obtained distribution in Table 9-1 from the theoretical distribution of random correlation coefficients.

his group (or feels liked and accepted), who has high position power, and who has a clear-cut task, has everything in his favor. His group members will be glad to follow him; those who are not compliant can be given specific directions and, if necessary, they can be coerced to perform the task according to the procedures the group is to follow. In fact, in many structured task situations, only the leader is given detailed instructions on the procedures the group is to follow. The liked leader, therefore, has "expert power" as well as "attraction power" and "coercive power." [2] Likewise, the situation in Octant VIII is not difficult to understand. The leader is not well liked, he has little legitimate or coercive power, and the task is so nebulous that one man's opinion is as good as another's. Under these conditions, the leader will find it very difficult to exert influence.

In attempting to order the intermediate octants, we encounter a number of problems. Is it better to be liked and to have low position power, or is it better to be disliked but to have a highly structured task?

We have here gone on the assumption that the leader-member relationship is likely to be most decisive in determining the favorableness of the situation for the leader. A leader who is liked, accepted, and trusted by his members will find it easy to make his influence felt. In fact, position power, under these conditions, may be somewhat redundant. The leader who is trusted and accepted does not need much position power to influence his group. We have, therefore, first classified all groups on the basis of leader-member relations.

The second most important dimension in this system seemed to be the degree of task structure. As we have said in Chapter 2, most groups exist for the purpose of performing tasks which are required by the organization of which the group is a subunit. The organization, therefore, has a considerable stake in assuring that the leader can get the tasks performed well and according to specifications.

One way in which the organization can assure compliance in task performance is by providing the leader with standard operating instructions, detailed manuals, and detailed step-by-step methods for performing certain jobs. The army's method of doing things "by the numbers" is the prototype of the highly structured task. There may well be "a right way and an army way" as is alleged by the uncounted privates of uncounted armies, but the fact of the matter is that the organization can increase reliable performance and output by insisting that step-by-step procedures be followed

For a more extended discussion of sources of power see French and Raven (1959).

even though there might occasionally be a way of doing the same task better and faster.

One important feature of the highly programmed or structured task is that the organization through the leader can maintain quality control over the process and over group behavior at every step. This also enables the organization to back up the leader whenever someone gets out of line. In effect, by structuring the task the organization is able to provide the leader with power, irrespective of the power of the position which he may occupy.[3] It is for this reason that we consider the leader's position power as somewhat less important than the task structure in providing the leader with influence. This is well illustrated in highly authoritarian organizations where low-ranking leaders occasionally may be used to supervise individuals of higher rank. One example is the noncommissioned officer or the junior officer who is given the job of training higher-ranking medical officers in military drill and ceremonials, or the aircraft commander with captain's rank who may be in charge of a crew in which the navigator and bombardier are majors.

While position power is here considered to be the least important of these three dimensions, we should emphasize that this hierarchy must not be seen as eternally fixed. Large differences in rank and position power may outweigh relatively slight differences in task structure. An extremely structured task (e.g., counting down a space probe) may outweigh the importance of poor leader-member relations. However, these examples are likely to be the exception rather than the rule.

Given the assumption that under ordinary conditions the leader-member relations dimension is the most important and the task-structure dimension the next most important of the three dimensions in defining the favorableness of the situation for the leader, we can then order the eight octant into a single array on the basis of their favorableness for the leader. We first order the octants according to whether the leader-member relation are relatively good or poor. We then order them according to high versus low task structure, and finally according to relatively strong versus weak position power. The resulting order is reflected in the numbering of octants, with Octant I being most favorable and Octant VIII being least favorable in this classification system. Octant I reflects situations in which

[3] Such other dimensions of the task as cooperation requirements, sequencing of functions, etc., may, of course, also play an important part in determining the favorableness of the situation (O'Brien, 1966). This needs to be considered in future studies.

the leader's job is very easy, in which he enjoys a great deal of influence. In this octant we have a well-liked or highly respected leader with high rank and power who directs his group members in a task which is well structured. This is also the case, to a somewhat lesser extent, in Octant II, in which the leader is liked and accepted and has a structured task, although he has little formal power to enforce his demands.

In contrast, there are some octants in which the leader's influence is quite low. Thus, in Octant VIII the leader is not well accepted nor does he have any sanctions at his disposal by means of which he can enforce his demands. Moreover, the task is ambiguous and unclear and he, therefore, is unlikely to know more about it than other members of his group. In fact, in a situation of this type, there is always the possibility that the group will simply fall apart. Such a situation tends to arise in volunteer committees which are saddled with a disliked or unacceptable chairman or in policy-making groups in which the chairman and his members are seriously at odds.

Of intermediate difficulty, as far as the leader is concerned, would be situations in which the well-liked leader has an unstructured task or in which the somewhat disliked leader has a highly structured task. In the former situation, typified again by the committee, or the creative group, the leader has no particular problem with the team he heads. He does, however, have a problem in defining the task, or in getting his group to work creatively on an ambiguous, vaguely outlined problem. The second case involves the somewhat disliked leader whose group has a structured task. Such situations occur in industrial groups or in military groups in which the leader may be mildly disliked or not highly respected.

It is now possible to plot the relations between leadership style and performance on the one hand, and the degree of favorableness which the situation has for the leader on the other. We shall indicate the favorableness of the group-task situation on the horizontal axis by ordering the octants from one to eight. We shall then indicate on the vertical axis the type of leadership style which promotes good performance. This is done by plotting the correlation coefficients between leader LPC or ASo scores and group performance at places on the horizontal axis which indicate the various octants. Points in the plot which fall above the midline (correlation of .00) indicate a positive correlation between leader LPC or ASo and group performance, i.e., that groups under relationship-oriented leaders (high LPC) tended to perform better than groups under task-oriented leaders (low LPC). Points below the midline of .00 indicate

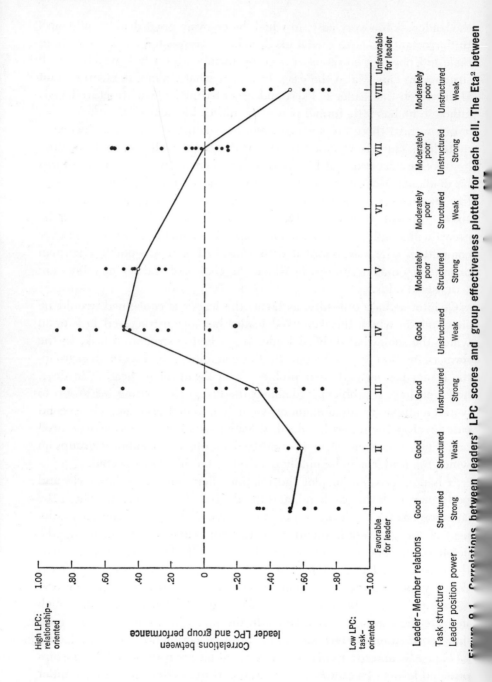

Figure 8.1 Correlations between leaders' LPC scores and group effectiveness plotted for each cell. The Eta² between

that groups under task-oriented (low-LPC) leaders performed better than did groups under the more considerate, relationship-oriented leaders (Figure 9-1).

As can be seen, when we connect the median correlations on this plot, we obtain a bow-shaped curve. This figure indicates that *the appropriateness of the leadership style for maximizing group performance is contingent upon the favorableness of the group-task situation.*

Group performance, then, is related to both the leadership style and the degree to which the situation provides the leader with the opportunity to exert influence. Task-oriented (low-LPC or -ASo) leaders perform best in situations which are highly favorable for them or in those which are relatively unfavorable. Considerate, relationship-oriented leaders tend to perform best in situations in which they have only moderate influence, either because the task is relatively unstructured or because they are not too well accepted although their position power is high and the task is structured.

This theoretical formulation, which has been called the "Contingency Model" of leadership effectiveness, by and large fits our everyday experience. In the very favorable conditions in which the leader has power, informal backing, and a relatively well-structured task, the group is ready to be directed, and the group members expect to be told what to do. Consider the captain of an airliner in its final landing approach. We would hardly want him to turn to his crew for a discussion on how to land.

In the relatively unfavorable situation, we would again expect that the task-oriented leader will be more effective than will the considerate leader who is concerned with interpersonal relations. Consider here the disliked chairman of a volunteer committee which is asked to plan the office picnic on a beautiful Sunday. If the leader asks too many questions about what the group ought to do or how he should proceed, he is likely to be told that "we ought to go home." This also reflects the old army adage that it is better in an emergency that the leader make a wrong decision than no decision at all.

In situations which are only moderately favorable or which are moderately unfavorable for the leader, a considerate, relationship-oriented attitude seems to be most effective. Under these conditions, in which the accepted leader faces an ambiguous, nebulous task, or one in which the task is structured but the leader is not well accepted, the considerate, relationship-oriented leadership style is more likely to result in effective team performance. Octant IV situations (accepted leader, low position power, unstructured task) are most commonly found in committees or creative groups. Here the leader must provide a nonthreatening, permissive environment if members are to feel free to make suggestions and to contribute to the discussion. The chairman or the leader typically is not in a position to enforce compliance with his instructions, nor would this contribute to the performance of the group. In fact, the committee chairman who imposes his own opinions and decisions on the group, or who forces decisions prematurely, in effect negates the potential benefits he could derive from the participation of his group members (Osborn, 1962; Parnes, 1962).

In the situation represented by Octant V (poorly accepted leader, high position power, structured task), the effective leader is apt to be diplomatic and indirect in his dealings with his group members. The leader who feels insecure or anxious is more likely to consult his group members, he is more likely to be cautious in making commitments for his group, and he will, generally, be concerned about the feelings of his group members. The highly task-oriented leader who is unaware of his status in the group, or who is made defensive by it, often tries to bluff his way through. This type of leader is likely to create resistance, and his group members may not put themselves out to assure good group performance.

LIMITATIONS OF THE MODEL

The plot in Figure 9-1 presents a two-dimensional picture of the relationship between leadership style and group performance on the one hand and the favorableness or difficulty of the group-task situation on the other. This two-dimensional picture is somewhat deceptive in suggesting that the groups are evenly distributed throughout the three-dimensional space described by leader-member relations, position power, and task structure. It is, therefore, instructive to present the same relations on a three-dimensional space (or rather, on two separate plots, of two dimensions each). Figure 9-2 shows the correlation coefficients (decimal points omitted) on two-dimensional coordinate systems, one for good leader-member relations, the other for moderately poor leader-member relations. The correlations are indicated in the space actually corresponding to the average ratings which each of the group-task situations received from our judges. While our system of classifying groups is admittedly tentative and rough, the figure shows quite clearly that some areas of the classification space are completely empty. This is the case, for example, of Octant VI, which should contain groups with high task structure and low position power.

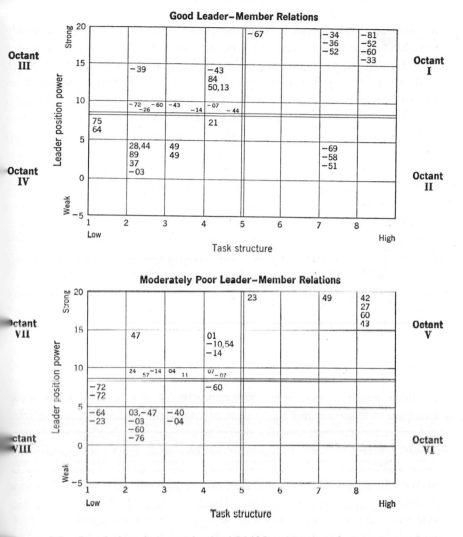

Figure 9-2   Correlations between leader LPC/ASo plotted against leader position power and task structure under good and moderately poor leader-member relations.

ikewise, groups with very high position power and very low task struc-
ure are absent from Octant III and Octant VII.

The thinly covered areas are either regions which our studies have not
mpled or those in which real-life groups and laboratory groups are
ther rare. For example, groups which would have a highly structured

task, very weak position power, as well as poor leader-member relations are not commonly found. As mentioned earlier, such groups are generally not able to maintain themselves over long periods of time since a disliked leader with low position power, or an emergent leader who is disliked, will soon be replaced. Likewise, a group with very strong leader position power but very low task structure is difficult to imagine in real life. An example would be a general and two enlisted men working on a creative task, such as a plan of strategy. Another example would be an archbishop working with two ordinary laymen on a church policy. One would guess that the group members might be so overawed that their contributions would be minimal unless the leader of the group is extremely nonthreatening and permissive. To behave in this fashion is often difficult for a leader with high position power.

In addition, as we mentioned previously, the classification system does not allow for the extremely poor leader-member relations which are sometimes found in real-life groups and which have been discussed in Chapters 5 and 6. The leader who is hated or strongly disliked will find the group situation very difficult since his influence attempts are likely to be rejected. In some instances, the disaffected members of his group may even subtly sabotage the task.

Because the leader-member dimension is so important we would expect that a group situation characterized by extremely negative leader-member relations would be quite unfavorable for the leader even when his position power is strong and the task is highly structured. We would anticipate that the task-oriented leaders who are strongly disliked or rejected would perform better than similarly disliked leaders who are relationship oriented. The effects of such very poor leader-member relations could be seen in the studies of bomber crews, antiaircraft units, open-hearth shops and farm supply companies. These studies indicate that the classification system needs to be extended and generalized to accommodate cases of this nature. We have done so by the expedient of adding another cell to the classification system, namely "Octant VIII-A," which contains groups with structured tasks and high leader position power but a strongly disliked or rejected leader.

This patchwork in our attempt to build a meaningful system for classifying group situations obviously points to the need for a simpler classification system that would lead to a more parsimonious and theoretically elegant solution. It should be emphasized, therefore, that the classification of groups according to the three dimensions of good and poor leader-member relations, strong and weak position power, and high and low task structure serves merely as a convenient interim basis for ordering group situations with respect to their favorableness for the leader. There are many other dimensions which should influence the favorableness of the situation for the leader. Thus, extremely stressful conditions, or an increase in the potential conflict among group members, should make situations less favorable. And such factors as member abilities and motivation, group heterogeneity, expertness of the leader and his familiarity with the task and with his group, should affect the degree to which he can influence the members of his group. Empirical research is clearly needed to develop a meaningful metric for indexing this situational favorableness dimension in terms which are absolute.

SUMMARY

We have here presented a theory, the Contingency Model, which states that the group's performance will be contingent upon the appropriate matching of leadership style and the degree of favorableness of the group situation for the leader, that is, the degree to which the situation provides the leader with influence over his group members. The model suggests that group performance can, therefore, be improved either by modifying the leader's style or by modifying the group-task situation.

The remainder of the present chapter is devoted to a methodological discussion concerning the statistical relations which this model implies. The reader who is not especially interested in these problems should turn to Chapter 10.

TECHNICAL NOTE

Multiple regression of the contingency relationship.[4] We obtained a curvilinear plot indicating the nature of the relationship between the leader's LPC and ASo scores and the performance of his group under varying conditions of favorableness. What part do the various components of the group-task situation play in determining performance?

In order to obtain a quantitative indication of the extent and nature of

The writer is indebted to Dr. Lee J. Cronbach for suggesting these analyses and to Dr. A. R. Bass, now at Wayne State University, who performed the statistical computations.

these relationships, a configural multiple-regression technique was employed (cf. Horst, 1954; Lubin and Osborn, 1957). The predictors in this multiple-regression equation were the three group dimensions, position power (PP), task structure (TS), and leader-member relations (LM), and the four interactions of these dimensions with one another (PP × TS, PP × LM, TS × LM, and PP × TS × LM). The latter terms were obtained from standard scores on the original dimensions and are, thus, nonlinear functions of these dimensions. A multiple regression was then computed for these seven predictors, the criterion being the correlation between the leader's LPC score and his group's performance. The number of cases for this multiple regression was sixty-eight, which is the number of individual correlations between LPC and performance reported in Table 9-2 plus those with intermediate values on the leader-member relations dimension. The validation data were not included in these analyses.

Table 9-3 shows the correlation among the predictors and their validities. This table also presents the beta weights for the predictors and the multiple correlation between the seven predictors and the criterion. The three dimensions taken alone are unrelated to the LPC-performance criterion. However, the two double interaction terms involving leader-member relations (PP × LM and TS × LM) are both significantly related to the criterion. Further, the triple interaction (PP × TS × LM), while having zero validity for the criterion, has the largest and only significant beta weight. This variable is a suppressor, having relatively high correlations with several other predictors which are components of it. It would appear, however, that this triple interaction is not a particularly important determinant of the LPC-performance correlations. Rather, its relatively large beta weight is a function of its necessarily large relationship with several of the other predictors.

The multiple correlation of all seven predictors and the criterion is .58 ($p < .01$). If we use only the three dimensions as predictors (PP, TS, and LM), the multiple R is negligible, namely, .15 (n.s.). However, if we add to these three predictors the single nonlinear term TS × LM, the multiple correlation increases to .45 ($p. < .05$). This increase from .15 to .45 is significant beyond the .01 level. Alternatively, if we add to the three original dimensions only the single interaction term PP × LM, the multiple R increases from .15 to .42, again a significant increase ($p < .01$) over the prediction obtained from the three linear predictors alone.

It will be noted that task structure and leader position power are highly correlated ($r = .75$). While this may be a peculiarity of the particular

A THEORETICAL MODEL OF LEADERSHIP EFFECTIVENESS   153

TABLE 9-3   Multiple Correlation Analysis of Group Dimension Variables as Predictors of the LPC/ASo–Group Effectiveness Correlation

	(1) PP	(2) TS	(3) LM	(4) PP×TS	(5) PP×LM	(6) TS×LM	(7) PP×TS×LM	Correlations between leader LPC and group performance
PP		.75*	−.09	.60*	−.08	−.17	.02	−.09
TS			.03	.43*	−.16	−.01	−.10	−.14
LM				−.17	.16	.15	.64*	.04
PP × TS					.08	−.15	.01	.08
PP × LM						.78*	.60*	−.34*
TS × LM							.49*	−.41*
PP × TS × LM								.01

Standardized Regression Coefficients

	Correlations between leader LPC and group performance
PP	−.39
TS	.05
LM	−.22
PP × TS	.22
PP × LM	−.40
TS × LM	−.39
PP × TS × LM	.59*

* $p < .01$ ($N = 68$)
Multiple R = .58
PP = position power; TS = task structure; LM = leader-member relationship

sample of tasks used in these studies, it is possible that this relationship is fairly general (i.e., that leader power is higher in those situations in which the task is more highly structured). The above findings may then indicate that the low-LPC leader has more effective work groups when either his position power or task structure is high *and* leader-member relationships are favorable. When leader power or task structure is low *and* leader-member relations are poor, then the high-LPC leader has a more effective group. This problem needs to be explored in future studies.

10 TESTS OF THE CONTINGENCY MODEL

The critical test of a theory is its ability to predict. The Contingency Model was inductively derived on the basis of data available in 1962. It is thus essential that we ask how well this model can predict group performance in entirely new studies and how well it allows us to extrapolate to other situations not specifically covered by the model.

One important set of relations predicted by the Contingency Model has already been described in Chapters 5 and 6. Data had been collected on groups having high position power and structured tasks. The original analyses (Fiedler, 1958) had yielded negative correlations between the leader's LPC or ASo scores and group performance when the leader-member relations were good, but positive or zero correlations for the remaining sets of groups.

The Contingency Model predicted that the correlations between leader LPC and ASo would be negative in situations which were very favorable for the leader in these groups in which the leader was sociometrically highly accepted (Octant I), and that they would be positive in groups in which the leader was only moderately accepted by his group (Octant V). It seemed reasonable to extrapolate from the model that these relations would again be negative in groups in which the leader was sociometrically rejected by members of his group (Octant VIII-A). All of these analyses supported the hypothesis derived from the model, as we have already shown in Figure 6-1. Since these data were collected prior to the development of the model, the results do not constitute completely "clean" validation evidence.

Two subsequent major investigations were specifically designed to test the Contingency Model. These two crucial studies are here described in some detail because they also provided data which will be discussed in later chapters. Also described are two less extensive studies which provide partial tests of the hypothesis.

THE BELGIAN NAVY STUDY

The first validation study [1] was conducted in cooperation with the Belgian

[1] This study was conducted while the writer was on a Ford Faculty Research Fellowship at the University of Louvain, Belgium, from 1963 to 1964. I wish to express my

naval forces (Fiedler, 1966a). In addition to testing the Contingency Model, this study also was designed to extend the Contingency hypothesis to linguistically and culturally heterogeneous groups. It tried to determine the effects of cultural heterogeneity on group performance.

Linguistic and cultural heterogeneity presents a serious problem in a surprisingly large number of modern nations. These, to mention but a few, include Canada, Finland, India, Israel, Italy, Mexico, Pakistan, Spain, Switzerland, Yugoslavia, portions of the United States, and practically all underdeveloped countries in the African and Asian continents. It is a ubiquitous and all-pervasive feature of Belgian life. Belgium is sharply divided into two population and geographical sectors. Roughly 50 percent of the population is Flemish and lives in the northern half of Belgium, with Dutch as the official language. Approximately 45 percent of the population is French-speaking. It consists of Walloons, who live in the southern part of the country, as well as the majority of the population of Brussels, which is predominantly French-speaking although officially bilingual. A small segment of the population is German-speaking. Only a small minority of Belgians are fluently bilingual, and relatively few French-speaking Belgians are able to speak Dutch.

Since its independence in 1830, the country has been enmeshed in the so-called "linguistic conflict," which has had far-reaching repercussions on Belgium's social, economic, and political life. In addition to the language barrier, the related cultural differences between the Flemish and French populations are considerable, in fact, almost as pronounced as the differences between the populations of Holland and France. In an effort to cope with this situation, the armed forces of Belgium have established, whenever possible, separate Dutch- and French-speaking units. Officers and petty officers are required by law to give orders, training, and instructions in the mother tongue of the men assigned to their units. A substantial number of important bilingual units do exist, and the effectiveness of these bilingual units is of critical concern to the Belgian armed forces.

The linguistic conflict of the country is of particular relevance for a test of the Contingency Model since heterogeneity in language and culture

particular appreciation to my close coworker, Professor Jozef M. Nuttin, Jr., Director of the Laboratory of Social Psychology at the University of Louvain, and to Mrs. Annie Janssen-Beckers, our research associate. We are deeply indebted to Commodore L. Petitjean, then Chief of Staff of the Belgian Naval Forces, for permission to perform the research, and to Capitaine V. Van Laetham, then Commandant of the Centre de Formation de la Force Navale, Ste. Croix, and to Dr. Urgiste Bouvier, Director of the Center for Social Studies of the Ministry of Defense, who actively consulted and cooperated with us in the planning and data collection phases of this study.

should substantially increase the difficulty of the leader's task (Fiedler et al., 1960; Katz and Cohen, 1962; Rombauts, 1962). A man who does not speak the leader's language well might accidentally or willfully mis-understand instructions and orders, leaving the leader little recourse but to assume that the difficulties were due to poor communication. Also, men with different cultural backgrounds tend to make different implicit as-sumptions about interpersonal relations (Hall, 1959). In addition, hetero-geneous groups tend to be less cohesive than homogeneous groups, and the participants tend to be under greater strain since the heterogeneity in language and culture is typically concomitant with antagonisms against members of the other groups (e.g., Rombauts, 1962). Differences in lan-guage and culture between the leader and his members were, therefore, expected to affect to a substantial degree the ability of the leader to influence his group, hence the favorableness of the situation with which he had to deal.

DESIGN OF THE EXPERIMENT

The test of the Contingency Model required that we determine the cor-relations between the leader's LPC score and performance in group situa-tions which vary from highly favorable to highly unfavorable. The model predicts negative correlations between leader LPC and group performance in very favorable and in very unfavorable situations, but positive correla-tions in situations intermediate in favorableness for the leader. In other words, task-oriented leaders should perform better than relationship-oriented leaders under conditions in which the situation gives the leader potentially much influence or very little influence over his members. Rela-tionship-oriented leaders should perform better than task-oriented leaders in situations in which the leader's influence is only moderately high.

Subjects.   The experiment was conducted at the Belgian naval training center in Ste. Croix-Bruges. The participants were selected on the basis of pretests to match Dutch- and French-speaking petty officers and men on the basis of intelligence, language comprehension, and attitude measures, as well as LPC scores.

The study involved 96 three-man groups consisting of 288 petty officers and recruits: 24 of these petty officers and 120 recruits came from French-speaking (Walloon) homes while the other 24 petty officers and 120 re-cruits came from Dutch-speaking (Flemish) homes.

The recruits ranged in age from seventeen to twenty-four years (mean age 20.17). Most of them had been in the navy less than six weeks at the time of the study.

Petty officers of the Belgian navy are career men who expect to remain in the service for twenty years or more. Typically, they are graduates of a petty-officer candidate school, which provides training in military specialties as well as in military leadership. Promotion to petty officer from the ranks is possible but unusual and the typical petty officer enjoys considerable prestige and power. His status is roughly comparable to that of a chief petty officer or that of a warrant officer in the United States Navy. The forty-eight petty officers in our sample ranged in age from nineteen to forty-five years, with a mean of 29.48. These men had an average of about ten years of navy leadership training and experience.

Composition of groups. The ninety-six groups were assembled to provide the widest possible range of situational favorableness for the leader. The favorableness of the group situation was operationally defined by four dimensions or facets. Three of these were basically identical to those in the original model.

We postulated that the group situation would be more favorable for the leader if (1) the leader had high position power rather than low position power; (2) the task was structured and clearly defined rather than unstructured and nebulous; and (3) the group was homogeneous in culture and language rather than heterogeneous in these respects. In addition (4) the group would provide a more favorable situation if the leader experienced the group climate as pleasant, accepting, and relaxed rather than as unpleasant, tense, and rejecting.

Three of these dimensions determining the favorableness of the situation could be experimentally built into the design of the experiment. These were the leader's position power, the structure of the task, and the group's heterogeneity. The fourth, the leader's relations with his members, had to be determined by means of postsession questionnaires, which were obtained after each of the task sessions.[2]

Although the procedure of assigning groups to cells on the basis of good or poor leader-member relations would have made for a better experimental design, experimentally manipulating this variable would have presented problems with which we could not deal in this study. It would have required assembling groups on the basis of sociometric preference ratings obtained in advance or having groups perform various tasks and then assigning them to appropriate cells on the basis of Group Climate scores in the previous interactions. Lack of time and personnel precluded these alternative methods.

Position power   This dimension was incorporated into the experimental design by assembling forty-eight groups with high leader position power. Leaders of these groups were petty officers who, as we mentioned above, have considerable legitimate power in the Belgian navy. Their power was further increased by giving them the final decision in all questions on which there might be disagreement. The forty-eight groups with low position power had recruit leaders matched with the petty officers in terms of intelligence, LPC, and language comprehension scores. These groups were instructed that the leader was to serve as chairman and that all group decisions had to be unanimous.

Task structure   Two structured tasks required the groups to route a ship, first through ten ports and then through twelve ports, by the shortest possible way. The unstructured task involved the composition of a letter urging young men to join the Belgian navy. Half the groups began with the structured tasks before going on to the unstructured task, while the other forty-eight groups began with the unstructured task. These tasks are described in greater detail below.

Heterogeneity   Forty-eight homogeneous groups consisted of a leader and two members from the same language and cultural background. In the forty-eight heterogeneous groups, twenty-four groups had a French-speaking leader and two Dutch-speaking members, while twenty-four groups had a Dutch-speaking leader and two French-speaking members.

Leader-member relations   Group Climate Factor scores were obtained from postsession questionnaires which the leader and the members completed at the conclusion of the structured and the unstructured tasks. The Group Climate Factor was defined by high factor loadings on the leader's Group Atmosphere scores, leader esteem for his members, leader satisfaction with his group, and member satisfaction with the leader.

Splitting the sample of ninety-six groups on the basis of heterogeneity, position power, and task structure resulted in eight cells. The groups within each of these eight cells were now further split into those with the leader's Group Climate scores above and those with his scores below the median for each cell. The final design consisted, therefore, of sixteen cells (Table 10-1). Each of these cells, in effect, defined a step on the dimension of the favorableness of the leader's situation. The most favor

TABLE 10-1   Design of the Belgian Navy Experiment * (Six Groups per Cell)

Leader's Language	High Position Power— Task Sequence		Low Position Power— Task Sequence	
	UT–ST–NVT	ST–UT–NVT	UT–ST–NVT	ST–UT–NVT
Homogeneous				
Dutch	D†	H	N	R
French	E	K	O	S
Heterogeneous				
Dutch	F	L	P	T
French	G	M	Q	U

* UT = unstructured task; ST = structured task; NVT = nonverbal task.
† Letters D through U identify cells in this study.

able leader situation would be a homogeneous group with high group climate working under the direction of a petty officer on a structured task. The least favorable situation would be a heterogeneous group with a low Group Climate score working under a recruit leader on an unstructured task. The general consensus of the research team and the staff officers at the training center was that the heterogeneity dimension would be most important in determining favorableness or unfavorableness and that the group climate dimension would be next in importance for these men.

Control variables. There was a considerable range in the intelligence scores of the men in our sample. It seemed highly likely, therefore, that very intelligent groups would perform more effectively than would relatively dull groups. It also seemed possible that leaders with high LPC scores would be overrepresented by chance in some cells of the design while leaders with low LPC scores might be overrepresented in other cells.

Further controls were, therefore, required. Each set of six groups within a cell was systematically assigned so that three groups within each cell would consist of men with relatively high intelligence scores while the other three groups would have men who fell into the lower half of the intelligence-score distribution. In addition, two of the groups within each cell (one with high and one with low intelligence scores) were assembled

TABLE 10-2   LPC and Intelligence Distribution of Groups within Each Cell

Intelligence of Group	LPC of Leader and Group Members		
	High	Medium	Low
High	One Group	One Group	One Group
Low	One Group	One Group	One Group

with high-LPC leaders, two with intermediate-LPC leaders, and two with low-LPC leaders (see Table 10-2).

Group tasks. As already mentioned, the groups were given one unstructured task and two essentially identical structured tasks. They were also given a nonverbal task in which all verbal communication was prohibited. This nonverbal task was always presented last.

In the unstructured task the men were told that they had been appointed to a committee which was to devise a recruiting letter for boys sixteen to seventeen years of age urging them to enlist in the Belgian naval forces. The letter, containing no more than 250 words, and written either in French or in Dutch, was to be completed in 30 minutes. The men were told that the letters would be judged on style and form as well as on persuasiveness and originality.[3]

The Dutch and French letters were rated by separate groups of judges, depending upon the language of the letter. The letters were rated by means of a manual on five criteria namely, well-written versus poorly written, sloppy, awkward; understandably presented versus confused, incomprehensible; interesting versus boring; persuasive versus unconvincing; and original versus trite, platitudinous, commonplace.

The reliability of the summed criterion ratings, based on interrater

---

[3] Our earlier studies in the United States and in Holland had required groups to invent a fable, tell a story, or prepare a skit. However, the officers of the naval training center believed that the petty officers and men would strongly object to working on a problem which did not appear directly relevant to the navy. For this reason, we chose the recruiting letter as an alternative even though a letter of this type constitutes a considerably more structured task than would have been desirable since it has a traditional form, a traditional beginning and end, and, in this case, a clearly defined content.

agreement (Cronbach et al., 1963) was .86 for the French-speaking judges and .92 for the Dutch-speaking judges.[4]

The two structured tasks required the groups to route a ship through a specified number of points.

To assure that all three group members would have to interact in working on the problems, the materials for performing these tasks were presented on three different sheets. One member of the group received a map of all the ports which were to be covered; a second member was given a mileage chart of distances between all ports; the third member was given a list of detailed instructions and a schedule for listing the ports and mileages for each leg of the journey. Each of the two structured tasks was to be completed in twenty minutes. The team which devised the shortest distance for the total route was given the highest score for the task. These scores, after being adjusted for errors made in routing the ship or in deleting a port, were then converted to T scores.[5]

The last problem presented to each group in this experiment was a nonverbal task. This task was included in the experiment so that we could determine the effect of cultural heterogeneity in situations which did not require verbal communication. Thus, if homogeneous groups performed more effectively than heterogeneous groups on the structured and unstructured tasks but not on the nonverbal task, it would suggest that difficulties in language rather than in cultural background accounted for the superior performance of the homogeneous groups. If, on the other hand, the homogeneous groups performed better on all tasks, including the nonverbal task, the inference could be drawn that the cultural differences, and perhaps antagonistic regional attitudes, degraded the performance of heterogeneous groups.

The nonverbal task was designed as a coacting situation. The group leaders had previously been instructed in field-stripping and reassembling

---

[4] Because the ratings of the French and the Dutch judges differed to some extent in means and standard deviation, the assumption was made that these differences were due to different response sets inherent in the culture. This assumption required that the ratings be converted to T scores.

[5] The first structured task turned out to be less satisfactory than the second task: nine of the groups obtained a perfect score and, therefore, had tied ranks. At the same time, on the first task sixty-two of the ninety-six groups made a total of 189 routing errors by "running out of fuel," forgetting to make required legs of the journey, or omitting one or more ports, as against forty-two groups with sixty-eight errors on the second structured task. Since the first task appeared to be a methodologically poor measure of group performance the analyses are based on the second structured task.

a .45 caliber automatic pistol. They were now asked to imagine that they were in charge of a NATO unit composed of men who did not speak their language. The leader's job was to train his two men in field-stripping and assembling the hand weapon in a ten-minute period without giving any verbal instructions. The group members were then given a blueprint of the various components of the weapon, and they were to indicate the order in which the parts were to be disassembled and reassembled.

The sum of the two members' scores constituted the criterion. However, because the correlation between the two members' scores was fairly low (.35), the data could be used only in some of the cruder analyses.

Task intercorrelations.   The tasks of this study were designed to span the range of required verbal interactions. The letter-writing task required a high level of verbal communication in which cultural and linguistic background would play an important part. The required level of verbal interaction was minimal in the pistol-assembly task in which no verbal communications were allowed to take place, and it was intermediate in the structured ship-routing problems.

The intercorrelation among the four performance scores is shown in Table 10-3. As can be seen, the performance scores for these four tasks were uncorrelated and, therefore, presumably independent. On the face of it, this set of results seems somewhat surprising, especially in the case of the two structured tasks which were essentially identical. These findings are, however, quite consistent with the hypothesis of the Contingency Model: we would expect different leader performance depending on whether the group-task situation is more or less favorable for the leader. The second structured task presented an easier situation for the leader since his previous exposure to the first structured task enabled him to

TABLE 10-3   Intercorrelations among Group-task Performance Scores *

	UT	ST I	ST II	NVT
Unstructured task	—	.20	.03	.14
First structured task		—	.14	.13
Second structured task			—	.10
Nonverbal task				—

* UT = unstructured task; ST I = first structured task; ST II = second structured task; NVT = nonverbal task.

direct the group more effectively. This is also shown by the fact that groups made more errors on the first task even though it was somewhat simpler than the second task. Since leadership style and the favorableness of the situation should interact, the model would predict low intercorrelations of group task scores.

POSTSESSION QUESTIONNAIRES

At the conclusion of each task session all participants completed a number of questionnaires and scales designed to measure the group members' reactions to the tasks and to permit some inferences about the group processes during the session. We will deal with these group process variables again in the next chapter.

Of major importance among the postsession questionnaires was the Group Atmosphere scale. The corrected split-half reliability of the scale was over .90. Leaders and members apparently tended to judge group atmosphere on the basis of different criteria since the correlations between group members' and leaders' scores were fairly low in each of the three tasks (.35, .31, and .43). Yet a group leader tended to give consistently good or poor Group Atmosphere scores in all task sessions, as indicated by the high intercorrelations among the three sessions, namely, .76, .73, and .83.[6]

Additional scales of importance were a twenty-item, eight-point Behavior Description Questionnaire (BDQ) and a sixteen-item Member Reaction Questionnaire of the same format. The former contained items designed to describe the leader's directive, structuring, task-oriented actions as well as person-oriented behavior labeled by Hemphill as "considerate" (1957). The second questionnaire was used to measure the leaders' and group members' reactions to the sessions. It included items

---

[5] Group Atmosphere scores are interpreted as conceptually related to good leader-member relations indices derived from sociometric preference questionnaires in real-life groups. However, the correlation between GA and sociometric indices was fairly low in this study. This may indicate that leaders in real-life groups only learn how well they are accepted as a result of interaction with group members over extended periods of time. In *ad hoc* groups, which meet at most for a few hours, the leader generally cannot obtain this feedback. He may, therefore, act on the basis of his own feelings toward the group, and the group is likely to go along with him for the duration of the experiment. This low correlation may also mean, however, that the leader's Group Atmosphere scores have a different meaning in this context than sociometric preference scores. This question deserves further study.

on the individual's feelings of interest, motivation, anxiety, and frustration with the task and his group. Finally, participants were asked to describe each of the other members of their group. These Interpersonal Perception scales, identical to those for obtaining LPC scores, yielded esteem scores for leader and fellow group members.

The items from the postmeeting scales and questionnaires given after the structured and unstructured task resulted in thirty-eight interpretable factors. A second-order factor analysis of these item clusters or factors yielded five clearly identifiable second-order factors in the case of the structured and the unstructured tasks and two in the case of the nonverbal task. Of major importance for testing the Contingency Model was the leader's Group Climate Factor, which was used to determine the effective leader-member relations as experienced by the leader. The scores most heavily loaded on the Group Climate Factors are listed in Table 10-4. They were here utilized to subdivide groups seen by the leader as pleasant and relaxed from those perceived by him as unpleasant and tense.

TABLE 10-4   Factor Loadings of Scales and Clusters of the Leader's Group Climate Factor

| | Factor Loadings | |
| | Unstructured | Structured |
Scale or Cluster	Task	Task
Leader's Group Atmosphere scale	.80	.81
Leader's esteem for members	.76	.89
Members' satisfaction with group	−.01*	.77
Leader's description of members as considerate	.69	.73
Leader's satisfaction with group	.66	−.08*

* These loadings were not included in the computation of factor scores.

TESTS OF THE CONTINGENCY HYPOTHESIS

The basic hypothesis of the model states that the leadership style required for effective performance of interacting groups is contingent upon the favorableness of the group situation. The critical problem of testing the model lies in ordering the group-task situations in terms of their favorableness for the leader. Once this is done, the leader's LPC scores can be correlated with the performance scores of the groups within each of the cells. Although we had started with the comparatively large sample of ninety six groups, the number of cases within each cell shrank rapidly with each variable that had to be incorporated in the design. We obviously had to divide the groups on the basis of the three original dimensions, namely, high versus low position power, task structure, and the Group Climate scores, which measured effective leader-member relations. A further division was required on the basis of homogeneity versus heterogeneity.

Several other variables in this study also had to be considered or statistically controlled. Since the size of the sample limited the number of comparisons we could make, it was essential to combine certain cells. For example, intelligent groups performed significantly better than did dull groups. These differences in performance could be statistically controlled by means of covariance adjustments. This procedure involved obtaining the mean difference between performance scores of the relatively bright and dull groups and adding this mean difference to the score of each dull group.[7]

A similar adjustment was needed to equalize mean differences in the performance of French- and Dutch-speaking teams where such extraneous factors as differences in scoring standards in the two languages and clarity in translating the instructions could have affected the results. Thus Cell D, containing Dutch-speaking groups, was merged with Cell E, containing French-speaking groups, Cell F was merged with Cell G, and so on.

To recapitulate, the classification procedure categorized the ninety-six groups on the basis of (1) homogeneity versus heterogeneity, (2) high versus low leaders' Group Climate scores, (3) high versus low leader position power, (4) task presentation order beginning with the structured or with the unstructured task. This classification generated sixteen cells with six groups per cell.[8]

Since the criterion tasks were uncorrelated and, therefore, presumed to be independent, correlations between the leader's LPC score and group performance were computed separately for each of the tasks. The resulting thirty-two correlations (two correlations for each of sixteen cells) constitute the basic data for testing the Contingency Hypothesis.

---

[7] This assumes, of course, that there would be no interaction between intelligence and other variables—an assumption which may not be correct, but which we had to live with. The most probable penalty for violating this assumption would be an increase in error variance, and it would, therefore, lead to conservative results, i.e., statistically not significant results, when the results otherwise would be significant.

[8] Two of the ninety-six groups had to be discarded for purposes of this analysis because of a clerical error, leaving five groups in two of the cells.

These data are presented in Table 10-5. Column 1 of this table indicates the cells which were involved in the analysis (see Table 10-1); columns 2, 3, 4, and 5 indicate the characteristics of the particular cell. Thus, Cell DE consisted of homogeneous groups (col. 2) with high position power (petty officers) (col. 3) and groups which began the experiment with the structured task (col. 4). (Dutch- and French-speaking groups were merged.) The twelve groups were then divided into the six in which the leader had high Group Climate Factor scores and the six in which he had

TABLE 10-5   Correlations between Leader LPC and Group Performance in Different Group-task Situations * ($N = 6$)

(1)	(2)	(3)	(4)	(5)	(6)	(7)	(8)	(9)
							Weights Indicating Situational	
					Tasks		Favorableness	
Cells †		PP	Order of Task Presentation	Leader's Group Climate	UT	ST II	UT	ST II
DE	Hom.	High	U	High	−16	−77	6	7
				Low	26	16	4	5
HK	Hom.	High	S	High	−54	−72	7	6
				Low	−27	03	5	4
NO	Hom.	Low	U	High	08	37	4	5
				Low	−37	07	2	3
RS	Hom.	Low	S	High	13	50	5	4
				Low	60	14	3	2
FG	Het.	High	U	High	20	03	4	5
				Low	−37	08	2	3
LM	Het.	High	S	High	−26	77	5	4
				Low	08	−19	3	2
PQ	Het.	Low	U	High	−89	77	2	3
				Low	−36	53	0	1
TU	Het.	Low	S	High ‡	70	−53	3	2
				Low ‡	−60	−90	1	0

* UT = unstructured task; ST II = second structured task; PP = position power; U = task presentation sequence beginning with the unstructured task; S = task presentation beginning with the structured task.
† See Table 10-1 for cell designation.
‡ $Ns = 5$.

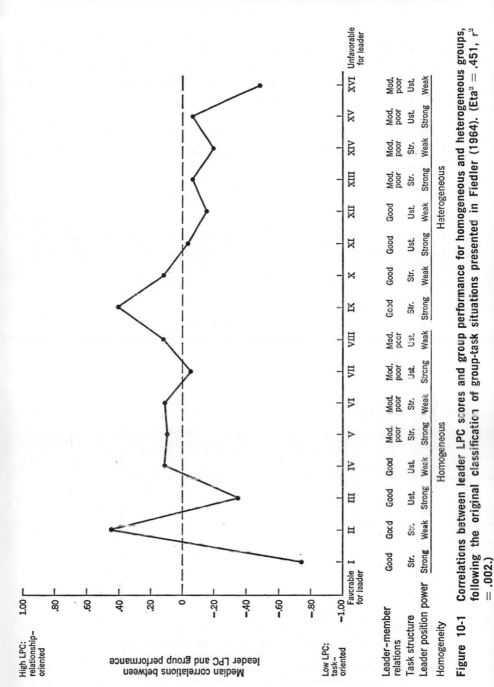

Figure 10-1 Correlations between leader LPC scores and group performance for homogeneous and heterogeneous groups, following the original classification of group-task situations presented in Fiedler (1964). (Eta² = .451, r² = .002.)

low Group Climate scores (col. 5). The correlations between the LPC of the leader and his performance on the unstructured task are listed in column 6, those on the second structured tasks in column 7. Two tests of the model, each based upon a different method of ordering, are here presented.

Test I. Replication of the original model.   The first test closely follows the method of categorization used originally. The test assumes that the dimensions of group climate, task structure, and position power have the same relative importance in the Belgian navy study as in previous studies conducted in the United States. It involved the categorization of groups on the basis of the three dimensions (using the unstructured and second structured task) in addition to the main variable of homogeneity versus heterogeneity. Figure 10-1 shows the performance curve based upon these

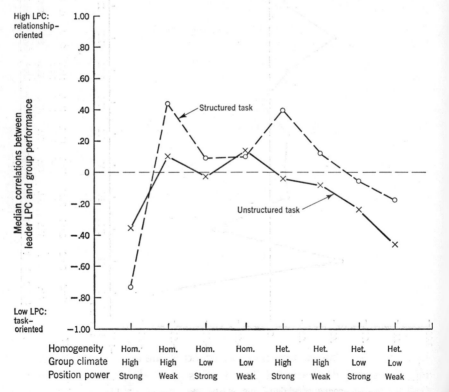

Figure 10-2   Median correlations between leader LPC and group performance in unstructured and second structured tasks. (Eta^2 ST$_{II}$ = .495, r^2 = .005; Eta^2 UT = .178, r^2 = .051.)

data abstracted for this purpose from Table 10-5. The curve is drawn through the medians of the correlations representing each cell.

Although the resulting plot is curvilinear (Eta^2 = .451; r^2 = .002) the F ratio between Eta^2 and r^2 is significant only for homogeneous groups, and the point-by-point correspondence with the predicted curve is far from satisfactory. The curve in the Belgian Navy study reaches its highest peak in Octant II, while the original curve peaked in Octants IV and V. Octant VIII of the original curve showed high negative correlations between leader LPC and performance, while the corresponding correlations in the present study do not become negative until the much more unfavorable situations presented by heterogeneous groups.

The difference between these two curves may well be due to the specific conditions under which this experiment was conducted. The difference in position power between petty officers and men was undoubtedly much greater in the Belgian military teams than in civilian groups or even in the American military crews which we had studied before. On the other hand, the difference between the structured and unstructured tasks was less than in previous studies. Plotting the results separately for each of these two tasks leads to curves which more closely approximate the predicted relationships (see Figure 10-2).

Test II. A generalized test of the Contingency Hypothesis. The basic hypothesis of the Contingency Model, as we emphasized before, is not tied to the definition of the favorableness dimension in terms of group climate, position power, and task structure. The hypothesis merely states that the task-oriented leaders will perform more effectively under very favorable and very unfavorable conditions, while the relationship oriented leaders will perform more effectively under conditions intermediate in favorableness. This makes the theory less brittle and hence less easily testable but it does take cognizance of the fact that other aspects of the group situation also may contribute to its favorableness, and that one factor may be completely overshadowed in importance by another in a particular situation.

The main question is always how to order situations in terms of their favorableness. The method here described is one alternative to the ordering which was the basis for Test I. This method avoids the assumption that leader-member relations are more important than task structure, and that task structure is more important than position power. Homogeneity of the group, position power, and group climate are each given equal weights of two points. Task sequence is given a weight of one point since it appears to have a smaller yet noticeable effect on making the situation more or less favorable. Thus, Group Climate scores were higher and responses indicating anxiety and tension were lower in the second half of the study than in the first half. This is likely because by that time the leader had gained experience and confidence in working with his group and because the experimental situation at first seemed strange and threatening to many of these men. The resulting weights are shown in columns 8 and 9 of Table 10-5.

The correlation coefficients between leader LPC and group performance are presented in order of the situational favorableness (Table 10-6). This ordering again indicates that the correlations have a tendency to fall in the

TABLE 10-6   Correlations between LPC and Group Performance Ordered on Situational Favorableness *

Degree of Favorableness	Unstructured Task			Structured Task			Predicted Direction of Correlations
7	−54			−77			
6	−16			−72			Negative
5	13	−27	−26	37	16	03	
4	08	26	20	50	03	77	
3	60	70	08	07	77	08	Positive
2	−37	−89	−37	14	−53	−19	
1	−60			53			Negative
0	−36			−90			

Observed Correlations	Predicted Direction of Correlations			
	Positive	Negative	Positive	Negative
Positive	6	1	6	5
Negative	0	9	0	5
	$p < .001$		$p < .06$	

Probabilities Computed By Fisher's Exact Test

* Weights, indicated on Table 10-5 in columns 7 and 8, were computed by assigning weights of two points each to homogeneity, position power, and group climate, and one point to task sequence—the task given later is considered more favorable than the task given immediately upon convening the group.

direction originally predicted by the model. Subdividing each of the arrays of correlations into an upper, middle, and lower third and applying Fisher's exact test to the fourfold tables of frequencies for observed versus expected positive and negative correlation coefficients yields probabilities of .001 for the unstructured test and of .06 for the structured test. It should be noted, however, that a different subdivision of these same data is also possible, and that one might well give different weights to the group climate, position power, and homogeneity factors, or to the task sequence. These alternative orders might or might not yield significant results. In no event can these or similar tests by themselves be taken as strong evidence for the Contingency Model. While we postulated in advance that the situation would be more favorable if the group is homogeneous, if the group climate is good, and if the position power is high, and while it is obvious from our postsession data that the second task presented a more favorable situation than did the first task in the study, the specific weighting was not spelled out in advance. The evidence which is here presented should, therefore, be interpreted in the light of the other validation evidence presented in this book.

Discussion. In general, the consistency of the data obtained in this experiment lends support to the major hypothesis of the Contingency Model, even though there are point-by-point discrepancies from the curve which was based on previous data. Whether these discrepancies in the shape of the curve are due to factors specific to the sample and the experimental conditions of the Belgian study or to the inadequacies of the theory will need to be determined. There can be little doubt that the Belgian Navy groups differed markedly in some respects from the groups with which we had worked in the United States, especially in terms of the difference in position power between the petty officer and his recruit group member. (However, this difference between petty officer and recruit is probably not specific to Belgium but is likely to be equally great between a Marine recruit and his drill sergeant.)

As mentioned before, the performance of heterocultural groups has become of considerable importance in recent years. It is not only critical in the large number of countries which have culturally and linguistically diverse populations, it is also a focal problem in business and industrial organizations as well as in intergovernmental agencies which are transnational in character.

When we speak of heterogeneity, it is obviously important to ask "heterogeneity in what?" Every group is heterogeneous to some extent. The problem is whether the heterogeneity is or is not task-relevant. Heterogeneity in height is quite irrelevant in scientific research, but it may be of considerable importance in assembling a basketball team or a troupe of chorus girls. In most groups, the members' communication problems, the degree to which the group members share relevant information and technical vocabulary, as well as a common cultural background will play an important part in determining their interaction (Triandis et al., 1964).

How, then, will heterogeneity in language and culture affect the leader's ability to deal with his group? Our common experience tells us that the interdisciplinary group or the interracial group presents a difficult problem in leadership. In the former, attitudes about work and technical vocabulary differ, and there are probably also some feelings about the value of one discipline or one method as against another. In the interracial group, the possibility of real and imagined slights, as well as suspicions about the motives of the others, creates a potentially explosive and therefore stressful situation.

A still more difficult problem exists in groups in which the members differ in language as well as in cultural background. Here the leader must bridge, in addition, the gap in linguistic competencies, and he must attempt to overcome the problems which arise when a member doesn't understand the leader's directions either by design or by accident. This problem will be especially acute when the group is relatively new and has not yet developed a tradition and a routine for cooperation. The leader of highly heterogeneous groups must provide some of the social glue to counteract the divisive forces that operate in such situations. He must attempt to make himself acceptable to different factions, none of which may fully trust him, and he must cope with the difficulties which arise because communications are more likely to break down. Heterogeneity may thus strongly affect the leader's relations with his group.

The organization enters the picture in assigning to the leader groups of greater or lesser heterogeneity and in being thus able to change his relationship with his group members to a correspondingly greater or lesser extent almost at will. While some leaders, by virtue of their personality, might well be able to handle highly heterogeneous groups with somewhat greater ease, such groups are likely to present a problem even to the most accomplished group leader. One important contribution of this study may be the suggestion that the group's heterogeneity may be treated—and perhaps manipulated—as a means for increasing or decreasing the favorableness of the group situation for the leader.

INDUSTRIAL WORK SITUATIONS

The Belgian navy study tested the Contingency Model in a setting in which the groups were specifically assembled for the purpose of the experiment. Since the groups existed only for a few hours, the leader's authority was extremely short-lived. It is, for this reason, of considerable importance to go beyond the laboratory and field experiment to determine whether the model will also predict group performance in real-life settings of ongoing organizations. Three sets of interacting groups, described below, were studied by Hunt (1966) as part of his dissertation research.

To measure task structure in these and other settings, Hunt developed a scale which involved carefully selected anchor points of various group tasks in business and industry. The scale was pretested by choosing one hundred jobs from the *Dictionary of Occupational Titles*. These jobs were then rated by eighteen business administration students on each of Shaw's (1963) four dimensions of goal clarity, goal-path multiplicity, decision verifiability, and solution specificity (see Chapter 2). Anchor jobs were chosen on the basis of this rating, and a Thurstone equal-appearing interval scale was developed. This scale (reproduced by permission in Appendix D) was then used by three or more raters within each company to assess the task structure of various groups within the organization. In addition, thirteen independent judges familiar with business and industrial organizations rated the jobs within all organizations in Hunt's study.

To obtain a scale of task structure, Hunt intercorrelated the four Shaw dimensions. These intercorrelations were .56 to .87 for company raters and .54 to .82 for independent judges. The intercorrelations for a sample of thirty-nine jobs evaluated by all raters averaged .86. The Group Atmosphere scale was used to measure the leader-member relations.

Research chemists.   One study was conducted in a large physics research laboratory which was part of a large nonprofit research organization. The laboratory's major effort was devoted to pure research, although a large number of groups are engaged in applied or service research designed to support the pure research groups.

Hunt obtained data on two sets of interacting groups composed of research chemists. These groups consisted of two to thirteen men; the leaders performed both research and supervisory functions. Most of the groups had two to three nonsupervisory professional members. Seven of these groups performed pure research and eleven performed service research.

Three executives of the organization classified all pure research groups and four of the service research groups as having low task structure, while the other seven service research groups were rated as having highly structured tasks.

All groups in the set were considered to have leaders with high position power. Thus, the pure research and the service research groups with low task structure fell into Octants III and VII, depending upon the leader's Group Atmosphere scores. The remaining seven service research groups were classified in Octant I, that is, as having high task structure and high position power and good leader-member relations.

Group performance based on productivity in research work was assessed by senior researchers and laboratory executives.

Supermarket meat departments. A second sample of groups came from a Midwestern chain of thirty-one supermarkets. The personnel of the meat markets in these stores perform tasks of an interacting nature involving unloading, various cutting operations, coordination of several employees in the operation of power tools and equipment, and maintenance of the display case. Journeymen meatcutters have the major responsibility for these functions in which apprentices and meat wrappers assist. The criterion of performance which the company uses is based on the dollar sales volume per man-hour.

Data were obtained from a total of twenty-one meat departments, with groups ranging in size from three to twelve employees. These groups were rated as having a highly structured task with detailed operating instructions and procedures prescribed by the store.

The formal position power of the meat market manager was rated as high since the manager is responsible for the work of the department as well as for personnel management. These groups fall, therefore, into Octants I and V of the model.

Heavy machinery manufacture. The third organization in Hunt's study was a farm and earth-moving machinery plant which employs several thousand workers. This part of the investigation focused on the performance of interacting groups consisting of the general foreman (or a superintendent substituting temporarily in that position) and his immediate subordinate foremen. These groups were from the manufacturing areas of the plant. All persons who participated in this study were male, and almost all foremen had worked their way up from the ranks. The foremen were the first-line supervisors who were here considered members of the general foreman's staff, or his asistants, supervising the work under the general foreman's direction. The situation is somewhat similar to that in the farm-supply companies which were described in Chapter 6.

The criteria of department performance were based on a ratio of expected production (computed on the basis of standard times for various tasks) to actual production. Average figures for these production criteria were available for three different six-month periods, with an estimated reliability, corrected for length, of .90.

The study involved ten production groups headed by ten general foremen. All groups were rated as having high leader position power and as having moderately low task structure. The groups were also considered to have interacting tasks since the work of one foreman was closely related to that of other foremen within his general foreman's department. These groups, therefore, fall in Octants III and VII, depending on the general foreman's Group Atmosphere score.

Results.   Least-preferred Coworker scores were obtained for each of the supervisors or foremen of each of the units in Hunt's study, and these LPC scores were then correlated with the criteria of group performance. The

TABLE 10-7   Rank-order Correlations between Supervisor LPC and Group Performance for Interacting Groups in Hunt's Study of Industrial Organizations

Organization	Octant I N	Octant I Rho	Octant III N	Octant III Rho	Octant V N	Octant V Rho	Octant VII N	Octant VII Rho
Research chemists (high task structure)	7*	−.64						
Research chemists (low task structure)			6	.60			5	.30
Meat departments	10	−.51			11	.21		
Heavy machinery plant (high task structure)			5	−.80			5	−.30
Median correlations		−.57		−.10		.21		.00
Predicted correlations		−.52		−.33		.42		.05

* This sample was not large enough to divide by group atmosphere. The whole sample was, therefore, classified as having good group atmosphere even though the sample included two groups with relatively low Group Atmosphere scores.

Figure 10-3   Correlations between Supervisor LPC and Team Performance in Various Work Situations obtained by Hunt (1966).

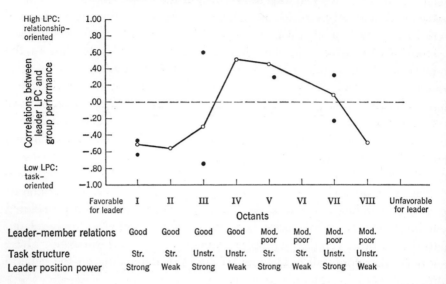

	Favorable for leader I	II	III	IV	V	VI	VII	VIII	Unfavorable for leader
Leader–member relations	Good	Good	Good	Good	Mod. poor	Mod. poor	Mod. poor	Mod. poor	
Task structure	Str.	Str.	Unstr.	Unstr.	Str.	Str.	Unstr.	Unstr.	
Leader position power	Strong	Weak	Strong	Weak	Strong	Weak	Strong	Weak	

results of these analyses are presented in Table 10-6. Also indicated in this table are the correlations expected on the basis of the original data presented in Table 9-2. Table 10-7 shows that Hunt's results very closely fit the expected curve, as can be seen in Figure 10-3. A test for overall significance, based on combined probabilities of the individual samples (Jones and Fiske, 1953), was significant at the .05 level (one-tailed).

Hunt's work supports the main hypothesis of the Contingency Model and thus provides further validation of the model for interacting groups in real-life business and industrial organizations. It is a particularly valuable contribution since the groups studied by Hunt are similar in nature to those on which the original model was based.

OTHER VALIDATION STUDIES

A number of studies have been conducted since the publication of the first paper describing the Contingency Model (Fiedler, 1963). These have provided validation evidence for various predictions derived from the theory. Two of these studies deserve particular mention.

Heterocultural groups.   Anderson (1964) conducted a study of thirty-six heterocultural teams each consisting of one graduate student from India and two American graduate students. One of the Americans served as leader and one served as the second group member. The leaders were selected so that eighteen of them would have high LPC and eighteen would have low LPC scores. Nine leaders in each set of eighteen were given thirty minutes of leadership training which was "redundant" and nine were given training "complementary" to their leadership style. In the redundant training conditions, the experimenters instructed the high-LPC leaders to be permissive, considerate, and nondirective, while they instructed the low-LPC leaders to be directive, structuring, and task-controlling. In the complementary condition the high-LPC leaders were trained to be structuring and directive, and the low-LPC leaders were trained to be considerate and permissive.

The groups worked on two tasks. The first of these was a discussion problem to determine criteria for selecting the residents of an Indian village for training in technical and managerial positions in a proposed industrial plant. According to the hypothetical problem, the village did not have enough eligible upper-caste males to fill the supervisory positions although many lower-caste individuals did qualify for the positions. The triads were asked to outline a policy statement resolving this dilemma in a way which would be acceptable to both the Indian villagers and to the American owners of the plant. The leader of the triad was to play the role of a corporation officer, and the American and Indian members were to be an industrial expert and a representative of the Indian government, respectively.

The group products were rated on acceptability and potential effectiveness by American and Indian judges. The reliability was, however, quite low: average intercorrelations for American judges was .29 (corrected to .74) and for Indian judges .21 (corrected to .57).

The second task consisted of writing two original stories based on TAT card 11 (dragon in the ravine). These were rated in the same manner as in previous studies. The average intercorrelation among judges was .95.

Since Group Atmosphere scores in this study correlated significantly with the leader's LPC score ($-.40$ in the first and $-.26$ in the second task) this measure could not be used to divide the groups on the basis of leader-member relations. The group situations could be ordered along a favorableness dimension by considering the relative amount of influence and rapport which the training instructions encouraged in the leader-member interaction and the difficulties which the intercultural task would engender.

The caste problem constituted the more difficult of the two leadership situations. It was an intercultural task which required each member to speak on a subject about which there was likely to be disagreement. It was also the first task on which the group worked. The leader was instructed to remain neutral, impartial, and not to contribute ideas to the solution of the problem. To judge from Group Atmosphere scores, this task seemed to produce a tense and unpleasant leader-member relationship in which the leader could wield relatively little influence. This was especially so in the conditions in which the leader was given initiation-of-structure training. This tended to increase the tension of the leader as well as of his group members. The consideration training instructed leaders to instigate a pleasant, friendly, and permissive group atmosphere in order to develop a more relaxed and congenial interaction.

While the TAT task was unstructured, it enabled the leader to contribute to the task and to exert some influence. This influence was enhanced by the fact that the TAT task came after the caste problem. The leader, thus, had had previous experience in dealing with his group members.

The group-task situations were then ordered from relatively favorable to relatively unfavorable in the following manner: TAT task with consideration training, TAT task with initiation-of-structure training, caste problem with consideration training, and caste problem with initiation-of-structure training. This particular ordering also corresponded to leader responses on postmeeting questionnaire items which indicated the degree to which the leader "felt somewhat anxious and tense in this session."

The results of the analysis, correlating leader LPC and group performance, are shown in Table 10-8. While the correlations are rather weak, in part perhaps because of the low reliability of criterion ratings obtained for the caste problem, they tend to support the Contingency Model hypothesis.

TABLE 10-8   Correlations between Leader's LPC Scores and Group Performance in a Study of Heterocultural Teams (Anderson, 1964)

Task	Training	Rank-order Correlation ($Ns = 18$)
TAT stories	Consideration	−.50*
TAT stories	Structuring	.21
Caste problem	Consideration	−.12
Caste problem	Structuring	−.22

* Significant at .05 level.

Experimental variation of task structure. A study by Shaw and Blum (1966) tested the effects of leadership style upon group performance when the structure of the task was systematically varied. This study used three types of tasks: (A) a discussion problem which required the group to list the five most important traits that a person needs for success in our culture (adapted from Cleveland and Fisher, 1957), (B) a discussion problem requiring the group to describe which of five possible courses of action would be best for a young politician who is burdened by an alcoholic wife (Bass, 1960), and (C) a task requiring the group to identify five objects by asking no more than forty questions (Smith, 1957).

Eighteen groups composed of five male students worked on every task in systematically varied order. The leader was appointed and the authors stated that all groups had good group climate.

The experimental manipulation in nine groups required the leader to be highly directive and autocratic in his approach while the leaders in the other nine groups were told to be nondirective and permissive.

On the basis of the Contingency Model the authors predicted that directive leadership behavior would result in more effective performance in the structured task, while nondirective leadership behavior would do so in the moderately unstructured tasks. The main results of the Shaw and Blum study are presented in Table 10-9. As can be seen, directive leadership was more effective than nondirective leadership only in Task C. On both Tasks A and B nondirective leadership was more effective. The leadership style $\times$ task interaction was highly significant ($F = 7.54$, $df = 2/32$, $p < .01$).

Shaw and Blum had expected to find that directive leaders would be more effective in the very unstructured task. As the authors point out, however, the group climate was favorable and the leader's position power

TABLE 10-9   Mean Time Scores (Minutes) for Leadership and Task Conditions *

Leadership style	Task		
	A	B	C
Directive	4.80	3.71	4.97
Nondirective	4.03	2.36	5.85

* This table was adapted from Shaw and Blum (1966). Scores were transformed by square-root transformation. Low scores indicate good performance.

was relatively high. In terms of the classification described in Chapter 2, the group-task situation was, therefore, no more than moderately unfavorable in the situation involving the least structured of the tasks (Octant V).

This study provides partial support for the model as well as a generalization beyond the LPC scores used in our previous research. If the Contingency Model is to have meaning beyond the very narrow operationalization of leadership style represented by the Least-preferred Coworker score, we must find behavioral correlates which will also predict leadership performance in a particular situation. Shaw and Blum have done this by prescribing the type of leadership behavior which would be most effective for the two group situations represented in their study.

SUMMARY

This chapter has presented data from four investigations which tested the Contingency Model. One was a field experiment conducted in collaboration with the Belgian navy, one was a study of three industrial and business organizations, and two studies were laboratory experiments. In all four studies the group situations were ordered on the basis of their favorableness for the leader, and each of these provided evidence that the task-oriented leader tends to perform best in situations which are very favorable while the relationship-oriented leader tends to perform best in situations intermediate in favorableness. Three of the studies also indicate that the task-oriented leader's style is relatively more effective in very unfavorable situations. The fourth study did not contain a situation which could be classified as very unfavorable on the basis of the system described in Chapter 2.

Since many of the cells in these studies contain very few sets of groups it is difficult to establish the statistical significance of the relationship between leadership style and performance within a particular cell or for a particular study. Taken as a group, the validation data here presented as well as those from additional studies which are as yet unpublished yielded highly consistent results which provide substantial support for the Contingency Model hypothesis. The next chapter is concerned with the underlying dynamics which account for these findings.

11 GROUP PROCESS AND GROUP PERFORMANCE

Chapter 9 presented a theoretical model of leadership that attempts to integrate the results which we obtained in our research over the years. Chapter 10 provided evidence that the measure of leadership style, LPC, correlates with group performance in predictable ways. However, the correlations by themselves give little insight into the underlying reasons for these results. What determines why a high-LPC leader will be successful in one situation and a low-LPC leader in another? We will here attempt to identify the processes which might explain the results the Contingency Model predicts.

Any attempt to interpret our findings requires that we understand three main aspects of the problem: (1) the meaning of LPC or ASo scores, (2) the significance of the "favorableness-for-leader" dimension, and (3) how LPC and the favorableness dimension interact in affecting group performance.

It may be well at this time to recall two important points and their major implications. First, we defined leadership as a process in which one person controls and influences others for the purpose of performing a common task. This relationship between the leader and his group members is typically a very important one for the leader; it is a relationship that tends to involve him deeply. Most leaders take their job very seriously, and most feel responsible for the group members as well as for the group's performance. This is true even in a role-playing situation in which short-lived teams are assembled merely for the purpose of a particular laboratory experiment.

Second, the prediction of group performance depends in part upon the favorableness of the group-task situations. We defined favorableness as the degree to which the situation enables the leader to exert influence and control over the group process. Let us now consider the nature of the interaction between leader LPC and situational favorableness.

LPC AND SITUATIONAL FAVORABLENESS

A situation in which we have influence and control implies that we can determine the outcome, that we can shape the situation to our liking. An important situation in which we are in control promises need gratification; we can, therefore, feel reasonably comfortable and relaxed. Feeling out of control and uncertain of the outcome will make us concerned and insecure. Having once tasted success, we generally work harder for rewards of which we are uncertain than for those of which we feel sure. A tennis champion will exert himself more when he is up against tough competition than when he plays a Sunday game with his children.

Similarly, the more unfavorable the group-task situation, the less the leader will feel in control and the less confidence he will have that he will be able to obtain gratification for his particular needs. A situation in which the leader has little control will be threatening, and it will, therefore, bring about increased attempts to control the group processes which can potentially provide need gratification. In highly threatening or extremely difficult group situations these efforts may become so intense and frantic that they become disfunctional.

The weight of the evidence, described in Chapter 3, shows that the high- and the low-LPC persons seek to satisfy different needs. The individual with a high LPC score obtains his need satisfaction and reinforcement by gaining recognition, by achieving a position of prominence, and by good interpersonal relations. These needs must be gratified by interacting with others.

The individual with low-LPC scores obtains his need satisfaction or reinforcement through his achievement in assigned tasks, or through the intrinsic satisfactions of the work he performs. He is less concerned with outside recognition and good interpersonal relations. Rather, his self-esteem and need gratification come from feeling that he has done a good job. Most leadership situations require good interpersonal relations or make them highly desirable if the task is to be accomplished. Hence, the low-LPC person is likely to seek good interpersonal relations with his group members if he feels these are needed in order to perform the task.

If our reasoning is correct, both types of leaders, those with high and those with low LPC, should react to a need-threatening (i.e., unfavorable) group situation by intensifying the kinds of behavior which will result in need gratification. But the threatening situation should trigger different behaviors corresponding to the differing needs the two types of leaders seek to satisfy. The high-LPC leader should increase the intensity of his interaction with group members, he should become more concerned with their opinions and feelings in order to increase his chances of gaining recognition and rewards as a person. The low-LPC leader should react by becoming more concerned with task-relevant aspects of the interaction so that he can experience the feeling of having done a good job.

We shall here juxtapose the behavior characteristics of high- and of low-LPC leaders in increasingly difficult or unfavorable group-task situations.

Very Favorable Group Situations (Octants I and II)

High-LPC Leaders	Low-LPC Leaders

The high-LPC person tends to be self-oriented in the sense of being concerned with gaining personal recognition and being considered successful as a person (Bass et al., 1965). He can gain this personal recognition and reward without too much difficulty in a situation in which he is accepted and liked by the group, in which he occupies a powerful position, and in which he is in control of the task. Just being liked or accepted and being powerful provide most of the need satisfaction the high-LPC leader seeks. He, therefore, experiences no particular threat, and he has little need to control the interpersonal relations which already give him what he wants. He does not have to exert himself either to obtain a good relationship or to perform well on the task. He can rest on his laurels and remain relatively passive, nondirective, and permissive.

The situation in which the group accepts the leader and in which he has power and a clearly structured task is excellently suited for the leadership style of the low-LPC person. He does not have to worry about his relationship with group members since he feels accepted, and he has all the influence he needs to perform the task. Since he gains satisfaction from the task, the leader will, with minimal apparent effort, direct and coordinate the task-relevant aspects of the group situation. Being less concerned with the feelings of his group members, the low-LPC leader is also less likely to have conflicts or misgivings about managing and directing his group. Since the task is structured and the leader knows what to do and how to do it, he will feel justified in rejecting and punishing group members who would hinder him in getting the job done (see, for example, Hawkins, 1962). The low-LPC leader is, therefore, also likely to be successful in directing the group task.

Somewhat Unfavorable Group Situations (Octants IV and V)

High-LPC Leaders	Low-LPC Leaders

As the favorableness of the situation decreases, so, by definition, will the leader's ability to influence and control the group. Hence he will sense somewhat greater difficulty in gaining rewards and recognition which he seeks. The leader may not be well accepted by his group, the task may be vague and unstructured, or the leader's position

In the somewhat more difficult situation (Octant IV) in which the task is less well structured, in which the leader's power is limited, or in which the group does not fully accept the leader (Octant V), the low-LPC person, like his high-LPC counterpart, is likely to become somewhat threatened. However, being task-oriented, the leader will become

Somewhat Unfavorable Group Situations (Octants IV and V) (*continued*)

High-LPC Leaders

may be weak. One consequence of this less favorable situation will be an effort on the part of the relationship-oriented high-LPC leader to interact more intensively with the members of his group. Wishing to be known as a good fellow, the leader will become somewhat more concerned with the feelings and opinions of his group members, hence more highly rated in consideration; he will become more responsive to the group, more permissive in his interactions, and more relationship-oriented.

This type of behavior is, of course, quite appropriate for chairmen of committees or leaders of creative groups falling into Octant IV. These must utilize and exploit the intelligence and creativity of the group members in order to be successful. It would also be appropriate for groups in which the task is structured but the leader is only moderately well accepted. Here the conciliatory, permissive, considerate leader who allows members a voice in the task and encourages member participation is more likely to get results than one who is impatient with the group.

Low-LPC Leaders

more tense and concerned about the task and hence more impatient to get it done. Since the task in Octant IV situations is unstructured and vague, his impatience to get on with the task will tend to cut off group discussion. His lesser concern for the feelings of the group members will inhibit them from free discussion of the problem and from venturing new and offbeat ideas. As a result, the leader will be unable to make full use of his group members, and the group productivity will suffer. In Octant V situations (in which the leader has position power, the task is highly structured, but the leader is not too well accepted) the low-LPC leader's behavior and attitudes are likely to alienate the members of his group and so reduce their motivation to work.

Relatively Unfavorable Situations (Octants VIII and VIII-A)

High-LPC Leaders

The style of the high-LPC leader will be less successful in situations in which he enjoys relatively little control. Here the members may be somewhat anxious and therefore less concerned with the task; the group may become less cohesive, and the leader's weak position power will no longer suffice to keep the members in line. The leader is likely to become quite threatened in these circumstances, and he will, therefore, tend to increase the rate and intensity of his interactions with his members in an effort to maintain his control over the group processes so that he can assure

Low-LPC Leaders

The leader who describes his least preferred coworker in very unfavorable terms tries to obtain satisfaction and social reinforcement through his involvement with the task. As Bishop's (1964) study has shown, he tends to experience an increase in self-esteem and adjustment if he feels that he has succeeded in the task, whether or not his interpersonal relations have been successful. In trying to control the situation low-LPC leaders, therefore, tend to become more task-oriented in group situations which are unfavorable. It is more important to them that the task be well

Relatively Unfavorable Situations (Octants VIII and VIII-A) (*continued*)

High-LPC Leaders

himself the recognition and rewards which he seeks. His anxiety may well lead to nonfunctional interactions with his group members. He may become demanding, dictatorial, and testy. He will, to a correspondingly lesser degree, attend to the task-relevant aspects of the group situation.

Low-LPC Leaders

done than that the group members be satisfied and enjoy good relations with the leader.

Very unfavorable situations do not allow the leader to exert much influence over the group, and the low-LPC person, like his high-LPC counterpart, will perceive a threat to his need satisfaction. However, the low-LPC person's needs are gratified by success in the performance of the task. The leader will, therefore, become more and more involved in activities related to the task and less in interpersonal relations with his group members. He will attempt to control task-relevant aspects of the group situation in order to compensate for the threat. Groups under more stressful or threatening conditions tend to be more tolerant of directive, even inconsiderate, leadership (cf. S. L. A. Marshall, 1959) which channels their activities into task-relevant behavior. The group members are, therefore, more likely to work effectively with task-oriented leaders than with leaders who are primarily concerned with their own status or with good interpersonal relations.

EMPIRICAL EVIDENCE

We have here spun out a fairly elaborate theory to conceptualize the group process. What is the evidence for these interpretations?

Support for the theory would require (1) that unfavorable group situations be more anxiety-arousing for the leader than favorable group situations, (2) that high-LPC persons tend to obtain need gratification primarily from success in interpersonal relations while low-LPC persons tend to obtain need gratification primarily from the performance of relevant tasks (some supporting evidence has already been presented in Chapter 3), and (3) that the unfavorable situations tend to make the high-LPC leaders behave in a relationship-seeking or controlling manner while they tend to make the low-LPC persons engage in task-concerned or task-controlling behavior.

Favorableness of the group situation and leader anxiety. While we did not obtain anxiety measures in all studies of group interaction, where these were available they present a very consistent picture that supports the hypothesis. This is no startling insight. When someone is asked to perform a task under conditions over which he has little control, he typically feels tense and anxious. In the Belgian navy study, for example, we found higher tension and anxiety scores in the heterogeneous groups than in homogeneous groups, higher anxiety scores for recruit leaders than for petty officer leaders, and higher anxiety scores for leaders who felt the groups were tense and unpleasant than for groups which the leaders experienced as pleasant and relaxed. Similar results were obtained in other studies (e.g., the Dutch creativity and ROTC studies).

Differences in need gratification of high- and low-LPC leaders. The crucial hypothesis concerns the way in which individuals with high and low LPC scores will behave under conditions which are favorable for the leader and conditions which are unfavorable for the leader. If the theory is correct, the unfavorable, threatening situation should trigger behavior in the high-LPC leader which is likely to satisfy his need to gain recognition and self-esteem in the interpersonal situation. The unfavorable, threatening situation should trigger behavior in the low-LPC leader which is compatible with his need to perform well in the task.

Data from several studies have been reanalyzed to test this hypothesis.

1. *The Dutch study*   As will be recalled, the Dutch creativity study used four-man groups which were composed either of four Dutch Catholic or Dutch Calvinist students, or of two Catholic and two Calvinist students. Leaders were either appointed by the experimenters or they were permitted to emerge in the groups (that is, leaders were identified after each session by means of sociometric questionnaires). The most favorable situations for the leaders in this study were groups in which the membership was homogeneous and the leader was appointed. These groups, being culturally homogeneous, experienced relatively little social strain, and the leader was given a position of legitimate power. The least-favorable situation was the heterogeneous group, in which the emergent, informal leader would have minimal power. The homogeneous groups with informal leadership and the heterogeneous groups with appointed leadership were considered intermediate in favorableness (see Chapter 7).

A content analysis was performed (Meuwese and Oonk, 1960) whic classified all statements into five categories. Four of these categories (converted to percent of total number of comments) could be used to test the hypothesis with which we are concerned. Two of the categories are indicative of attempts to control interpersonal relationships. The first of these concerns procedural statements "you start," "let's not work on . . .," etc., which in effect, regulate who talks to whom, about what, and when. These behaviors, therefore, control the interpersonal relations within the group. The other category subsumes task-irrelevant statements which consist of personal remarks, pleasantries, and tension-relieving comments and jokes. We would expect the rate of relationship-oriented statements to be increasingly higher in the high-LPC groups, and we would expect the rate of task-oriented statements to be increasingly higher in low-LPC groups, under unfavorable rather than under favorable conditions.

The tasks of the Dutch groups consisted in developing stories based on Thematic Apperception Cards. Statements introducing, criticizing, and elaborating new ideas are, therefore, the main categories which would materially affect the success of the group. We would expect the rate of these two task-oriented categories to be increasingly higher in the groups led by low-LPC leaders than in those led by high-LPC leaders under correspondingly unfavorable conditions.

Table 11-1 presents the rate with which statements in the relationship- and task-oriented categories occur in groups led by high- and by low-LPC leaders. These rates, for relationship-oriented comments, are plotted in Figure 11-1. The curves are as the theory would predict. In situations which are unfavorable for the leader, and therefore threatening, the relationship-oriented high-LPC leader and his group members devoted a higher proportion of comments (and concern) to relationship-oriented

TABLE 11-1   Proportion of Task- and Relationship-oriented Comments by Groups in Three Conditions of Situational Favorableness

Type of Group	Relationship-oriented Categories		Task-oriented Categories	
	High LPC	Low LPC	High LPC	Low LPC
Homogeneous—formal	24.3	33.3	75.3	65.9
Homogeneous—informal Heterogeneous—formal	32.9	32.7	67.2	67.1
Heterogeneous—informal	29.8	23.8	61.5	76.0

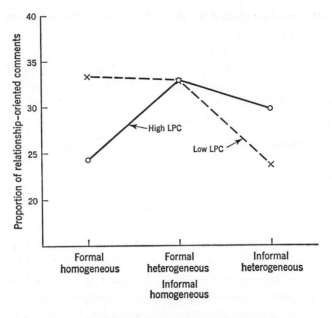

Figure 11-1   Proportion of relationship-oriented comments by high-LPC and low-LPC groups
under three different conditions of favorableness in the Dutch study.

statements than did the task-oriented leaders and their members. Exactly
the reverse was the case for task-oriented statements. Here, the groups
led by the task-oriented leaders made more comments in the task-related
categories than did groups led by the relationship-oriented leaders (Figure 11-2).

In the moderately favorable group situations (Octant IV) we note that
the relationship-oriented leader, who has his needs gratified by the good
relationships and position which he enjoys, devotes more of his energy to
the task. The task-oriented leader, in this same situation, devotes more of
his and the group's energies to relationship building. It should also be
pointed out that the high-LPC leader in the more favorable situation—
here Octant IV—is more effective than the low-LPC leader. The latter
is more effective in the less favorable group situations of the Dutch study,
that is, in heterogeneous groups and/or groups with emergent leadership
(Octant VIII).

That these relationships are not peculiar to the Dutch study can be seen from data obtained in other investigations.

2. *The ROTC study*   This study has already been described in Chapter 8. It used three sets of eighteen groups, with each group composed of three ROTC cadets. The groups worked under conditions of low stress, stress generated by conflict within the group, and external stress generated by having a high-ranking military officer closely observing and rating the team. Each set of eighteen groups was further subdivided into three sets of six groups rated by the leader as having relatively high group atmosphere, intermediate group atmosphere, or low group atmosphere. These scores indicate the subjective feeling of tension experienced by the leader.

Observer ratings were obtained in the control and external-stress conditions. The first six indicated the degree to which the leader (1) promoted group participation, (2) exhibited democratic leadership behavior, (3)

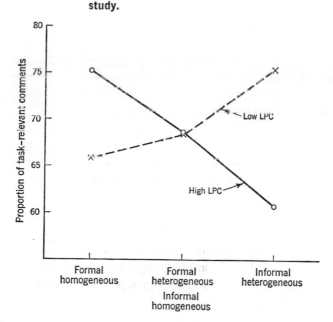

Figure 11-2   **Proportion of task-relevant comments by high-LPC and low-LPC groups under three different conditions of favorableness in the Dutch study.**

TABLE 11-2   Percent of Comments by Leader in Task- and Relationship-oriented Categories—ROTC Study

Ratings of Leader Behavior	Average Percent	Leader LPC	Low Stress Leader GA Scores			External Stress Leader GA Scores		
			High	Med.	Low	High	Med.	Low
Group participation	16.0	High	9.6	19.5	11.7	17.5	12.5	25.3
	16.9	Low	24.4	10.5	10.7	22.9	13.3	19.3
Democratic leadership	12.3	High	11.8	15.8	18.1	8.5	9.6	9.8
	13.3	Low	16.0	19.3	16.6	16.3	6.6	4.8
Group cohesiveness	3.8	High	.8	8.3	2.5	3.9	3.5	3.7
	2.9	Low	4.4	2.2	4.0	.6	4.2	2.0
New ideas	17.6	High	18.1	14.9	20.4	22.4	18.3	11.6
	18.2	Low	16.2	12.6	14.1	21.7	22.5	22.3
Integrated ideas	47.6	High	55.3	40.5	43.9	47.0	53.4	45.2
	45.9	Low	38.5	53.9	49.3	38.1	48.7	46.6
Authoritarian leader	2.9	High	4.3	1.8	3.5	.7	2.7	4.6
	2.7	Low	.3	1.2	5.1	.4	4.8	4.4
Total activity		High	63.9	58.0	75.0	53.0	72.7	63.3
		Low	84.0	70.0	63.0	72.2	72.2	75.0

promoted group cohesiveness, (4) produced new ideas, (5) integrated ideas by others, and (6) exhibited authoritarian leadership. Finally (7), ratings of the total activity of the group were obtained.

We classified the ratings into those reflecting relationship-oriented or task-oriented leadership behavior. Two of the categories were clearly relationship-oriented. These were "promotes group participation" and "democratic leadership." Two categories were clearly task-oriented. These were "production of ideas" and "integrates ideas."

Total group activity could not be classified in either of these categories. Categories three and six were not used in the analyses since less than five percent of leader comments fell into category three (promotes group cohesiveness) and category six (authoritarian leadership). They are, however, indicated in Table 11-2.

The relationship-oriented comments have been plotted in Figure 11-3 and separate curves have been plotted for high- and for low-LPC leaders. Each point on the curves represents the average percent of comments made by the leaders of three different groups on both tasks.

As in the Dutch study, high-LPC leaders made fewer relationship-oriented comments than low-LPC leaders in group situations which they

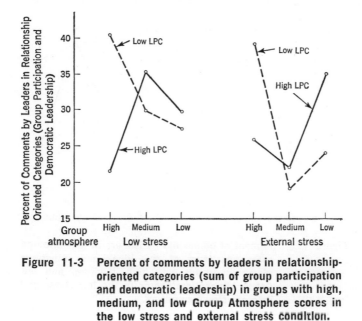

Figure 11-3   Percent of comments by leaders in relationship-
oriented categories (sum of group participation
and democratic leadership) in groups with high,
medium, and low Group Atmosphere scores in
the low stress and external stress condition.

considered relatively free of stress and relatively pleasant. However, high-
LPC leaders made more comments of this type than low-LPC leaders in
the more stressful situations. Thus, when the high-LPC leaders felt under
stress or tension, they made a greater effort to develop good interpersonal
relations in their group. Low-LPC leaders, in contrast, made fewer relationship-oriented comments in situations which were relatively stressful
and tense.

The opposite is the case with task-oriented comments. As can be seen
in Figure 11-4, the low-LPC leaders made relatively fewer task-oriented
comments than high-LPC leaders in the relatively relaxed group situations.
Low-LPC leaders made more task-oriented comments than high-LPC
leaders in the relatively more stressful group situations. These data again,
therefore, support our interpretation.

Similar results are reported by Sample and Wilson (1965) in a study
of groups which performed highly structured laboratory experiments.
These investigators found no differences in the performance of high- and
low-LPC leaders under relaxed conditions, but low-LPC leaders performed
more effectively on the assigned task when the group was under stress.

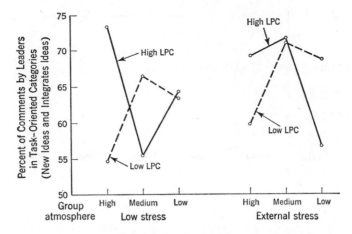

Figure 11-4   Percent of comments by leaders in task-oriented categories (sum of new ideas and integrates ideas) in groups with high, medium, and low Group Atmosphere scores in the low stress and external stress condition.

3. *The Belgian navy study*   This experiment compared homogeneous and heterogeneous teams with powerful and weak leadership using structured and unstructured tasks. The study provided an unusual opportunity to investigate group processes in experimentally created groups in which group situations ranged from very favorable to very unfavorable. Group processes could be inferred from the ratings which group members made of the leader's behavior after the conclusion of the structured and unstructured tasks.

We will here focus on two questions. The first of these concerns the relationship of LPC to leader behavior under different group-task situations. The second question concerns the leader behavior which most effectively contributes to the group's performance.

The primary data which are the basis of the discussion came from a Behavior Description Questionnaire. The items of this questionnaire included statements identical or similar to those of the Leader Behavior Description Questionnaire developed by the Ohio State Group under C. L. Shartle (Stogdill and Coons, 1957) as well as other items which were likely to indicate important aspects of leader behavior. The items in this questionnaire, as well as all other items from posttask measures, were

factor analyzed. The Behavior Description Questionnaire led to six identifiable item clusters [1] which are listed below:

Behavior Description Questionnaire:

1. *Involved and structuring*

    He participated well in the work with the other members of the group.
    He encouraged the group to complete the task.
    He made several suggestions which were useful in doing the work.
    He helped to clarify the situation by giving useful information.
    He insisted that the members of the group concentrate their efforts on
        arriving at the best possible group solution.

2. *Critical*

    He interrupted when others were speaking.
    He criticized those he did not agree with.
    He often opposed and was aggressive toward the other members of
        the group.
    He criticized bad work.

3. *Directive*

    He was the real leader of the group.
    He led with an iron fist.
    He established a definite plan of action, and he insisted that the group
        members follow it.
    He assigned special tasks to group members.

4. *Consideration behavior*

    He listened attentively to the others.
    He treated all the members of the group as his equals.
    He was friendly and it was easy to talk to him.
    He put the members at ease when he talked to them.

5. *Real leader*

    He was the real leader of the group.

6. *Focus of group discussion*

    The group discussion focused on him.

   None of these cluster scores was significantly related to LPC. The correlations ranged
from .02 to .18, with a median of .08.

The postmeeting measures and questionnaires led to a total of thirty-eight identifiable clusters. The interpretation of this number of variables was quite unmanageable and required further reduction of the data. A second-order factor analysis was, therefore, necessary. This analysis led to five clearly identifiable factors for the structured and for the unstructured tasks. These are (1) the leader's group climate factor, (2) the members' group climate factor, (3) the members' ratings of the leader, (4) the members' ratings of each other, and (5) the leader's ratings of his members' behavior. We shall here concern ourselves with the members' descriptions of the leader which indicate differences in leader behavior under different group situations (3 above).

It should first be pointed out that neither this second-order factor nor any of the other four was significantly related to group performance or to LPC. Second, all of the six first-order factors derived from the Behavior Description Questionnaire, on which members described the leader, were intercorrelated and constituted one second-order factor.

The next steps in this analysis are somewhat complex. The results are, however, sufficiently important to be considered with care. To recapitulate, we have a factor score based on item clusters labeled "involved and structuring," "critical," "directive," "considerate," "real leader," and "focus of group discussion." What will be the result if we now obtain the correlations betwen leader LPC and the second-order factor scores under various difficulty or favorableness levels in group-task situations? Using heterogeneous groups as well as homogeneous groups yielded a correlation of .27 (not significant). This correlation, based only on homogeneous groups, was .62, which is significant at the .02 level. (It should be noted that the homogeneous groups provide a more reliable estimate of the relationship since the ratings of leaders by some men in heterogeneous groups were confounded by feelings of regional antagonism between Flemish and Walloon population sectors.)

What do these correlations indicate? They suggest that the low-LPC leaders are relatively more directive, critical, considerate, motivating, and structuring, and in the forefront of the group discussion when the situation is favorable for the leader; the high-LPC leaders are more directive, critical, considerate, etc., when the situation is increasingly more unfavorable for the leader. The fact that the factor score contains items which deal with considerate behavior as well as critical, aggressive, hostile behavior seems to show that we are really dealing with a factor which measures *the intensity with which the leader interacts with the group*, that is, be haviors which make the leader highly salient and visible to the members of his group. This result is consistent with previous findings. The high-LPC leader seeks a prominent place in the group and close interpersonal relations with his members. As the situation becomes more threatening he tends to interact with increasingly greater intensity, becoming both more considerate and human-relations oriented and more critical, task-oriented, and structuring even though this behavior results in less effective task performance and even in less cordial interpersonal relations.

Let us now consider briefly a further question, namely, what behaviors are characteristic of successful and unsuccessful leaders. We did find low positive median correlations between group performance on the structured task and factor scores on "involved and structuring" (.25), "considerate" (.25), and "directive" (.29) leader behavior. These findings are in accord with findings from various studies with the Ohio State scales (Stogdill and Coons, 1957). However, the corresponding median correlations between leader behavior ratings and group performance on the unstructured tasks were only .08, .07, and .07. These findings suggest that these leader behaviors tend to contribute to group performance only in some situations but not in others. The data obtained in the Belgian navy study show that the successful leaders tended to be "involved and structuring" and "directive" in relatively favorable situations, but they were described as quite low on both of these behaviors in the relatively unfavorable situations, and especially so in heterogeneous groups with unstructured tasks. Similarly, the successful leaders tended to be less considerate in the less favorable situations than were the unsuccessful leaders. Not surprisingly, therefore, behaviors which tend to contribute to success under one set of conditions will not necessarily contribute to success under other conditions. This supports the Shaw and Blum Study (1966) as well as the hypothesis of the Contingency Model.

SUMMARY

One of the most stubborn and difficult problems in our research program has been the development of a theoretically sound explanation of group processes which underlie effective and ineffective group performance. Such a theory must take account of the leadership style and its interaction with the favorableness of the group-task situation.

We have interpreted high LPC as indicating relationship-oriented and self-oriented needs, and low LPC as indicating task-oriented needs. The high-LPC person thus is seen as obtaining need gratification from achieving a prominent position and success as a person. The low-LPC person obtains need gratification from performing relevant tasks.

In situations which provide little influence and control over the group, the leader experiences a threat to his need gratification and he, therefore, exerts greater effort to achieve his goal. Under these conditions which are unfavorable for the leader, the high-LPC leader will intensify his interaction with his group, and his attempt to gain prominence in the eyes of his group members. The low-LPC leader will become more concerned with the task-relevant aspects of the interaction and less concerned with maintaining pleasant, rewarding relationships. The group will perform successfully to the extent to which the group-task situation calls for task-oriented or relationship-oriented behavior. A comparison of behaviors of successful and unsuccessful leaders shows that the successful leaders decrease in the intensity of their interaction with group members, that they become less directive, less involved and structuring, and less considerate in unfavorable group-task situations.

IV This section presents studies which extend the Contingency Model (1) to groups under varying types of stress, (2) to coacting and counteracting groups, and (3) to leadership at the second and third levels of organizational management.

The work in these areas has been of more recent origin than that described in previous parts of this book. Although the evidence and conclusions are considerably more tentative than those based on earlier research, the dearth of adequate data on stress, coacting groups, and leadership at higher management levels makes it desirable to cover those topics at this time.

Chapter 15 discusses the implications of our research for management and leadership selection and training. It proposes a new approach to the upgrading of group performance which envisages the engineering of group-task situations to fit the job to the leader as an alternative to current methods which focus primarily on attempting to fit the leader to the job.

12 EFFECTS OF LEADER ATTITUDES AND ABILITIES ON PERFORMANCE UNDER STRESS

How a group performs in emergencies and under stress frequently determines its eventual success and survival. This is obviously the case for military combat crews which must operate under conditions involving physical danger. To a lesser extent this is also true of business and industrial organizations. A work group or a business which cannot function adequately under emergency conditions, or which cannot recover quickly from a crisis, is not likely to remain viable.

There is little doubt that the leader plays the decisive role under disruptive and trying conditions (Edgerton, 1953; Sells, 1962; Torrance, 1958). He contributes to group performance by reducing the anxiety of his men and by preventing and alleviating stress-produced maladjustment among his team members. He also provides the main thrust and direction for extricating the group from the stressful situation.

We shall here define situational stress as a condition in the environment which is experienced as threatening and therefore as anxiety- and tension-arousing. We distinguish between situational stress and the stress due to subjectively felt anxiety which the individual cannot refer to a stimulus or situation outside himself (the typical neurotic anxiety). It is also important for our purposes to distinguish between conditions of situational stress which arise from within the group and the stress which originates outside the group, that is, from a stress-producing environment within which the group operates. Intragroup stress arises as a result of conflict among group members or as the result of potentially threatening interpersonal encounters typical of groups in which members come from highly divergent and mutually antagonistic population sectors. Externally originating stress may be caused by a hostile and dangerous physical environment such as arctic or desert climates, it may be due to harassment by superiors, pressure of time, or to the fear of failure generated by unusually difficult tasks (see Sells, 1962).

We shall here consider three main questions which deal with the effect of stress on the behavior of interacting groups. The first of these is the leader's influence on the morale of his group and on the personal adjustment of group members. Second, we shall attempt to determine how leadership style affects performance in stressful situations. Third, we shall ask about the contribution which the leader's and the members' abilities and intelligence make to group performance under various conditions of stress and degrees of anxiety. Coincidentally we shall also ask about the effect of stress on group performance, specifically, whether groups perform more poorly under stressful than under stress-free conditions.

THE LEADER'S EFFECT ON GROUP ADJUSTMENT

There can be little doubt that the leader plays an important role in influencing the morale and adjustment of his group members (Brayfield and Crockett, 1955; Sells, 1962). Studies conducted during and since World War II have shown that the morale of the group depends in large measure on the relationship between the immediate leader and his members (Stouffer et al., 1949; Clark, 1955). We shall consider these adjustment-promoting relations between leader and members in the first part of this section.

Quasi-therapeutic leadership functions.   The leader of interacting task groups affects his members' adjustment in two important ways: (1) through his interpersonal relations with individual group members and with the group as a whole, and (2) through his organizational role which allows him to influence morale as well as group performance.

The leader plays a large part in the life of the group members and he potentially affects the adjustment of his members through his relations with them. This is particularly true of real-life groups in which the individual's career or even his life and safety are at stake (Torrance, 1958; Marshall, 1958). Not only do the leader's esteem and approval influence the individual's chances for promotion and his status in the eyes of others, but, as Freud (1922) suggested in his analysis of leadership, they also deeply affect his self-esteem and his feeling of psychological well-being. To be liked and accepted by a powerful figure represents security for the individual group member whose control over his own fate may be relatively weak. The task leader is, therefore, frequently exhorted to consider the adjustment of his group members as one of the most important facets of his job.

On the other hand, the leader who becomes involved with the personal problems of his members may precipitate difficulties for himself, since his therapeutic role is not always compatible with his organizational role as a disciplinarian and taskmaster. Although the armed services as well as most industrial organizations encourage the subordinate to discuss his personal problems with his supervisor, such a policy may also have undesirable side effects. A therapeutic relationship not only requires a sympathetic ear, but also acceptance and permissiveness which will encourage the individual to speak freely about his feelings and concerns. It is easy to see that the information which is likely to emerge in a quasi-therapeutic interaction may conflict with the evaluative, critical, and task-oriented requirements of the supervisor's job. It is a very unusual executive who could remain accepting and nonjudgmental about the employee who tells him that he is sabotaging his superior's efforts to meet his production quota.

This dilemma has been explicitly recognized by Roethlisberger and Dickson (1938), Rogers (1951), Traxler (1945), Caudill (1958), and others, who recommend splitting the therapeutic functions from the administrative functions of leadership. This division of responsibility is implicit in the organization of the armed services. Officials in whom the individual may freely confide, such as chaplains, medical officers, or inspectors general, are outside the regular command channels and do not have disciplinary responsibilities for their "clients."

There are, however, many day-to-day interactions between leader and subordinate which affect adjustment. For example, overt leader behavior such as that which Hemphill and Coons (1957) subsumed under the dimension of "consideration" includes the leader's concern that the men have adequate food and shelter, that their interests are protected, and that they get a sympathetic hearing and fair treatment.

Clark (1955) has discussed such functions of infantry squad leaders at the Korean front. The men who performed this function were described by squad members as follows:

He's easy to talk to. He listens to our gripes and helps set things straight. He helps me write letters, I couldn't ask just anyone to do that, but with him I don't mind. He stands guard with the new guys and they just forget the jitters. He just seems to understand things.

Clark stated that:

> The sustaining function seemed to have a decided therapeutic value in the squads in which it operated. Interpersonal problems came out into the open and were settled. The squad members developed more confidence in each other and seemed to be a closer, more harmonious group.
>
> The men who fulfilled the sustaining function were warm and understanding. Their fellows trusted them. But they were more than listeners, more than sympathizers. . . . They helped squadmates obtain more individual satisfactions, and at the same time helped them make more of a contribution to the group. More than other leadership functions, the sustaining function was related to the development of "groupness.". . . Squads with group goals and squads with a standard of combat aggressiveness had more sustainers than did other squads.

A number of studies have also shown that relatively permissive, accepting attitudes on the part of the leader result in greater member satisfaction and personal adjustment. The permissive, nondirective, and considerate leader fulfills some of these quasi-therapeutic functions (Hutchins and Fiedler, 1960; Fiedler, Meuwese, and Oonk, 1961). Leaders with high LPC scores tend to have groups which have lower anxiety scores and more satisfied group members (Chemers et al., 1966).[1] This does not necessarily mean, however, that the considerate, permissive leader will also be more effective. Nor can it be assumed that quasi-therapeutic attitudes are essential for the adjustment of men in task groups.

Individuals who are working on group tasks in which they are deeply involved will experience a feeling of personal satisfaction and an increase in self-esteem when their group is successful (Myers, 1962) whether or not the leader's attitudes are quasi-therapeutic. Hence, the group's effectiveness itself can be quasi-therapeutic for the members.

To quote General S. L. A. Marshall (1958), who says of factors in military organizations that affect adjustment:

> I used the word therapy. I think it fits. In combat or out of it, once an organization gets the conviction that it is moving to higher ground and some distinction will come of it, then all marginal problems begin to contract. Discipline and standards of courtesy tighten of themselves because pride has been restored. Malingering in the form of too many men on sick call, A. W. O. L's

[1] Some of our recent unpublished work suggests that high-LPC leaders are able to act as buffers for their group members, making objectively more stressful situations less anxiety-arousing.

(absences without leave), and failure to maintain proper inspection standards becomes minimal through a renewed confidence and an upgrading of interpersonal relationships at the lower levels. When the group gets the feeling of new motion it centrifugally influences anyone who tries to stand still. It can even make good soldiers out of potential bad actors.

The leader's task-related behavior becomes especially important in times of emergency. The military group which performs poorly or in a disorganized manner is in imminent danger of sustaining battle casualties and capture. Where danger threatens, the men must depend upon the leader's ability and judgment. Torrance (1958) in a discussion of survival-training research concluded that the power exercised by the leaders constituted one of the most important forces in maintaining adjustment. ". . . when this power was not exercised, panic, disorganization, loss of life, and other unfavorable conditions ensued . . . failure on the part of the official leader to exercise power and organize things results in dangerously long periods of shock or lack in overcompensation and adaptation. Ultimately, someone will emerge as a leader, but it may be too late." And Edgerton (1953), in his report on personnel factors in polar operations, emphasizes the importance of effective leadership. He states,

> There is evidence in the literature on leadership in the Arctic regions that psychological adjustment in this region is not governed by the severity of the cold itself, but relates to the success or failure of leadership provided by officers in dispelling effects of isolation which the cold produces. When there is good leadership at a base, even very poor living conditions appear to have no serious effect on the morale of the men.

One of the important adjustive functions which the leader fulfills is to provide structure and stability in group relations. Torrance (1958) notes four such functions which identify the leader: "(1) He exercises his power; (2) he maintains the communication linkages of the group; (3) he rapidly restructures the situation; and (4) he maintains the group's goal orientation." Insofar as possible, the group should remain stable. The leader of a small isolated group under stress should be the same as the official leader under normal operating conditions. Interviews of flying personnel showed that only 13 percent would accept a highly skilled survival instructor as leader in a survival situation in preference to their aircraft commander.

A study by Dusek (1961) reported that low-morale groups lacked clear-cut leadership. These groups did not have one member who was consistently rated high on peer nominations. And men having low morale differed most from those with high morale in characterizing their groups as being "low in structural clarity." The members did not know what they were there for; some did not have a clear idea of what they were supposed to be doing.

A number of writers (Bass, 1960; Carp, 1961; Torrance, 1954; and Ziller, 1955) have pointed out, therefore, that groups under stress should perform better under leaders who structure the situation and who, in our terms, are task-oriented. This seemed to be the case in the study of group creativity in Holland. While the relatively tension-free and relaxed group climate appeared to call for a permissive, considerate leader (that is, one with high LPC), the more stressful heterogeneous groups, or those under informal leadership structure, called for a task-oriented (low-LPC) leader.

The point we are trying to make is that quasi-therapeutic leader attitudes are essential in some stressful situations and task-oriented attitudes are essential in others. The problem again is to specify which situations require which kind of leadership.

THE EFFECT OF LEADERSHIP STYLE
AND STRESS ON GROUP PERFORMANCE

The second church leadership study.   This study was conducted within the context of a leadership training workshop of a religious association.[2] Participants were nineteen men and thirty-eight women, ranging in age from twenty to sixty-seven years, most of them with a college education. The participants included both ministers and lay leaders of the church.

All fifty-seven participants completed Least-preferred Coworker (LPC) scales and a short intelligence test. They were then assigned to 19 three-person groups, with leaders selected from among those falling into the upper and lower thirds of the distribution of LPC scores. The remaining participants were roughly matched on intelligence and randomly assigned to the three-man groups.

The assembled groups were told that they would work on two successive tasks. The first of these was presented as a "warm up" exercise, for which they would be given sufficient time (thirty-five minutes) "to

[2] I am indebted to Mrs. Nelson Burgess and Mr. Royal Cloyd, of the Universalist-Unitarian Association, for their cooperation in enabling us to conduct this study.

acquaint the group members with each other and with the task." The second task was described as a "real test of leadership" and "much more difficult." Only twenty minutes were allowed for its completion. It, therefore, placed the groups under externally stressful conditions generated by limited time and a difficult task.

The first task read:

> The local schools have instituted a policy of starting each day's class in primary grades with a short prayer. Children of your church members cannot understand why their parents object to this practice and why they discourage participation in this class activity. You have been asked to compose a statement which will explain and justify the parents' position to the children.

The second task was:

> The local Congregational Church is sponsoring a series of programs on various religious faiths. You have been asked to prepare the part of these programs which presents the Unitarian-Universalist viewpoint. Write material on "What we believe" in a form suitable for 8 to 10 year old children of all faiths.

After each task session the leader and his members completed a short Group Atmosphere scale and postmeeting questionnaire describing their reactions to the session.

Following the two experimental sessions the groups were disbanded and all participants were asked to read and evaluate the written products of each group except their own.

The main results of this study are presented in Table 12-1. The permissive, considerate, high-LPC leaders had significantly better performing groups than did the task-oriented, low-LPC leaders in the low-stress condition; no difference was found between groups of high- and low-LPC leaders in the second, presumably more stressful, situation.

These results are reminiscent of the findings we obtained in the Dutch study with heterogeneous groups under informal leadership. They suggested that a stressful situation may weaken the relation between leadership style and group performance, perhaps because the leader loses control over task performance under conditions of stress.

The church leadership study had several major limitations. Above all, the sample consisted of only nineteen groups. Secondly, analyses of postmeeting questionnaires showed that a surprisingly large number of the

TABLE 12-1 Participant's Rankings of Group Products in the Church Leadership Study †

| | | Condition | |
LPC of Leader	N	Low Stress	External Stress
High	10	7.3*	9.9
Low	9	12.9	10.1

† Mann-Whitney U = 18.5. $p < .025$ (one-tailed test).
* A low score indicates high rank, hence good performance.

leaders reported experiencing greater stress in the first than in the second task situation. The interviews with participants suggested that this experience of stress may have been caused by their unfamiliarity with the first task situation which required the leaders to work with relative strangers on a difficult task. Thus, the experimental manipulation in this study was at best only moderately successful. Finally, this study attempted to deal only with externally generated stress. A more extensive investigation, using a more sophisticated design with better controls, was therefore undertaken.

The ROTC study. This experiment (Meuwese and Fiedler, 1964) was designed to check the previous findings and to extend the research to situations in which the source of stress was intrinsic to the task. This study has been mentioned before in Chapter 8 and is here only briefly reviewed.

The participants in the study were seniors in the army and navy ROTC programs at the University of Illinois. All were candidates for regular or reserve commissions in their respective services.

The experiment involved 54 three-man groups, each of which performed two tasks in succession. The groups were randomly assigned to each of three experimental conditions: a control condition, one internal-stress, and one external-stress condition. Within each condition, nine groups had leaders with high-LPC scores, and the other nine had low-LPC leaders.

All subjects completed a battery of pretests (including LPC scales) prior to the experiment, and Group Atmosphere scales and various post-session questionnaires after completing each of the two tasks.

As will be recalled, the first task, the Pay Proposal, required the groups to devise a new system for providing financial support for army and navy ROTC programs. This task required the group members to cooperate in finding a single solution based on available information about the pay of

ROTC students in the various programs. It was, in effect, a problem-solving effort.

The second task, the Fable, required the groups to invent a fable for children to illustrate the need for a peacetime army. This task required divergent thinking. In contrast to the constraints set by the first problem, the second task neither was based on available information nor did it require a reconciliation of interests. It set a premium on originality and interesting presentation rather than upon logical analysis and problem-solving abilities.

A summary of the main results is presented in Table 12-2. A significant interaction between leader LPC and conditions of stress affecting group performance was obtained for the Proposal task. The task-oriented (low-LPC) leaders performed better in the low-stress condition; the inter-personal relations-oriented (high-LPC) leaders performed better in the internal-stress condition. There was no substantial difference in performance due to different leadership styles in the external-stress condition.

On the Fable task, the low-LPC leaders performed better, not only in the control and internal-stress conditions, but also in the external-stress condition. This may have been either because the task was more manageable or because the leader had learned how to manage his group by the time of the second task.

It is interesting to note, in this connection, that the level of group performance did not materially deteriorate under stress. Performance in the most stressful condition was roughly as good in quality as it was in the low-stress condition. Thus, the stressfulness of the situation per se

TABLE 12-2   Mean Performance Scores for Groups with High- and Low-LPC Leaders under Different Stress Conditions

Criterion	LPC	Low Stress	Internal Stress	External Stress	F	p
Proposal	High	86.1	95.9	91.9	3.49*	.05
	Low	113.4	80.7	89.3		
Fable	High	96.9	96.0	97.7	5.63†	.025
	Low	108.8	110.2	115.2		

* Interaction between condition and LPC. $df = 2/36$.
† Main LPC effect. $df = 1/36$.

did not lead to a deterioration of performance, as has sometimes been assumed.

The relationship between leadership style, measured by LPC, and group performance is obviously complex. Can we integrate the present results with the Contingency Model? This may be possible by construing the stressfulness of the situation as one factor affecting favorableness. Scaling the situations on the basis of their presumed stressfulness should then yield curves similar to those obtained in previous applications of the Contingency Model.

Two components of favorableness were examined. These are (1) the stressfulness of the three situations and (2) the leader's perception of group atmosphere as being high, medium, or low in pleasantness.

We assumed that the overall level of stress would be greatest in the condition of external stress, less in the internal-stress condition, and least in the low-stress condition. This was supported by data from the postsession questionnaire showing that leaders in the external-stress condition reported considerably more subjective stress than did leaders in the other two conditions. There was, however, relatively less difference between the Group Atmosphere scores of leaders in the low-stress and internal-stress conditions.

As in our other studies, high Group Atmosphere scores were assumed to reflect good leader-member relations. Medium and low Group Atmosphere scores were taken to indicate a correspondingly less favorable group-task situation. The analyses were then designed to indicate the type of leadership style which would be most appropriate under different degrees of favorableness as indicated by the stress condition and by the leader's Group Atmosphere scores.

The simplest classification of group-task situations is probably one which first classifies groups on the basis of the stress situation and secondly on the basis of the leader's Group Atmosphere score. Barron (1967) conducted a study of leader behavior under different conditions of stress which utilized the Meuwese and Fiedler (1965) typescripts. The results of her analysis correlating leader LPC and group performance (combined over tasks) are presented in Table 12-3, and the correlations are plotted in Figure 12-1. The two curves are remarkably parallel, even though the correlation between the two tasks was only .33. The pattern of correlations is very similar in shape to the curve which is characteristic of the Contingency Model.

As the Contingency Model would predict, the low-LPC leaders per-

TABLE 12-3   Correlations (*r*) between Least-preferred Coworker Scores and Group Effectiveness in the Two Tasks of the ROTC Study (Barron) ($N = 6$)

Stress Condition	Group Atmosphere	Index of Group Stress	Task Pay Proposal	Fable
Low	High	I	−42	−71
Low	Medium	II	−56	−59
Low	Low	III	−32	+69
Internal	High	IV	+67	+41
Internal	Medium	V	−08	−15
Internal	Low	VI	−01	−20
External	High	VII	−53	−47
External	Medium	VIII	−72	−61
External	Low	IX	+18	−14

formed most effectively in the relatively relaxed, tension-free condition, the high-LPC leaders performed best in the intermediate situations, and the low-LPC leaders again appeared to perform better than the high-LPC leaders in the situation of relatively high stress.

Figure 12-1   Correlations between leader LPC scores and group performance plotted for various conditions of situational stress and leader Group Atmosphere scores.

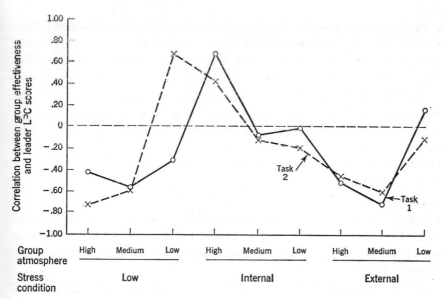

It should be noted that the intermediate stress condition was identical to the condition in which the stress was interpersonal in nature. It is, therefore, not clear in this case whether the high-LPC leader performed more effectively because he was best able to handle interpersonal stress or because the situation was intermediate in favorableness. Further research will be needed to answer this question.

THE EFFECT OF LEADER AND MEMBER ABILITY ON GROUP PERFORMANCE UNDER STRESS

Let us now consider the question of how the stress of the situation, or the anxiety of the leader, affects his or his members' ability to contribute to the task. This section is predicated on the working assumption that we can infer the leader's contribution to the task on the basis of the correlation between the leader's intelligence score and the group performance measure. While this assumption is far from axiomatic, it leads to reasonable working hypotheses for interpreting the data. For example, if the correlation were 1.00 we would infer that the leader's intelligence determines task performance. The more intelligent the leader the better the performance of the group. If the correlation is zero we must assume that the variables are unreliable or irrelevant, that they are nonlinearly related, or that the leader's ability does not play a noteworthy part in determining group performance.

We generally expect a simple monotonic relationship between intelligence and group performance. A group consisting of highly intelligent members is expected to perform better than a group consisting of dull members. Likewise, a group with a very intelligent leader is expected to outperform a group with a dull leader. This common assumption is not strongly supported. Mann's (1959) review of the literature reported a median correlation between the intelligence score of the leader and his group's performance as being about .25.

Fiedler and Meuwese (1963) were able to show, however, that the leader's intelligence and ability scores in four different studies correlated highly with group performance when the internal group environment was relatively pleasant and free from stress, that is, when the leader was accepted by his group and/or when the group was cohesive. In groups in which the group climate was presumably stressful, that is, where the leader was not accepted or where the group was uncohesive and divisive, the correlation between leader intelligence and group performance tended to be low and slightly negative (Table 12-4).

TABLE 12-4   Correlations of Leader's Ability with Group Effectiveness

Study	Ability Score	Effectiveness Criterion	Cohesiveness Criterion	Correlation (Rho)			
				Cohesive Groups	N	Uncohesive Groups	N
Army tank crews	AGCT †	Probability of winning a battle	Sociometric	.26	8	−.21	8
Army tank crews	Proficiency rating	Probability of winning a battle	Sociometric	.94**	8	−.21	8
B-29 bomber crews	Ground school grade	Radar bomb score	Liking for the group	.67	6	−.40	4
Antiaircraft artillery crews	AGCT	Ratings	Leader's army adjustment score	.84*	6	.23	9
Antiaircraft artillery crews	AGCT	Ratings	Member's army adjustment score	.57	8	−.05	8
Dutch creativity study	Analogies score	Creativity ratings	Presence of destructive critic	.54*	14	.24	17

* $p < .05$.
** $p < .01$.
† Army General Classification Test.

Further light is also cast on the generality of these findings by Anderson and Fiedler's (1964) investigation of 30 four-man teams. These teams consisted of a senior navy ROTC student who served as leader and three freshman or sophomore ROTC men who were assigned as team members. In fifteen of these teams, the leader served as chairman and fully participated in the work of the group. In the other fifteen groups, the leader was limited to purely supervisory functions. He was prohibited from contributing substantive ideas which might assist in solving the problem or completing the task, although he could veto suggestions, make procedural comments, and structure the interaction (see Chapter 8).

The groups performed four different tasks. One of these consisted in devising two stories from a Thematic Apperception Test; the second required that the group prepare arguments in favor of and against dangerous military training in peacetime; the third problem consisted of finding unusual uses for two common objects (Guilford et al., 1954), a ruler and a wire coat hanger; and the final problem required the group to think of ways in which a man of average ability and average means could gain fame and immortality (Triandis et al., 1963). All creativity tasks could be scored by means of manuals and yielded acceptable interrater reliabilities.

As we mentioned previously, this study was conducted under the supervision of navy officers, and the men were aware of the fact that these exercises were part of their course in naval leadership. They were fairly tense during the session; in addition, the Group Atmosphere scores were quite low.

Leaders had been given intelligence tests prior to their participation in the study, and a wide variety of ability tests had been administered as part of the Naval Reserve Officer Training Corps program. These included also military aptitude ratings by NROTC instructors, buddy ratings by NROTC classmates, a mechanical aptitude test, a mathematical aptitude test, and a verbal aptitude test given as part of the NROTC battery. As can be seen in Table 12-5, most correlations were low. While all of the ratings and measures are not equally good intelligence indicants, all have been related to intelligence and ability.

The importance of these data does not lie in individual results which show that some leader intelligence or ability scores correlate in a positive or in a negative direction with performance. Rather, the relations between leader ability and group performance were very variable, and no less than 26 of the 54 correlations were in the negative direction in these groups in which the leader was under tension and presumably experiencing anxiety.

TABLE 12-5   Correlations of the Leader's Aptitude Scores, Ability Scores, Peer Ratings, and Group Performance

Aptitude	Leadership Condition	
	Participatory	Supervisory
Leader's military aptitude ratings (by NROTC instructors):		
TAT stories	.19	.13
Unusual uses	.24	−.12
Argument construction	−.08	.09
Fame problem	−.37	.26
Leader's NROTC "buddy ratings" (by NROTC classmates):		
TAT stories	−.17	.01
Unusual uses	.40	−.43
Argument construction	−.37	.03
Fame problem	−.48	.34
Mechanical aptitude (NROTC battery):		
TAT stories	−.25	.26
Unusual uses	.21	−.60*
Argument construction	−.34	−.26
Fame problem	−.17	−.45
Mathematical aptitude (NROTC battery):		
TAT stories	−.09	.32
Unusual uses	.15	−.38
Argument construction	−.13	−.04
Fame problem	−.02	−.32
Verbal aptitude (NROTC battery):		
TAT stories	.15	.13
Unusual uses	.01	−.38
Argument construction	−.61*	.57*
Fame problem	.16	−.10
Verbal intelligence (Cureton):		
TAT stories	.61**	−.01
Unusual uses	.40	−.16
Argument construction	−.19	.65*
Fame problem	.25	.03
Median correlations	−.08	.00

* $p < .05$.
** $p < .01$.

The study by Meuwese and Fiedler (1965) provided an opportunity to conduct a more extensive investigation of the effects of stress and anxiety on group performance. We had obtained intelligence test scores (Cureton Multi-Aptitude Test) [3] from all leaders and members who participated in the ROTC study. At the time of the pretest we had also obtained

[3] Copyright, The Psychological Corporation, New York.

anxiety scores using the Alexander and Husek anxiety differential (1962). This same measure was again obtained at the end of the experiment, permitting us to determine not only the general anxiety level of the individuals who participated, but also the change in anxiety level which occurred as a result of working in a more or less anxiety-arousing condition.

As will be recalled, the design of the ROTC study called for three conditions (low stress, internal stress, and external stress), and eighteen groups were randomly assigned to each of these conditions. Nine of the groups in each condition had high-LPC leaders and nine had low-LPC leaders. This design therefore involved six cells with nine groups per cell. Mean intelligence scores within each of these six cells were approximately equal.

We shall here consider three questions. These are: (1) How is the correlation between leader (and member) intelligence and group performance affected by the experimentally induced stress conditions? (2) How does the leader's anxiety affect the correlation between leader intelligence and group performance? (3) What are the effects of the general anxiety level, as measured by pretests, on his and his members' contribution to the group performance?

Consistent with the results of previous research, the leader's intelligence score was expected to correlate positively with group creativity under conditions of low stress, but the correlations were expected to be near zero or slightly negative under more stressful conditions; secondly, the average intelligence score of group members was expected to correlate negligibly with group performance under the low-stress condition but high and positively under stress.

Table 12-6 shows the correlations obtained on both tasks as well as the mean correlations. The correlations are listed separately for high- and low-LPC leaders in each of the experimental conditions. As can be seen, the results were in the hypothesized direction for both leaders and members.

The findings shown in Table 12-6 suggest that the stress of the situation caused the leader to be anxious and that the leader's anxiety, in turn, interfered with his ability to concentrate his efforts on the task. Thus we would expect that the leaders' anxiety caused by the experimental manipulation would lessen the leaders' contribution to the task while it would increase the members' contribution.

This hypothesis was tested by obtaining the difference (that is, the change) in leader anxiety scores between pretest and posttest. This score, in effect, indicates the situational anxiety associated with a particular

TABLE 12-6   Correlations between Leader's Intelligence Scores and Qualitative Criterion Scores ($N = 9$)

| | | | Condition | |
Task	LPC	Low Stress	Internal Stress	External Stress
Leaders:				
Pay proposal	High	.40	.20	.08
	Low	.35	.35	−.03
Fable	High	.43	.01	.13
	Low	.46	.38	.28
Mean correlations †		.41	.24	.13
Members:				
Pay proposal	High	−.37	−.27	.76*
	Low	.07	−.03	.80*
Fable	High	.31	−.42	.45
	Low	−.11	−.30	.43
Mean correlations *		−.03	−.26	.64

† Means were obtained by converting to z.
* $p < .05$.

experimental condition. The correlation coefficients between leader in
telligence and group performance given in Table 12-6 were computed for
each of the nine groups within a set (for example, the set consisting of
the nine groups with high-LPC leaders in the low-stress condition). These
correlation coefficients were then correlated with the average change in
leader anxiety between pretest and posttest for each of these six cells.
Similar correlations were obtained with member intelligence and group
performance.

The results are shown in Table 12-7. All four of the correlations were in
the hypothesized direction, indicating that the contribution of the leader's
intelligence became relatively *less* as the situation became more anxiety-
arousing for him. Conversely, the members' intelligence contributed relatively *more* to the task when the situation was more anxiety-arousing for
the leader. Although the correlation between the Proposal and Fable tasks
was low (.32), it was not appropriate to combine the probabilities of the
four correlation coefficients. The pattern of correlations suggests, however, that we are not dealing with random effects.

TABLE 12-7   Correlations between Change in Anxiety of Leaders and Correlation Coefficients between Intelligence and Group Performance ($N = 6$)

Correlations between Change in Leader Anxiety and	Proposal	Fable
Leaders' IQ and perform.	−.64	−.49
Members IQ and perform.	.46	.26

This still left open the question of whether the general anxiety level of the leader, *irrespective of the experimental situation,* would affect his ability to apply his intelligence to the solution of the task and at the same time free his members' ability to contribute to the task. This question could be answered by dividing the fifty-four groups into six sets of nine groups purely on the basis of the leader's pretest anxiety, that is, without regard to the experimental treatment which they received. In other words, we asked here whether leaders who were generally anxious people would contribute less to the task solution than leaders who generally tended to be free of anxiety. Conversely, we could also ask whether group members would contribute more when the leader was a generally anxious person and relatively less when he was free of anxiety.

The correlations between (1) leader intelligence and group performance and (2) member intelligence and group performance for each of the six subsets of nine groups are indicated in Table 12-8. As can be seen in Figures 12-2 and 12-3, we found that leader anxiety depressed the correlation between leader intelligence and group performance while it

TABLE 12-8   Correlations between Leader and Member Intelligence Scores and Performance under Different Levels of Leader Pretest Anxiety

Leader Anxiety	N	Leaders		Members	
		Pay Proposal	Fable	Pay Proposal	Fable
Very low	9	.50	.40	.03	−.42
Low	9	.36	.61	−.18	.11
Somewhat low	9	.53	.66	.37	.06
Somewhat high	10	.19	.06	.00	−.29
High	8	.29	.12	.47	.34
Very high	9	−.34	−.39	−.08	.43

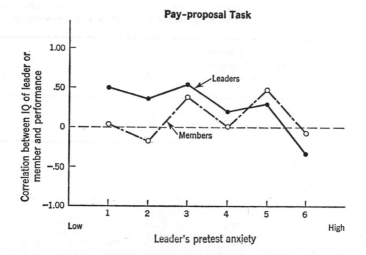

Figure 12-2   Correlations between leader and member intelligence and group performance on the Pay Proposal task under increasingly anxious leaders.

raised the correlation between member intelligence and group performance. Table 12-9 presents the correlations between the leader's pretest
anxiety and the intelligence–group performance coefficients.

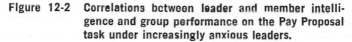

Figure 12-3   Correlations between leader and member intelligence scores and group performance on the Fable task under increasingly anxious leaders.

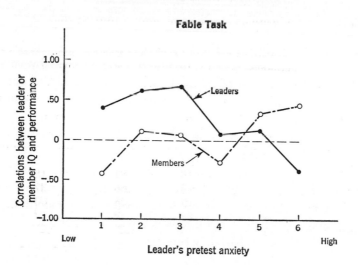

TABLE 12-9   Correlations between Pretest Anxiety Level of the Correlation Coefficients between Intelligence and Group Performance ($N = 6$)

Correlations between Leader Pretest Anxiety and	Proposal	Fable
Leaders' IQ and perform.	−.77*	−.72
Members' IQ and perform.	.09	.77*

* $p < .05$, one-tailed.

Interestingly enough, it made little difference in group performance whether or not the members were basically anxious people, as indicated by their anxiety scores obtained in the pretest, or whether they became anxious as a consequence of the situational stress (indicated by the difference between pretest and posttest anxiety scores). Rather, it appeared to be the leader's anxiety level which determined his and his members' contribution to the task. These findings are all the more interesting since the performance of groups led by anxious leaders was neither significantly better nor poorer than that of the relatively anxiety-free leaders. In groups with anxious leaders, the members appear to have carried the main burden of task-relevant activities since their intelligence correlated with group performance.

A group consisting of both highly intelligent leaders and members will obviously tend to perform better than a group of both dull leaders and members. The data indicate, however, that the degree of stress determines whether the group will utilize the leader's or the members' intelligence in performing the task. The major importance of our data is that the leader's intelligence or task-relevant abilities are utilized by the group primarily under conditions of minimal stress. Under stressful conditions, especially those involving external harassment, the leader's intelligence is not substantially related to performance and it may, in fact, be detrimental. In contrast, the average member's intelligence or ability is essentially unrelated to performance under ordinary conditions, while it is related to performance in situations of stress and anxiety. Whether these findings are applicable only to creative tasks or whether they are generalizable to other tasks needs to be determined in future studies.

The findings suggest that conditions of stress or general leader anxiety threaten the leader more than they threaten his members, perhaps because the leader feels primarily responsible for the group's performance. If he is unable to concentrate on the task because of his anxiety, the members' contributions will determine the success of the group.

Where the leader is a specialist with rare task-relevant talents, it seems, therefore, well worth considering that he might be unable to use his talents unless he can operate in a tension- and stress-free environment. The study also suggests that highly intelligent or expert members will not contribute to the task in proportion to their abilities unless the conditions within the group are especially unfavorable. While our study indicates that member contributions will be high in tense and anxiety-arousing situations, other conditions may well be found in future research which permit the group to utilize the leader's ability while allowing more effective member contribution to the task performance at the same time.

SUMMARY

This chapter has considered the effects of stress on leader behavior and group performance. In general, we found (1) that low-stress conditions tend to require relatively managing, controlling leaders, while situations of moderate or interpersonal stress tend to require permissive, considerate leaders, and that task-oriented leaders perform better in highly stressful conditions; (2) that leader intelligence correlates with group performance primarily under low-stress conditions or under conditions which are free of anxiety for the leader, while group member intelligence contributes to group performance under high-stress conditions and those which are anxiety-arousing for the leader; (3) finally, that total group performance does not appear to be strongly affected by the range of stress present in the laboratory studies which were discussed here.

13 COACTING GROUPS AND COUNTERACTING GROUPS

The bulk of the leadership literature has dealt with interacting groups. These correspond most closely to the classical definition of the group as a set of individuals who interact in the pursuit of a shared goal. Yet a substantial proportion of groups in our society—perhaps even a majority— are coacting in nature. These are groups in which each individual performs his own job in relative independence from his coworkers.

A typical example of a coacting team is found in bowling in which one team member at a time steps forward to bowl his inning. He contributes to the group effort by adding his own score to that of his teammates. To be sure, he may be influenced to some extent by the moral support of his fellow team members (Whyte, 1943), but this influence will be relatively minor. Analogous situations exist in a business organization where each representative is assigned to a different territory, in retail stores or real-estate offices where each salesman works on a commission basis, and in the many industrial concerns which operate on individual piecework wages. In addition, practically all classroom situations fall into the coacting category. We shall here try to isolate the factors that affect the performance of these teams, and we shall attempt to determine whether the contingency theory will enable us to understand more clearly how coacting groups operate.

One major difference between interacting and coacting groups is clearly apparent. Since the members of coacting groups work on individual tasks, the leader will not need to concern himself greatly with coordinating the activities of his subordinates. While there will be some interacting activities, such as shifting supplies, loading a truck, or deciding on a work schedule, the overwhelmingly large portion of the individual worker's time is spent in activities which require little or no help from others and little or no interaction with them. As a result, the leader of the coacting group will, to a large extent, interact separately with each of his group members. The coacting group may thus be conceptualized as a set of two-man teams consisting of the leader and his several subordinate group members. An understanding of these diadic relations may be critical for understanding certain aspects of coacting teams.

Let us ask, first of all, what leadership functions in coacting groups determine group performance. Three important functions can be tentatively distinguished (although these are not exclusively found in coacting groups). These consist of motivating and supervising individual group members, of training, and of performing quasi-therapeutic functions.

Motivation and supervision of group members.   This leadership function is essential to all types of formal task groups, be they coacting or interacting. It will be as important in organizations in which the members work on an individual piece or commission basis as it will be in classroom situations. The supervisor or leader in coacting groups must see that each individual meets his quota and that he is properly motivated to perform his task according to specifications.

The leader of the interacting group can very often work through the group as a whole because he may be able to count on the group to prod the worker who does not pull his share of the load. The leader of the coacting group must, to a much greater extent, motivate each individual separately.

Training.   A second leadership function, important in many groups, consists of training or teaching individual group members. Typical is the apprenticeship system, in which the supervisor oversees and guides the work of one or more novices who are assigned to him for on-the-job training. It is also typical of the classroom situation, in which each individual works on the same problem or attempts to learn the same material. The performance of a group of this type is generally measured by the average progress scores made by the several group members. In most of these situations the formal leader has relatively high position power. The structure of the task will depend upon the content of the subject matter and is likely to influence the type of leadership style which will be most appropriate.

Quasi-therapeutic functions.   Finally, an important function of leaders in many coacting groups appears to involve quasi-therapeutic interactions. These serve to lessen the anxieties stemming from an inhospitable external environment or from stress-inducing tasks. Quasi-therapeutic relations, as we indicated earlier, are defined as interpersonal interactions among group members or between the leader and a group member which serve to increase the individual's ability to adjust.

It seems highly probable that the importance of quasi-therapeutic leadership functions is greater in coacting than in interacting group situations. The interacting group demands that the individual relate closely to others in the performance of the shared task and that he interact with them in a wide variety of activities. Each member will, therefore, tend to be seen and valued as an important contributor to the common task and as essential to group success. This interdependence among group members typically results in positive, accepting, and supportive interpersonal relations which are adjustive in nature (Fiedler, 1962b). The coacting group by definition is less dependent upon each individual group member. In fact, interaction among group members is neither required nor in many situations welcomed since it interferes with the work. As a result, the individual tends to be psychologically isolated and, therefore, more vulnerable to maladjustive processes in the situation (Fiedler, 1962b; Fiedler, 1966b; Julian, Bishop, and Fiedler, 1966c).

As we pointed out in Chapter 3, Assumed Similarity scores were originally developed in studies of psychotherapeutic relations (Fiedler, 1951). Therapists with high Assumed Similarity (who perceived little difference between themselves and their patients) tended to be more effective than were therapists who perceived patients to be dissimilar to themselves. We have found since then that the perception of others as similar or as having highly valued attributes also has quasi-therapeutic effects (Fiedler, 1951; Kipnis, 1961). Likewise, a high-LPC score, that is, perceiving even one's least-preferred coworker in a relatively favorable manner, seemed to result in higher adjustment indices among group members and lower anxiety scores. We are hypothesizing that these quasi-therapeutic relations, as indexed in part by high-LPC scores, will importantly contribute to the performance of coacting teams which operate under anxiety-arousing situations.

We are proposing, as a first step toward the development of a more general theoretical framework, that coacting groups can be divided into two major classes, namely, the typical coacting *task* groups and groups in *training* and *teaching* situations. These groups may be further subdivided into those which are relaxed and relatively free of tension and those which are stressful and anxiety-arousing. The latter presumably require the leader to interact with his subordinates in a quasi-therapeutic manner.

Where quasi-therapeutic interactions are required, we would expect that the relationship-oriented leader will perform more effectively than the task-oriented leader. Where the situation does not require quasi-therapeutic leader attitudes, the structure of the task, the position power of the leader, and the group's climate are likely to determine the appropriateness of the leadership style, as would be expected for interacting team situations.

INDUSTRIAL WORK SITUATIONS REQUIRING MOTIVATING LEADERS

Hunt's study (1966), in part described in Chapter 11, involved not only interacting groups but also two sets of coacting work groups. Hunt hypothesized that the Contingency Model could be extended to these coacting work units and that the correlation between the leader's LPC score and the group performance criteria would be in the same direction and of the same order of magnitude as the corresponding correlations for interacting task groups in the same octant.

Industrial workshops. One set of coacting groups, obtained in the physics research laboratory, consisted of eleven workshops. The men in these shops were highly skilled craftsmen who were assigned individual tasks. Most of these jobs were highly structured. Their work required the repair and fabrication of equipment for basic research projects. Included in the sample were welding, optics, machine repair, and sheet metal shops as well as several service shops for first echelon maintenance. Also included were an inspection department and a tool and stock room. Each of the shops may be considered a small department supervised by a foreman. The position power of the foreman in these groups was rated as relatively high, and the groups were divided on the basis of the foreman's Group Atmosphere scores. These groups, therefore, fell into Octants I and V, depending upon the foreman's rating of the group climate.

The effectiveness of the crafts shops was judged by three raters familiar with their work. Ratings were made on (1) quality of the output, considering working conditions, equipment, and other relevant factors; (2) quantity of output in terms of required deadlines; (3) attitudes of workers and grievances; and (4) an overall evaluation of shops based on the order in which supervisors would be selected if the evaluators had their own businesses. The interrater correlation among the three judges was quite high (.86 to .92 corrected for number of raters).

Supermarket grocery departments. Data were collected from twenty-six stores in the supermarket chain described in Chapter 11. The group is here considered to be the entire store, exclusive of the produce departments and meat markets, which are managed separately.

The jobs performed by store employees are primarily coacting in nature. Food is unloaded, stored, marked, and shelved; customers are checked out and groceries are sacked and placed in customer cars. In addition, the store must be kept clean and neat, and display shelves and cases must be kept attractive. Most of these jobs are performed by employees working alone. Where interacting tasks are required the groups tend to be of very transitory nature.

The leader position power of the store managers was judged to be high and the tasks were judged to be highly structured. Depending upon the store manager's rating of the group climate, these groups again fell into Octants I and V.

The grocery departments were evaluated on the same basis as were the interacting meat departments, namely, the amount of sales per man-hour, which appears to be a valid index for comparing stores of this supermarket chain.

Results.   As in other studies, Hunt correlated the LPC scores of shop foremen or of store managers with the performance ratings of their work units. The correlations are in the expected direction and of approximately the same magnitude as the corresponding correlations predicted by the Contingency Model (see Table 9-2). While three of the individual correlations failed to reach an acceptable level of significance, taken as a group the results shown in Table 13-1 are highly significant. (Joint probabilities were computed by Fisher's exact test, see Gordon et al., 1952.)

TABLE 13-1   Rank Order Correlations between Supervisor LPC Scores and Group Performance for Coacting Groups in Octants I and V *

Sample	Pleasant Group Climate (Octant I)		Tense, Unpleasant Group Climate (Octant V)	
	N	Rho	N	Rho
Foremen of crafts shops	6	−.48	5	.90*
Store managers of supermarkets	13	−.06	11	.49
Obtained median correlations		−.27		.69
Expected median correlations		−.52		.42

* Combined probability $p < .01$ (one-tailed).

Hunt's work suggests that the interaction between leadership style and the group situation in determining performance is very similar in coacting and interacting work teams and that it may be possible to extend the Contingency Model predictions to coacting task groups.

COACTING TASK GROUPS WITH WEAK LEADER POSITION POWER

Whether the Contingency Model can be generalized to all coacting task groups is questionable. Where the position power of the leader is very weak his influence over individual members of the group and hence over their work performance is likely to be minimal. This is suggested by a study (DeZonia, 1958) of sixteen teams participating in a recreational bowling league. The correlation between the elected (hence accepted) team captain's ASo score and team performance turned out to be only .06.

Similar results were found in an investigation of rifle teams. Myers (1962) compared 30 three-man teams which were in competition with one another and 30 three-man teams in which competition was discouraged and deemphasized. The leaders were identified by sociometric questionnaires administered during and after the study. Here, again, the correlations between leadership style and team performance scores were low and insignificant. The leader's control over his team members may be simply too weak in these situations so that we cannot obtain meaningful relationships between performance and his leadership style. Nor are bowling and rifle marksmanship in the context of recreational activities sufficiently anxiety-producing to force team members to turn to the leader for quasi-therapeutic interactions.

COACTING GROUPS IN ANXIETY–AROUSING TRAINING SITUATIONS

Naval aviation cadets. One major investigation was carried out in 1955 at the Naval Air Station at Saufley Field, Florida (Fiedler and Hutchins, unpublished).[1] Naval aviation cadets were assigned to this naval air station as part of their officer candidate course after completing basic individual pilot training.[2] Saufley Field provided the training in formation flying.

We are indebted to Drs. W. B. Webb and J. de Rivera who made this study possible.
The flights also contained a small number of junior officers and cadets from foreign countries. These were given no special treatment.

Students were assigned in order of their arrival to squadrons of sixteen men, and each of these squadrons was further subdivided into eight-man squads or "flights" which were the basic units of instruction. The formation flying maneuvers were taught according to a very detailed set of standards, and the instructors followed a highly structured syllabus.

Tight formation flying is potentially dangerous, and it was especially anxiety-arousing for these inexperienced student pilots. In addition, of course, the high failure rates typical of officer candidate schools further contributed to the anxiety of the cadets in the program.

Since the flight's performance was based on the average performance scores of each of the student pilots, rather than on the evaluation of the entire flight, the groups were considered to be coacting. In fact, the emphasis in training the pilot was on his ability to fly formation with any other pilots. Team performance, as such, was not stressed.

A group of five or six instructors was assigned to each squadron. The senior instructor, who was designated by the school on the basis of his flying ability and past experience as instructor, was in charge of the squadron during its six-week training course. The senior instructor was, thus, the formal leader of the squadron and, in view of his responsibilities and control over group activities, he can be considered to have high position power.

In addition, we also identified an informal leader of each flight by means of two sociometric preference questions which asked each student pilot to name the man in his squadron whom we would most prefer a combat leader and whom he would most prefer as his wingman in combat. These informal leaders were identified at the termination of training they had no formal authority or assigned functions in their flights. Their leader position power was, therefore, extremely weak.

A number of criterion measures were available. The most reliable of these was a combination of two scores: (1) the sum of "check-flight" score which the student received from base examiners with whom he had no previously worked, and (2) the number of so-called "non-check down indicating the standard flight maneuvers the student performed satisfactorily after each phase of training and for which he, therefore, did no require additional training.

The reliability of flight scores was quite low. It was obtained by a varia of the odd-even method of correlating the individual performance score of one half of the men in each flight with the performance scores of the other half of the flight. We obtained two samples several months apa

The performance scores obtained in the first sample had a reliability of .47. The reliability of the second sample was .32. Further inquiry about this discrepancy in reliability revealed that there had been a shortage of flight instructors at the time of the data collection for the second sample and that the range of scores for this second sample was considerably smaller than that of the first (40.4 versus 51.0).

Assumed Similarity between Opposites (ASo) scores were obtained from all available student pilots and instructors at the beginning of each training cycle. These scores were then correlated with the average performance score of each man in the flight or in the squadron.

The first sample consisted of twenty-two flights. The ASo score of the flight's informal leader (that is, the man who was sociometrically most chosen by his fellow group members) correlated with the flight performance score .55 ($p < .02$) exclusive of the informal leader's own performance score. (The ASo of the informal leader and his *own* performance correlated .10.)

These flights suffered considerable attrition since a substantial number of students failed the course, resigned, or were set back because of illness or emergency leave. A correlation was, therefore, computed for the subsample of seventeen flights in which the attrition rate was less than 50 percent. The resulting correlation between informal leader ASo and the flight's performance was .70 ($p < .01$).

A correlation was also computed between the ASo score of the formal leader of the squadron, that is, the senior flight instructor, and the performance of the squadron which he supervised. This correlation was .45 for fifteen squadrons ($p < .10$).

A second sample of fifteen flights was obtained later during that year, and as already indicated, the performance scores were of lower reliability. Hence, the correlations between leader ASo and performance would also be expected to be lower. The correlation between the informal leader's ASo score and the flight's performance was .28 (not significant). Using only the twelve flights with less than 50 percent attrition, the correlation rose to .32 (not significant). The correlations between the senior instructor's ASo score and the squadron criterion for sixteen squadrons was .17, which is, of course, not significant, although both validation results were in the hypothesized direction.

If we consider the joint probability of the results obtained in both samples, the data indicate fairly clearly, especially in the case of informal leaders, that the men in the flights performed more effectively if the leader was relationship-oriented (high ASo) and presumably quasi-therapeutic in his interactions.

COACTING TRAINING GROUPS IN RELATIVELY TENSION–FREE SITUATIONS

There are very few studies thus far which relate LPC and ASo scores to the instructor's performance in classroom or training situations. One small study by J. E. Marse (unpublished) used instructors of various sections of an undergraduate physics course and an undergraduate rhetoric course. Only those instructors were selected who were accepted (that is, rated highly) by their students. Their performance was evaluated by senior faculty members who had overall supervision of these courses.

The samples consisted of six accepted physics instructors and eighteen accepted rhetoric instructors. The correlation between the physics instructors' ASo scores and their rated effectiveness was −.70; the correlation between the ASo scores of eighteen accepted rhetoric instructors and their effectiveness ratings was −.36. Neither of these is significant. Since the results obtained by Marse were based on very small samples the correlations may well be due to chance fluctuations. The findings suggest, however, that further research along this line may be fruitful.

A second investigation of teaching effectiveness was conducted by DeZonia (1958), who worked with student teachers from eight different subject matter areas (foreign language, English, mathematics, speech, agriculture, home economics, physical education for women, and science). The university faculty members in charge of these sections were asked to evaluate the performance of these student teachers. The degree to which the student teachers were accepted by their own pupils could not be established. None of the correlations was significant.[3]

DISCUSSION OF COACTING GROUPS

While our understanding of coacting groups obviously leaves much to be desired, the relations which have been obtained between leadership style and group performance are beginning to form a meaningful pattern. A

[3] Two of the correlations, speech (.57) and English (−.55), were significant when teaching performance was correlated with a variant of ASo which required the student teacher to describe the most- and the least-preferred pupils he ever had. It is difficult to assess the results obtained with this measure.

TABLE 13-2   Summary of Results Obtained in Studies of Coacting Groups— Correlations between Leadership Style (LPC or ASo) and Group Performance

| | Group Climate | | | |
	Pleasant	Nonstressful	Unpleasant	Stressful
High Position Power	N	Correlation	N	Correlation
Task groups				
Workshops	6	−.48	5	.90*
Supermarkets	13	−.06	11	.49
Training or teaching situations				
Physics instructors	6	−.70		
Rhetoric instructors	12	−.36		
Anxiety-arousing training situation				
Navy pilot instructors—sample I			15	.45†
Navy pilot instructors—sample II			16	.17
Low Position Power				
Task groups				
Bowling teams	16	.06		
Rifle teams	30	.18	30	−.19
Anxiety-arousing training situation				
Informal navy flight leaders—sample I			22	.55**
Informal navy flight leaders—sample II			15	.28

** $p < .01$.
* $p < .05$.
† $p < .10$.

summary of results obtained in coacting group-task situations is presented in Table 13-2.

As can be seen, we have divided the groups on the basis of the leader's position power and on the basis of the presumed stressfulness of the situation. It is not yet clear whether the more typical work groups and the training or teaching situation in which the instructor holds a position analogous to the leader should be combined. We have done so here, although pooling of these groups may have been premature.

The table shows that the effective leaders (or instructors) of groups with high position power and pleasant, nonthreatening group climate tended to be task-oriented, low-LPC or low-ASo persons. While the individual correlation coefficients were low and insignificant, all were in the negative direction. In contrast, all five correlation coefficients in groups having tense or anxiety-arousing group climate and high position power were positive. This suggests that the relationship-oriented, quasi-therapeutic leaders perform better under these conditions. This is also suggested by the results from groups in which the leader position power was low.

The relationships in groups with pleasant group climate but low position power were negligible. This, in retrospect, does not seem too surprising. The leader who has little or no authortiy is not in a position to direct or advise; he cannot even train people or give them special instruction. Only when the group members' anxiety rises to the critical point where help is urgently sought and gladly accepted is the group likely to turn to the leader with low position power for assistance in reducing tension and anxiety.

The formal leader with high or moderately high position power can assist the group under stressful and tension-arousing situations by creating a nonthreatening, permissive group climate. This could also be seen in the study of naval ROTC cadets who participated in creative group tasks under supervisory and participatory leadership. Performance on the task which required the group to invent unusual and unique uses for common objects, namely for a wire coat hanger and a ruler, correlated .63 ($p < .05$) and .31 (n.s.) in the participatory and supervisory conditions respectively (see Chapter 8). These problems were very similar to coacting tasks, and the group members and leaders felt under considerable pressure since they were constantly watched by their ROTC officers. It seemed likely under these conditions that the group members felt more at ease and, therefore, more able to think of original and unusual uses for these articles when the leader was relationship-oriented (high LPC) in his approach.

Since most correlations obtained in this and other studies here reported were not significant taken singly, the results have to be interpreted with considerable caution. The consistency of the relationships and their correspondence with existing theory indicate, however, that these findings can serve as hypotheses for more intensive explorations of coacting groups.

COUNTERACTING GROUPS: NEGOTIATION AND BARGAINING

A very small number of studies relating leadership style to performance of counteracting groups has been completed. Counteracting groups, as we indicated earlier, consist of members who pursue the common goal of seeking a compromise, while at the same time representing a point of view or position to which they adhere or which they advocate in opposition to other members of the group. While the members of the coacting group work side by side, "in parallel" so to speak, the members of counteracting groups are in opposition to each other on one or several relevant issues.

McGrath (1965) has proposed a very insightful model of negotiation situations which spells out the various forces which impinge upon the individual members of these groups. The group member, or representative, has the task of obtaining an advantage over other members of the group, as is the case in bargaining. He may also have the task of having his own or his constituency's point of view adopted by the entire group. In addition, however, a negotiation situation cannot be considered successful unless some agreement is reached. This agreement must not only satisfy both sides to the controversy but it may also have to satisfy the demands of society at large as represented by a community or a small group of other persons who set standards and whose judgment needs to be respected.

One study in our program, conducted by McGrath and Julian (1962), dealt with counteracting groups consisting of members from three religious organizations and one neutral moderator. One person represented the viewpoint of the Catholic Newman Foundation, one the viewpoint of the Southern Baptist Student Foundation, and one the viewpoint of the Unitarian Channing-Murray Foundation. These points of view were outlined in position papers prepared with the assistance of the clergymen heading the three religious foundations. The student members were told that it would be their task to represent and advocate these viewpoints. They would be rated on a *multiplicative* scale based on the product of points they received from their reference group, that is, the clergymen of their foundation, and on points the entire group obtained for the constructiveness of the solution. The individual could earn a total of $25 if he obtained the maximum of five points for incorporating his foundation's point of view into the group solution and if he obtained the maximum five points for the constructiveness of the solution. Each subject participated in three different negotiation sessions. In two of these he was in the majority, in one situation he was in the minority, position.

The moderators were graduate students from the Institute of Labor and Industrial Relations or from the Law School. The particular aspect of importance here is the relationship between the moderator's leadership style and the constructiveness of the solution. Group Atmosphere scores indicated the degree to which the moderator experienced the group as pleasant or unpleasant.

TABLE 13-3   Relationship between Leadership Style of the Moderator and the Performance of Negotiation Groups (Constructiveness of Solution)

Topic	N	All Groups	Moderator's Group Atmosphere Score		
			N	High GA	Low GA
King James Bible	20	.02	10	−.56	.44
Federal aid to parochial schools	20	−.12	10	−.39	.27
Censorship for TV	20	.03	10	.46	.18

The three topics for discussion were (1) a program advocating the reading of the King James Bible as literature in public schools; (2) federal aid to parochial schools; and (3) government censorship of television and radio. These topics placed the Catholic, Baptist, and Unitarian participants consecutively in a minority role. The order of presenting the topics was counterbalanced. Twenty students from each foundation and twenty moderators participated. There were, thus, twenty sessions on each topic, with participants rotated so that each group represented a completely new combination of participants.

Table 13-3 shows the correlations obtained between the moderator's LPC and his groups' performance scores for each of the sessions. As can be seen, these correlations were negligible when all groups were included in the analysis. Somewhat more systematic results appeared when the authors took into consideration the Group Atmosphere score of the moderator. In two of the three topics, the task-oriented moderator (low LPC) tended to perform better than did the relationship-oriented moderator, provided he felt accepted by his group. In all groups with low Group Atmosphere the relationship-oriented moderator tended to be more effective.

Results similar to those obtained for groups with low Group Atmosphere scores were obtained in a recent study which was conducted with culturally heterogeneous groups consisting of one American leader, one American member, and one Arab member. A total of twenty-seven teams participated; half of these had leaders with high-LPC and half had leaders with low-LPC scores. One of the problems with which these groups dealt was a simulated negotiation problem to decide the percentage of Arab and Moslem workers to be employed in an Arab-American enterprise in the Middle East. The Arab students were instructed to bargain for the highest possible percentage of Arab and Moslem as against foreign workers; the Americans were instructed to work out a compromise which would allow the company to hire as many men as possible on the basis of merit, irrespective of religion and nationality. As in all situations involving culturally heterogeneous groups, the group climate tended to be strained and tense, leading us to expect positive correlations between leader LPC and group performance.

The results (Chemers et al., 1966) showed that the groups under relationship-oriented, high-LPC moderators obtained somewhat better solutions on the basis of both Arab and American standards. Groups with high-LPC moderators also achieved a better group climate and better relations between Arab and American participants.

Discussion. Far too few data are available at this time to permit more than a few tentative hypotheses about the leadership style required for negotiators. Our present data suggest that the task-oriented, low-LPC moderators perform relatively better in situations in which they feel or are well accepted. Moderators with relationship-oriented, quasi-therapeutic leader attitudes (high LPC) appear to perform better in groups which are unpleasant or tense, or which are difficult to handle because they involve culturally heterogeneous participants.

If our results are representative they suggest that the leadership requirements in coacting and in counteracting groups may be quite similar in some respects. In both types of groups, the relationship-oriented, quasi-therapeutic, considerate leader performs more effectively when the situation is tense, unpleasant, and difficult for the leader. Under these conditions, the relationship-oriented, quasi-therapeutic leader is likely to reduce tension and anxiety to permit the group members to perform their jobs more effectively, whether this job consists of acquiring skills under anxiety-producing conditions or whether it consists of negotiating a mutually acceptable agreement. The results suggest that the task-oriented leaders perform better in task groups which are free of stress, although these results are less consistent.

SUMMARY

This chapter presented data on coacting and counteracting groups, that is, groups in which members either interact only minimally with one another in performing a common task or in which group members represent different and partially incompatible viewpoints and therefore work against other members of the group.

While relatively few data are available, they suggest that coacting and interacting task groups with high leader position power require similar leadership styles. In coacting groups with training functions, the task-oriented (low-LPC) mediator appears to perform better in situations which are relatively pleasant and free from anxiety while the relationship-oriented leader or mediator tends to perform better in situations in which tension or anxiety is relatively high. These findings have been discussed in terms of group-member requirements for quasi-therapeutic interactions in groups which typically provide little psychological support for the individual group member.

14 LEADERSHIP AND ORGANIZATIONAL MANAGEMENT

There is a widespread and probably justified belief that the success or failure of an organization is determined in large part by the quality of its leadership. The strength of this belief is well demonstrated by the high monetary rewards and honors which are bestowed on the leader. Top executives may earn as much as ten, twenty, or more times the salary of nonsupervisory employees. It is the general who is decorated for the success of his army and the plant manager who gets the praise and bonus for outstripping his production quota or for reducing his operating expenses. According to this assumption, a man who is a successful business executive or army general should also make a successful university president, government administrator, or railroad manager.

Moreover, in the layman's view managerial skills and abilities are independent of the type and function, as well as of the level, of the organization. A good first-level supervisor is expected to make a good second-level manager; a man who performed poorly as a first-line supervisor is not likely to get promoted to a second-level management position.

Unfortunately, there are no adequate box scores on the number of the successes and failures which occur when an executive shifts from one organization to another. While the triumphs are well publicized and celebrated, the songs are more muted about those who did not make the grade. Nor do we have adequate information about the degree to which managers who were highly successful at one level of the organization tend to succeed or fail at successively higher levels.

A number of writers have questioned whether organizational leadership is really as independent of the situation as is frequently assumed. Pfiffner and Sherwood (1960) have pointed out, for example, that a person who performs well at one level of the organization may not perform equally well at another, because his abilities may not be sufficient for the higher job or because he fails to adapt his behavior to meet the demands of the new job. Argyris (1964) points out more specifically that the effectiveness of the first-line supervisor, as compared with managers at higher levels, is significantly influenced by the technology and controls systems.

The higher the manager climbs in the organizational hierarchy the less the technology and organizational controls influence his behavior and the more will job objectives and interpersonal factors influence his effectiveness. The second-level management position may, therefore, require not only different skills and task-relevant knowledge but also relations with subordinates that differ from those required by first-level supervision. It is important to ask, in effect, whether the leadership style which contributes to effective performance at one level of the organization will be equally appropriate at other levels.

First, however, we must ask whether and to what extent the leadership style of the manager at the second and higher levels of the organization will, in fact, influence organizational effectiveness. Being two or three steps removed from the operating level should make it more difficult to affect the work of the nonsupervisory employee, and hence also the productivity of the organizational subunit which the second- or third-level manager heads.

We generally credit the overall performance of an organization to the leadership and administrative abilities of its executives. We also find a substantial body of evidence which demonstrates that the first-line supervisor plays an important role in determining group performance, group morale, and job satisfaction. He is in direct, day-to-day contact with his men, and his relationship with them is considered by many writers to be one of the most important factors in determining group productivity and morale. This was one of the important implications of the Hawthorne study (Roethlisberger and Dickson, 1939) or Meyer's (1951) study of supervisory success. It is also implicit in the results of many field and laboratory studies which social and industrial psychologists have conducted in the last two decades (see Likert, 1961; McGrath and Altman, 1965). However, organizational leadership functions, as Katz and Kahn's (1965) highly sophisticated analysis has emphasized, must be carried out by executives at all managerial levels. This is true even in mature and smoothly operating organizations in which managerial and work functions are well established. Since the leadership of the second-level manager has to be mediated by the first-level supervisor, it is of considerable theoretical interest as well as of practical consequence to determine the relative contribution of the second-level manager to the performance of the operating group.

THE LEADERSHIP INFLUENCE OF SECOND-LEVEL MANAGERS

The executive at the level above that of the first-line supervisor can exert control in at least two ways. He can select subordinates who will perform their leadership and supervisory functions in accordance with his implicit or explicit expectations; or he can influence by his own style of leadership the leadership style and administrative behavior of his subordinate supervisors. Both of these modes of exerting influence may play a part, although the second- or third-level manager in large organizations very rarely has a strong voice in choosing his first-level supervisors. Unless his subunit is newly established he is typically expected to work with the subordinates he inherits from his predecessor or with those whom the organization assigns to him. This is almost always the case in such organizations as the military or the civil service. Thus, the influence of the middle-level manager over his work groups is more likely to be due to his own leadership style than to his ability to select and replace subordinate managers.

In attempting to compare the relative leadership influence of first-level and second-level managers we shall again make the assumption that a measure of personality or behavior which correlates with group performance provides one indication of the leader's influence over group performance. The logic underlying this assumption has been discussed in Chapter 12. It should be pointed out, however, that we cannot assume the opposite: a low correlation does not necessarily mean that a leader has little or no influence since we have no assurance that we have exhausted all other relevant personality variables which might relate to group performance. On the other hand, a high positive or a high negative correlation between the manager's leadership style score, ASo or LPC, and performance can provide a rough indication of the strength of the manager's influence over group performance.

Open hearth shops.   The best example of groups which permit a comparison of leader influence by managers at two levels of the organization is provided by the open hearth study (Chapter 6). As pointed out, each shift had a senior melter foreman in charge of steel production and one or two junior melter foremen who directed the work of the furnace crews. The junior melters were thus first-level supervisors while the senior melters were at the second level of management. The foremen's ASo scores were correlated with the primary steel production criterion of tap-to-tap time. The correlations between the senior melters' scores and the average tap-to-tap time was $-.54$ ($N = 15$, $p < .05$); the correlation between junior melters' ASo scores and tap-to-tap time for their units was only .10 ($N = 10$, not significant). See Table 6-2. The correlations between leadership style and the tap-to-tap time computed separately for groups with good, intermediate, and poor leader-member relations also were somewhat higher for senior than for junior melters.

The differences between the two sets of correlations is not significant and these results have to be interpreted with caution. If the results are not due to chance it appears that the leadership influence in these shops extended at least to the second level of management and that it may, in fact, have exceeded the influence of the first-line supervisor.[1]

Farm supply companies. Similar results were found in the study of farm supply companies (Chapter 6). Each of the thirty-two companies had a board of directors, a general manager, and many companies had two or more assistant managers. The organization consisted, therefore, of a superordinate policy- and decision-making group, a second-level manager, and first-level supervisors who headed the departments of the company.

It is, unfortunately, impossible to assign the portion of the company's net income which was due to the performance of a particular assistant manager. The best we could do was to have the general manager identify his right hand man among his assistant managers, that is, the assistant manager on whom the general manager relied most heavily for implementing his decisions. We could then compare whether the general manager's or the key assistant manager's leadership style was more closely related to company performance. While the general manager's ASo score correlated between $-.39$ ($p < .05$) and $-.74$ ($p < .01$) with company net income, the comparable correlations between the main assistant manager's score and company performance were quite low (.10) and insignificant.

---

[1] It should be noted, however, that these relations depend upon the specific situation. The pit foreman who supervises tapping the furnace and pouring the ingots appears to be relatively independent of the general foreman's direct supervision. Here the correlation between the pit foreman's ASo score and shift performance was $-.72$ ($p < .01$), indicating that this particular first-level supervisor played a substantial role in determining organizational efficiency.

The farm supply company study does not permit us to make as neat a comparison as did the open hearth steel shop study. Because many companies have several assistant managers it is much more questionable whether the criterion of company effectiveness can be influenced by the one key assistant manager to the same degree that the tap-to-tap criterion can be influenced by the junior melter foreman in open hearth shops. However, the data leave little doubt about the importance of the second-level manager's leadership style in influencing company performance.

Various writers (including the author) have shown that the first-line supervisor's attitudes and leadership style or behavior influence the output, morale, job satisfaction, and personal adjustment of his men (Kasl and French, 1962; Neel, 1955; Pelz, 1951; Seashore, 1955). These previous findings are not incompatible with the findings on middle managers. Most relationships between leadership style and group performance in field studies account for a comparatively small portion of the total effect. It is, therefore, logically and mathematically possible for the second-level manager to exert influence over and beyond that which is generally attributed to the first-level supervisor.

In most laboratory studies and field experiments which utilize *ad hoc* groups, the issue of second-level management is, of course, moot to begin with. Groups of this type are typically established as if they were completely independent of one another or of a higher organization. Under these conditions it is not surprising that the leadership of the first-level supervisor or leader emerges as preeminent. And even here there is reason to believe that the experimenter, in his unwitting role of second-level manager, may affect the outcome of the research, as recent studies of demand characteristics have shown (Orne, 1966).

What determines whether leadership influence will extend to the second-, third-, or even higher levels of the organization presents an interesting problem. While we have very little evidence which can be brought to bear on this question, a number of factors in organizational structure are likely to affect the influence penetration of higher level management. One of these factors is the degree to which the organization is centralized. The middle-manager of an assembly line operation is more likely to influence performance than is the middle-manager of a company whose crews work many miles away from headquarters. Related to this is the degree to which the organization is tall or flat. The manager at the second or third level will tend to have less influence over the work group if he supervises ten or twenty crews or departments than if he supervises only two or three. A third factor may be the level at which a suborganization can successfully isolate itself from the total organization. Some suborganizations are practically autonomous of the parent organization (as is the FBI of the Department of Justice) while others are closely tied to it. The nonsupervisory employee's reference to the "big boss" may be a good indication of the level at which the source of leadership influence is located.[2]

LEADERSHIP REQUIREMENTS AT DIFFERENT MANAGERIAL LEVELS

The second major problem with which we are here concerned deals with the differences in leadership styles required by different management levels and functional specialties. We shall ask whether effective managers at the first and second supervisory levels of the same organization tend to have similar or different leadership styles, and whether these differences in leadership style are related to the manager's functional specialty.

Differences in leadership style of first- and second-level managers. Our studies have shown that effective and ineffective leaders differ in their style of interacting with subordinates. It now seems reasonable to ask whether individuals with a higher or with a lower LPC or ASo score are more likely to be found in higher management positions.

Our studies have not shown major differences in LPC or ASo scores between first- and second-level managers. The average scores of senior melters and junior melters in the open hearth study were almost identical, as were the average scores of general managers and assistant managers in the farm supply company study. Similarly, Nealey and Blood (1967) did not find significant differences between nurses at the first and at the second level of supervision. These data and scattered findings from other studies provide little encouragement for the belief that executives tend to be selected for higher management positions on the basis of their leadership style scores.

A psychologically more interesting question is whether managers at adjacent levels in the organizational structure should have similar or different styles of leadership. Should a task-oriented second-level manager

[2] Personal communication, W. McConnell, U.S. Civil Service Commission.

work with a subordinate who also is task-oriented or with one who is relationship-oriented?

Our limited data indicate that organizations differ widely in this regard. The type of organization and the type of functional specialty of the manager appear to influence the particular style of leadership that will contribute to effective group performance.

Again we lack sufficient data for broad generalizations. However, a brief review and discussion of the available evidence provides some clues about the factors which might determine the combination of first- and second-level leadership which the organization requires.

It will be recalled that the ASo score of the accepted general manager in the farm supply study correlated negatively with company performance while the ASo score of the board's leader correlated positively with performance in these companies. In other words, harmonious companies tended to operate most effectively with a task-oriented general manager and a relationship-oriented leader of the board of directors. (We found no systematic relations between the leadership style of the general manager and that of his assistant managers.)

It will be recalled that the effective production foremen in the open hearth study tended to be task-oriented in groups which accepted them, relationship-oriented in groups which were neutral, and task-oriented in groups which were rejecting in their sociometric choices. This was the case both for senior melters and for junior melters. These data suggest, therefore, that the same type of leadership style is required of first-level and second-level managers in open hearth shops. It should also be recalled at this point, however, that the foremen of open hearth shops have highly structured tasks even at the second managerial level.

Similar findings were obtained by Hunt (1967) on general foremen who were the second-level managers in the heavy machinery plant (see Chapter 10). The effective second-level managers tended to be task-oriented, especially in departments which the foremen described as having high Group Atmosphere.

A recent study by Nealey and Blood (1967) investigated the nursing organization of a large Veterans Administration hospital. The authors obtained criterion ratings for various psychiatric wards on physical care of patients, the staff's information about patients, the interpersonal relations between patients and staff, and the general effectiveness of the wards supervised by each of twenty-one head nurses. The head nurses were first-

TABLE 14-1   Correlations between Measures of Nursing Staff Performance and LPC Scores at Two Levels of Supervision

	Level of Supervision	
	First Level	Second Level
Performance	Head Nurses	Unit Supervisors
Criteria	$N = 21$	$N = 8$
Physical care of patients	−.40	.58
Information about patients	−.37	.66*
Interpersonal relations	−.06	.82**
General effectiveness	−.22	.79**
Median correlation	−.30	.72

* $p < .05$.
** $p < .01$.

level supervisors in direct charge of the staff nurses and psychiatric aides. The second-level managers in this organization were eight "Unit Supervisors" whose responsibility extended over a semiautonomous section of the hospital.

Table 14-1 presents the correlations between the LPC scores of the first-level and the second-level supervisors in this organization and the rated performance of their respective units. As can be seen, the effective first-level supervisors tended to be more task-oriented than the ineffective first-level supervisors. In contrast, the effective unit supervisors who were at the second management level were more relationship-oriented than the ineffective unit supervisors.

These findings make sense when we consider that the unit supervisor in the nursing organization oversees the work of professional colleagues who have essentially the same training that she does. A highly task-oriented, structuring nursing supervisor is likely to be resented by her subordinate supervisors who will feel that their professional competence and judgment are being questioned. They will respond more favorably to a more permissive, relationship-oriented supervisor who will give policy guidance and who will encourage decision making of her subordinate supervisors. Moreover, the second-level supervisor in this organization may simply not have the necessary information which structuring management requires.

The nursing supervisor at the first level is in charge of the day-to-day operation of the ward and she supervises subprofessional nursing aides who require and welcome clear and precise directions on how to perform their assignments.

Likewise, the board of directors in the farm supply companies, which meets only once every month, cannot give detailed instructions to the general manager. Its major function is to provide broad policy guidance and general instructions which are then to be implemented by the general manager and his staff. Detailed operational instructions are likely to interfere with sound management.

This group of findings suggest a number of hypotheses. One of these relates to the structure of the second-level manager's task. Where the manager is removed from the day-to-day operations of the working group task-oriented leadership is likely to be ineffective. To the extent to which the second-level manager must depend upon the judgment and willing cooperation of the first-level supervisor he must share decision making with the first-line supervisor and he must be willing to see his first-level supervisor as a partner in the undertaking. Under these conditions it seems likely that a relationship-oriented leadership style will be more effective. The leadership style required by the first-level supervisor depends in part upon the favorableness of the group situation. The favorableness of the group situation may well be strongly influenced by his relationship with the second-level manager, as well as the task structure, position power, and relations with his own subordinates (see the farm supply study, Chapter 0).

Leadership style and functional specialty. Also of importance will probably be the functional specialty of the second- or higher-level manager. Here again we can point to the difference in the functions of the board of directors and the management of the farm supply companies, and the differences in functions of the unit supervisor and of the head nurse in the Nealey and Blood study.

An even clearer example of this point is provided by data from an investigation of chemical processing companies (Lawrence and Lorsch, in press). This study compared the performance of six very similar organizations, each of which had four major divisions: fundamental research, applied research, sales, and production, with a senior executive in charge of each division.

The authors obtained performance measures for each organization and then correlated these with the LPC scores of the division executives. These correlations, obtained from data which the authors kindly made available,

TABLE 14-2   Rank-order Correlations between Organizational Performance and LPC Scores of Division Managers in Different Functional Specialties ($N = 6$) *

Functional Specialty	Task Structure	Correlation between Organizational Performance and LPC
Production	High	−.46
Sales	Medium	.01
Applied research	Medium	−.19
Fundamental research	Low	.72
Average of managers	—	.24

* Adapted from Lawrence and Lorsch, in press, by permission.

are shown in Table 14-2. As can be seen, the results are in line with our expectation that the unstructured tasks involved in fundamental research would require a relatively relationship-oriented director while the structured tasks of production management would require a task-oriented executive. These findings support Hunt's (1967) study of research groups and production foremen. It should also be noted that the average LPC score of managers did not correlate with organizational performance since the functional specialties required different leadership styles.

There are, however, some organizations in which the average leadership style of executives seems to correlate with organizational effectiveness. This was the case in the open hearth study in which ASo scores of the foremen in the same shift were averaged and this average ASo score was correlated with the "tap-to-tap time" criterion. This correlation based on sixteen shifts turned out to be −.71 ($p < .01$). Thus, shifts with task-oriented foremen tended to perform significantly better than did shifts with relationship-oriented foremen.

The average of LPC scores of executives also correlated with organizational performance of sixty-two savings and loan associations in the Chicago area. All companies were independent organizations serving various districts in Cook county. The criterion of performance consisted of the rate of growth of assets and additions to surplus over a three-year period (Stafford and Becker, 1967).

There is thus an inconsistency in the results obtained in the open hearth shops and Stafford and Becker's study of loan associations on the one hand and the farm supply study, the Lawrence and Lorsch study, and the nursing supervisor study on the other. One fairly obvious hypothesis to account for these contradictory findings is that the functions of managers within the open hearth shops are relatively similar, as are those within the savings and loan associations. Most open hearth foremen in a shop are directly concerned with steel production; most executives in savings and loan companies are involved with the assessment of credit risks and the granting of loans and related transactions. The executives in these organizations thus have considerably more homogeneous assignments than do executives in farm supply companies with their general managers, sales managers, warehouse managers, office managers, etc. Likewise the functions of the executives in the chemical processing companies were quite dissimilar, as are the functions of the supervisors at the first and the second level of management of the nursing organization. We would anticipate, therefore, that the average leadership style scores will predict organizational success only in organizations which are very homogeneous in terms of the managers' functional specialties.

The data which this chapter has presented provide only the most tentative answers and some interesting hypotheses for further study. These data serve to indicate, however, that the area of second-level management is a potentially very rich source for the investigator who wishes to explore leadership in organizations at the middle management level.

SUMMARY

This chapter dealt with the leadership requirements of complex organizations. The discussion was confined to studies of organizational leadership in which LPC and ASo scores served as predictors of leadership performance.

We have been concerned with two specific questions. These are (1) whether, and to what extent, the manager at the second or higher level of the organization determines the productivity of the basic work group, and (2) whether certain organizational levels of management and certain managerial functions call for particular styles of leadership.

An attempt was made to determine the comparative influence of first-level supervisors and second-level managers on work group or suborganizational performance. The data, while highly tentative, suggest that the second-level manager's leadership influence over work performance is considerable and that it may be greater than that of first-level supervisors in many organizations.

The available data also suggest that different functional specialties may require different leadership styles. Structured tasks, as exemplified by production management or the day-to-day supervision of relatively unskilled work groups, appear to call for task-oriented leadership; relatively unstructured second-level management functions or higher management, as exemplified by policy making groups and research units of organizations, seem to call for a relationship-oriented leadership.

15 CREATING EFFECTIVE ORGANIZATIONAL LEADERSHIP

The Contingency Model postulates that leadership effectiveness depends upon the appropriate matching of the individual's leadership style of interacting and the influence which the group situation provides. What are the implications of this theory and our findings for the selection and recruitment of leaders for training and for the management of organizations?

The major point of this theory is that leadership effectiveness—that is, effective group performance—depends just as much on the group situation as it does on the leader. If the theory is right this means that a personnel program that deals only with the personality aspects of the leader or only with the situational aspects of the organization is bound to fail. One style of leadership is not in itself better than the other, nor is one type of leadership behavior appropriate for all conditions. Hence, almost everyone should be able to succeed as a leader in some situations and almost everyone is likely to fail in others. If we want to improve organizational performance we must deal not only with the leader's style but also with the factors in the situation which provide him with influence. While one can never say that something is impossible, and while someone may well discover the all-purpose leadership style or behavior at some future time, our own data and those which have come out of sound research by other investigators do not promise such miraculous cures. And if leadership performance is in fact a product of both the individual's leadership style and the leadership situation then it is logically impossible that one leadership style could serve in every context. On the other hand, it also follows from this theory that we can improve group or organizational performance either by changing the leader to fit the situation or by changing the situation to fit the leader.

Industrial psychologists and personnel men typically view the executive's position as fixed and immutable and the individual as highly plastic and trainable. When we think of improving leadership performance we generally think first of training the leader. Yet, we know all too well from our experience with psychotherapy, our attempts to rehabilitate prison inmates, drug addicts, or juvenile delinquents—not to mention our difficulties with rearing our own progeny—that our ability to change personality has its limitations.

A person's leadership style, as we have used the term, reflects the individual's basic motivational and need structure. At best it takes one, two, or three years of intensive psychotherapy to effect lasting changes in personality structure. It is difficult to see how we can change in more than a few cases an equally important set of core values in a few hours of lectures and role playing or even in the course of a more intensive training program of one or two weeks.

On the other hand, executive jobs and supervisory responsibilities almost always can be modified to a greater or lesser extent both by the incumbent of the position and, even more readily, by his organization. In fact, organizations frequently change the specifications of a management job to make it more appealing to the executive whom the organization wishes to attract or whom it wishes to retain. If anything, many organizations change executive jobs and responsibilities more often than might be necessary.

Executives at higher echelons are well aware of the fact that they must take account of the strengths and weaknesses of their subordinate managers. One man may operate most effectively when his authority is strictly defined and circumscribed while another must be given considerable leeway and discretion. Some executives excel in staff work while others perform best in line positions; some are known as specialists in troubleshooting who thrive on turmoil and crisis while others perform best as administrators of well-running subunits of the organization. Our theory provides a conceptual framework and a preliminary set of guidelines for determining how to match the leadership situation and the man. While cookbook prescriptions are still a task for the future we can indicate here some of the major directions which our theory indicates. The basic methods in managing executive and managerial talent has been by leadership recruitment and selection and by leadership training. We shall add to these an organizational engineering approach and discuss these three approaches in light of the theory and the data which this book has presented.

LEADERSHIP RECRUITMENT AND SELECTION

The classical and "time-tested" method for maintaining a cadre of executives calls for the recruitment of men who not only have the technical experience and background which the job requires but also the personality attributes and abilities which will make them effective leaders. Given a candidate who has the technical and intellectual qualifications, the recruiter then tries to predict the individual's leadership potential from his background and possibly from psychological tests.

However, previous leadership experience is likely to predict future performance only if the past leadership situation was nearly identical to the leadership situation for which the individual is to be selected. And all too frequently the recruiter knows very little about the leadership situation the individual is likely to face. He knows next to nothing about what he will do two or five years later. And no system of leadership selection is likely to work without this knowledge as long as leadership performance varies from situation to situation or from task to task. That this is the case has been amply demonstrated. To mention but a few studies, Knoell and Forgays (1952) showed that the same aircrew might perform excellently on one task and quite poorly on another. Flanagan's (1949) study of naval officer performance showed that highly rated naval officers did not necessarily obtain high ratings in officer candidate school and that officers' efficiency ratings for sea duty were uncorrelated with their efficiency ratings for shore duty. And our own data on bomber crews, tank crews (Chapter 5), and Belgian navy teams (Chapter 10) further support this statement. If the performance of the same group can be excellent on one subtask and poor on another it is obvious that we cannot hope to predict how the leader will perform with a single leadership test. This is even less likely when neither his future group nor his future tasks are known.

Some studies have shown consistency of leadership performance. These include studies by Bass (1954), Carter (1953), Gibb (1947), and Bell and French (1955). However, all of these studies were conducted in highly controlled laboratory settings in which the leadership situations were quite similar from task to task. Where tasks differed, as they did in a study by Carter, leadership performance was similar within families of tasks but dissimilar from one task family to another. In Gibb's study, groups were given widely different tasks. However, leadership performance was assessed by members' ratings of their fellow members, and these ratings are likely to be highly influenced by halo effect.

Also worth mentioning are the important studies which indicate that peer ratings can be used to predict future leadership performance (for example, Anderhalter et al., 1952; Hollander, 1956). These demonstrate respectably high relations between peer ratings obtained in officer candidate school and subsequent efficiency ratings by superior officers several years later. Do these indicate that leadership ability is a personality attribute that remains constant over situations? Sociometric studies cannot be interpreted this way. These studies are important contributions in their own right. It should be noted, however, that the predictions are based on ratings of men who performed highly similar tasks as students in officer candidate school and as junior officers. The men were rated *as individuals* and not strictly in terms of the performance of their groups. The man who looks and acts like the stereotype of a good officer while in officer candidate school will probably still look and act this way several years later. This is not to say that ratings of this type may not be extremely useful for various purposes. In fact, leadership style measures make sense only if the basic personality remains constant over situations, but it is unlikely that these ratings can serve as generalized predictors of leadership ability as measured by group performance.

We must emphasize that management and administrative functions, or being a "good executive," are not identical with leadership. Management is more than leadership. It includes routine administration and the maintenance of communications with other departments or other agencies; it requires knowledge of organizational procedures and regulations. It usually involves negotiating and bargaining functions between the manager and his own superior or with others at his level to maintain the status of his department within the total organization (see for example Barnard, 1938; Katz and Kahn, 1965). It also requires the motivation to seek and accept executive responsibilities. Some of these factors of administrative skill may well be predictable by personality and achievement tests. Leadership ability—the knack of getting any group to perform in a highly efficient manner—is not currently predictable. Considering the fact that years of effort have failed to produce any generally valid leadership tests, and that these tests would fly in the face of all currently available evidence, it seems safe to say that they are not likely to appear in future.

If our theory is correct then the recruitment and selection of leaders can be effective only when we can also specify the relevant components of the situation for which the leader is being recruited. There is no reason to believe that this cannot be done, or that this should not be done in specific cases. Difficulties arise because leadership situations change over time. The organization must then be aware of the type of leadership situations into which the individual should be successively guided, but this is basically no different than seeing that an electrical engineer does not get assigned to bookkeeping duties.

LEADERSHIP TRAINING

Because the leader is seen as the key to organizational success, be this in government, in educational institutions, in sports, in the military, or in business and industry, it is not surprising that these organizations have unstintingly devoted substantial time and money to leadership training. These training programs, supervisory and leadership workshops, and residential courses have enjoyed widespread popularity for many years both in the United States and abroad.

These programs frequently provide instruction in administrative procedures, in organizational policy, and such various other fields as accounting, cost control, and legal responsibilities of the organization. As before, our discussion deals only with leadership training per se, that is, with the skills that can be measured in terms of group and organizational effectiveness. We recognize that these training programs often provide a number of other benefits. These may range from giving the executive a welcome break from his routine or widening his intellectual horizon to raising his own morale and that of his subordinates. Whether or not an executive development program or a leadership training workshop can be justified in these terms is a matter of administrative judgment.

Of relevance is the fact that many of these programs are primarily designed to increase the individual's leadership skills. It might also be pointed out that the yearly amount expended for training programs of this sort in the United States is likely to stagger the imagination. It is all the more unfortunate, therefore, that the development of these programs, as well as the utilization of other leadership selection devices, has not been matched by an appropriate number of adequate evaluation studies. Organizations have been more than happy to spend money on training programs but they have been considerably less eager to find out whether the training really does any good. Moreover, personnel research has been severely handicapped by the fact that the criteria of group and departmental effectiveness are only vaguely spelled out and defined in many organizations, and even less frequently are they measured with any degree of reliability.

This is not to say that the problems in assessing the value of an executive training program or of a leadership workshop are minor. As Jaques (1961) and Martin (1959) have pointed out, the manager's job is necessarily one which requires a longer time perspective than does the job of the nonsupervisory employee. It takes longer, therefore, and it is correspondingly more difficult to obtain accurate measures on the effects of managerial training the higher we go up the executive ladder.

There are, in fact, very few studies which evaluate leadership training research under controlled conditions and with objective performance measures. Those which have been reported throw considerable doubt on the efficacy of these training programs for increasing organizational and group performance. Thus, Fleishman et al. (1955) compared the performance of a group of trained and untrained foremen in the International Harvester Company before and after training. While these authors reported some changes in attitudes and behaviors they found no evidence that the training program had increased departmental effectiveness. Similar findings have been reported by Carter (1953) and Tyler (1949). Newport (1963) recently surveyed a large number of major business organizations in the United States which conducted executive development programs for middle managers. While most of the companies reported themselves to be satisfied with the results of these programs, he found no objective evidence that the training programs had increased leadership performance.

Equally discouraging are the findings from our Belgian navy study (Chapter 10; Fiedler, 1966). We compared the groups led by forty-eight new and inexperienced navy recruits with a matched sample of forty-eight Belgian petty officers who had received two years of training in petty officer candidate school and who had an average of ten years of navy experience. The tasks were designed with the assistance of navy officers at the training center, and they were similar to tasks which a group of enlisted men might be expected to perform. Yet, the groups led by trained and experienced petty officers did not perform significantly better on any of the four tasks than did groups led by raw recruits who had had less than six weeks of experience in the navy. Moreover, when we correlated the group performance scores of petty officers with the number of years of navy leadership experience of these petty officers, the correlations were essentially zero. Thus, neither the leadership training nor the leadership experience, tantamount to on-the-job training, had enabled the men to perform more effectively in these leadership situations.

A relatively new method of leadership training was developed in the late 1940s. This method, variously called T-group, sensitivity, or laboratory training, is built around unstructured group situations which provide the participant an opportunity to explore his own motivations and reactions, and his relations with other participants in the group. Excellent descriptions of this method are now available, e.g., Schein and Bennis (1965); Blake and Mouton (1961); Bradford (1961); Argyris (1964). Here again, however, the evaluation research which deals with group performance leaves much to be desired. Schein and Bennis (1965) introduce their chapter on research on laboratory training outcomes by noting ". . . that the evidence is meager."

Unfortunately very few studies of laboratory training deal with group performance as the measure of outcome. Argyris (1962) found an increase in a top management team's decision-making processes although no evidence is available on the effect of these decisions on organizational performance. Blake and Mouton (1963) report an investigation to evaluate the effects of an idea laboratory. But here again the performance criteria consisted of measures indicating better listening ability, greater readiness to face conflict, and increased rejection of compromise as the basis for decision making. Research of this nature is important and these outcomes are intrinsically interesting and valuable as are the changes in individual values and attitudes. But this research does not indicate whether the work performance of groups with trained leaders was significantly greater or better than the work performance of groups with untrained leaders.

Laboratory training methods potentially provide one important avenue for introducing the individual to leadership situations in which he can perform well and to those in which he is likely to fail. Laboratory training might also provide the environment in which the individual can experiment with attempts to change the leader-member relations or his position power vis-à-vis his fellow group members. Whether laboratory training can effect changes in the individual's leadership style is considerably more doubtful.

While we can offer no more than speculation to account for the lack of positive results of leadership training programs, a few comments may be appropriate. There is, first of all, evidence that leadership training programs result in some behavioral and attitudinal changes (Shartle, 1956; Schein and Bennis, 1965) even though these may not be lasting unless the organizational climate is conducive to these new behaviors and attitudes. Likewise, the more elaborate T-group and laboratory training may assist the leader in developing a more favorable group climate and more positive member attitudes. Training, therefore, has some effect on the trainee and on his group.

Most leadership training programs are designed either to change the trainee's attitudes and behaviors in the direction which will make him more task-oriented, managing, and directive, or in the direction which will make him more human-relations oriented, permissive, and nondirective. If we assume that these training programs are effective in changing the behavior in the desired direction, and if the Contingency Model is an accurate mapping of reality, then about half the trainees would have come out with an inappropriate leadership style no matter which type of program they attended. Those trained to be directive, managing, and task-oriented would be well suited for leadership situations which are very favorable or else very unfavorable, but they would be unsuited for the situations intermediate in favorableness. Those trained to be relationship-oriented, permissive, and nondirective would be well suited for the situations intermediate in favorableness but poorly suited for the very favorable or the very unfavorable situations. This assumes, of course, that a training program actually can effect more than temporary modifications in the individual's leadership style and concomitant behavior, which still remains to be established.

If leadership training is to be successful, the present theory would argue that it should focus on providing the individual with methods for diagnosing the favorableness of the leadership situation and for adapting the leadership situations to the individual's style of leadership so that he can perform effectively. It should be relatively easy to develop methods which would indicate to the leader whether or not the situation fits his particular style. As we have shown in Chapter 2, scales for measuring leader position power and task structure are already available. (See also Hunt's scale in Appendix C.) It should also be possible to construct a measure which would indicate to the leader how good his relations are with his group members. We can then instruct the leader in making the necessary modifications in the leadership situation so that the situation will match his style. While this sounds simple in principle a number of difficulties will need to be resolved before a procedure of this type can be put into general practice.

The alternative method would call for training the leader to develop a flexible leadership style and to adapt his leadership style to the particular situation. The author is highly pessimistic that this training approach would be successful. There may well be some favored few who can be effective in any leadership situation, and some unfortunate few who would even find it difficult to lead a troop of hungry girl scouts to a hot-dog stand. However, our experience has not enabled us to identify these individuals. Nor have we found it possible to identify those who can switch their leadership style as the occasion demands. It would seem more promising at this time, therefore, to teach the individual to recognize the conditions under which he can perform best and to modify the situation to suit his leadership style.

ORGANIZATIONAL ENGINEERING

The Contingency Model suggests one important alternative method for improving leadership performance. This is predicated on the belief that it is almost always easier to change a man's work environment than it is to change his personality or his style of relating to others. Experienced managers have long been aware of the fact that an executive who performs poorly in one situation might be excellent in another. However, there has been no rationale for changing an executive from one job to another, nor for changing the dimensions of a given job in order to make him more effective. The comment is often heard that one manager has too much responsibility, that another needs more rank in order to function effectively, or that a third is an excellent staff officer but a poor line executive. The Contingency Model permits us to place these evaluations into a theoretical frame of reference and to determine a priori what kinds of changes might be required to obtain maximum performance from various men in positions of leadership.

It might appear at first blush that it would be a very formidable task to change the situation so that it will fit the man's leadership style; that we surely cannot reorganize a company every time a new manager is hired; and that such organizations as military units simply cannot be changed at all. It may indeed be impractical or impossible to modify some situations to fit them to the leader's style. Yet, in the overwhelming number of cases, including military organizations, it should be possible to make some relevant changes. Here again our conjectures far outstrip our data but it seems profitable to indicate the ways in which various leadership situations could be modified.

1.   In some organizations we can change the individual's task assignment. We may assign to one leader very structured tasks which have implicit or explicit instructions telling him what to do and how to do it, and we may assign to another the tasks which are nebulous and vague.

The former are the typical production tasks, the latter are exemplified by committee work, by the development of policy, and by tasks which require creativity.

2. We can change the leader's position power. We not only can give him a higher rank and corresponding recognition, we can also modify his position power by giving him subordinates who are equal to him in rank and prestige or subordinates who are two or three ranks below him. We can give him subordinates who are expert in their specialties or subordinates who depend upon the leader for guidance and instruction. We can give the leader the final say in all decisions affecting his group, or we can require that he make decisions in consultation with his subordinates, or even that he obtain their concurrence. We can channel all directives, communications, and information about organizational plans through the leader alone, giving him expert power, or we can provide these communications concurrently to all his subordinates.

3. We can change the leader-member relations in the group. We can have the leader work with groups whose members are very similar to him in attitude, opinion, technical background, race, and cultural background. Or we can assign him subordinates with whom he differs in any one or several of these important aspects. Finally, we can assign the leader to a group in which the members have a tradition of getting along well with their supervisors or to a group which has a history and tradition of conflict.

The concept of organizational engineering requires that the average performance of groups be independent of the favorableness of the group situation. When we correlate leader LPC and group performance for various levels of group favorableness, we are dealing with group performance scores in relative terms. However, we must also consider group performance in absolute terms if we hope to improve group performance by increasing or by decreasing the favorableness of the group situation.

It would seem reasonable to expect, on a commonsense basis, that the average level of group performance will be lower as the favorableness of the group situation decreases. That is, we would expect poorer performance of groups in which leaders have very little influence than in groups in which they have much influence. If this is the case there would be little advantage in changing the leadership situation to make it fit the leader. We would only need to make the situation as favorable as possible, whatever the leadership style of the executive.

As already indicated in previous chapters, this typically is not the case: the average level of group performance is very little affected by the favorableness of the situation. This point is sufficiently critical to warrant a look at data from several studies.

As one example, the Dutch creativity study contained groups which could be classified into three levels of favorableness. The homogeneous groups with formally appointed leaders presented the most favorable situation, followed by homogeneous groups with informal leaders or heterogeneous with formal leaders, and finally by heterogeneous groups with informal leaders. The average performance scores of these three sets of groups have been plotted on Figure 15-1, based on data in Table 7-1. As can be seen, there was no systematic decrease in group performance as the favorableness of the situations decreased, nor were the differences among mean performance scores significant.

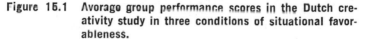

Figure 15.1   Average group performance scores in the Dutch creativity study in three conditions of situational favorableness.

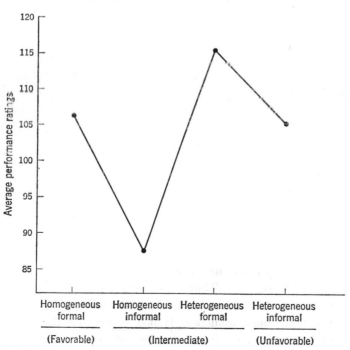

Figure 15.2   Average group performance scores on the Proposal and Fable tasks in the ROTC study under three conditions of stress.

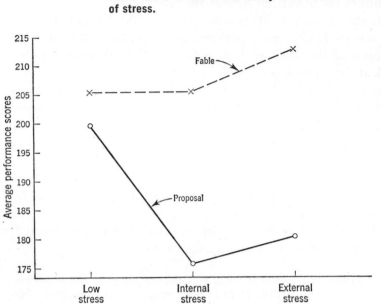

A second example is taken from the ROTC study described in Chapter 12. The low stress condition was considered to be more favorable than the internal stress condition, and the external stress condition was considered least favorable. Again, the average performance scores of groups in these three conditions did not differ markedly (Table 12-2) nor did they decline as the favorableness decreased (Figure 15-2).

Finally, let us consider the Belgian navy study (Fiedler, 1966a) in which groups differed in homogeneity, group climate, and position power. Figure 15-3 presents the average performance scores for the structured task, the unstructured task, and the nonverbal task for each of eight levels of favorableness. There were no significant differences between groups with high and with low position power, or between groups with high or with low group climate scores. Only in the unstructured task did the homogeneous groups perform significantly better than did the groups in which the men were heterogeneous in language and cultural background. Only in the unstructured task is there a trend indicating that the favorableness of the situation correlated with the average performance level of the group and this is the only study in which this trend has appeared, and even here on only one task. In other studies, and in the two other tasks of the Belgian navy study, the performance of groups in unfavorable situations was on the average as good as the performance of groups in favorable leadership situations. The data suggest, therefore, that it should be possible in most cases to improve the effectiveness of a leader even though this may require making the leadership situation less favorable.

In fact, the leader, himself, may sometimes change the leadership situation in a less favorable direction. A leader may decide to work on a vague and unstructured assignment before tackling a highly structured task; he may voluntarily relinquish or not fully utilize the power of his position by seeking the group's advice or by announcing that he will not make decisions without his group's concurrence. If the leader is made aware of his strengths and weaknesses as well as possible remedies, he may not only be able to modify group situations to match them with his leadership style, he may also learn how to avoid group situations which are incompatible with his style and seek out those in which he is most likely to succeed.

Figure 15.3   Average group performance scores on three different tasks in the Belgian navy study in eight conditions of situational favorableness.

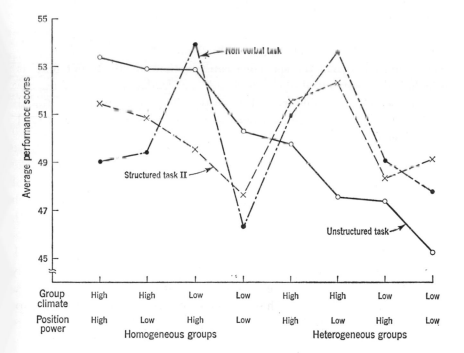

A man who is able to avoid situations in which he is likely to fail is likely to be a success.

A major potential advantage of the organizational engineering approach is that it enables the manager at the second or third level of the organization to provide a situation for his subordinate managers which will utilize their leadership potential to the fullest. It should be possible to train the higher level manager to diagnose the leadership situation of his subordinates and, knowing his subordinates' leadership style, to modify the task, the position power, or the group relations in a way which will make it compatible with the leadership style of the executive. While we are admittedly speculating on the basis of very incomplete evidence, these modifications could be accomplished by the organization without fanfare and on a basis sufficiently gradual to provide close control over the effects.

When a valued executive performs poorly in his position, or when the outstanding specialist, the expert in his field, or the particularly knowledgeable member of the organization is unable to deal with his leadership responsibilities, the organization is faced with the dilemma of getting rid of the man or shifting him to another job in the hope that he may improve in time. It is essential that we realize that poor performance in a leadership position is likely to be as much the function of the leadership situation which the organization provides as it is the function of the individual's personality structure. An alternative to discarding the poorly functioning leader is then to engineer the organizational dimensions of the leadership job so that the specialist can function effectively not only as a technical expert but also as a manager and leader. In view of the increasing scarcity of highly trained executive manpower, an organizational engineering approach may well become the method of necessity as well as of choice.

16 IN CONCLUSION

A few concluding statements are in order to summarize some of the main points of the research and the theory which this book has described, and to indicate, above all, some of the major problems which lie ahead.

This book presented a theory of leadership effectiveness which takes account of the leader's personality as well as the situational factors in the leadership situation. We have known for some time that the same type of leadership style or leadership behavior will not be suitable for all situations. This theory attempts to specify in more precise terms the conditions under which one leadership style or another will be more conducive to group effectiveness. The theory thus reconciles the sometimes conflicting claims and results which would favor one style of leadership over another.

Our research has developed two measures of leadership style, the Least-preferred Coworker (LPC) scale and the closely related Assumed Similarity between Opposites (ASo) score. It has also introduced the concept of situational favorableness, that is, the degree to which the leadership situation provides the leader with influence. The theory postulates that the leadership style is determined by the needs the individual seeks to satisfy in the leadership situation and that the increasingly less favorable leadership situation represents a corresponding increase of threat to the leader's need gratification. Individuals with different leadership styles seek to satisfy different needs and thus respond differently to the threat which the unfavorable situation presents. The performance of interacting groups and organizations is therefore contingent upon the favorableness of the leadership situation as well as upon the executive's leadership style.

Leadership performance depends then as much on the organization as it depends upon the leader's own attributes. Except perhaps for the unusual case, it is simply not meaningful to speak of an effective leader or of an ineffective leader; we can only speak of a leader who tends to be effective in one situation and ineffective in another. If we wish to increase organizational and group effectiveness we must learn not only how to train leaders more effectively but also how to build an organizational environment in which the leader can perform well.

The immediate problems for future research are neither few nor minor. A number of the more prominent of these problems are here briefly indicated.

1. Above all, we require a better method for measuring the favorableness of the leadership situation. It should be possible to develop an absolute scale which is sufficiently general so that it can be applied to any leadership situation. We require a scale which is based not only on the presence or absence of good leader-member relations, homogeneity, leader position power, and task structure, but which takes account also of the other factors that are likely to affect the favorableness of the situation. These may need to include the leader's and his members' intellectual abilities and technical qualifications, the motivation of the group, and the conditions of stress under which the group is forced to operate.

2. The present method of measuring situational favorableness implies that certain equivalencies exist among the various components which determine the favorableness dimension. We need to determine how many units of a leader's position power equal how many units of task structure; how good a leader-member relationship must be to equal a certain degree of position power; how much task structure can be traded for good leader-member relations. These questions imply that the categorization of good versus poor leader-member relations, strong versus weak position power, and high versus low task structure must be replaced by a scale which indicates the *degree* to which position power is high, the *degree* to which the task is structured. One important problem for future research will be the adequate scaling of each of the various dimensions singly as well as in conjunction with others.

3. Such situational components as position power, task structure, and homogeneity are inherent in the situation and therefore largely beyond the leader's direct control. In contrast, the relationship between the leader and his members is in part a function of the leader's own personality and interpersonal behavior. We need to learn what determines a good or a poor leader-member relationship, and to what extent this is a product of the leader's personality and behavior, on the one hand, and a product of the situational context, on the other. While the leader's Group Atmosphere scores reflect the leader's perception of his group, to what extent is this perception based on the reality of the situation? In the Dutch creativity study, the research on military crews and farm supply studies, or on basketball teams and surveying parties, leader-member relations were measured by

means of sociometric preference scores. The fact that we obtained similar results in studies which measured leader-member relations by means of leader Group Atmosphere scores and sociometric ratings would suggest that the two types of measures are conceptually related. The nature of this relationship still needs to be explicated.

4. There is a large and important gap in our knowledge about the effects which leader and member intelligence have on group performance. We know that these relationships are complex and that intelligence and ability factors interact in important ways with leadership style, anxiety, and situational factors. Considering the importance of intelligence and technical training in most task groups, it is necessary to determine how to utilize to the fullest the intellectual resources which members can potentially contribute to the group task.

Nor do we know as yet how the intelligence of leaders and members affects the situational favorableness. Is it easier to be a leader of a group in which intelligence is evenly distributed or is it easier to lead a group if the members are duller than the leader and hence intellectually less resourceful? Is the leader's job easier when his members are experts or is his job easier when his members look to him for expert knowledge?

5. Our studies have shown that such behaviors as leader consideration, criticalness, tension relieving and supportive behavior, or initiation of structure, change with changes in the situational favorableness. In view of the importance which these and similar measures have played in leadership research of other investigators it would be highly desirable to reanalyze or replicate studies, but with sets of groups classified on the basis of the situational favorableness dimension. This would allow us to determine whether group performance can be predicted with other leadership measures when these are considered in the context of situational favorableness.

6. In measuring the favorableness of the group situation we have been concerned only with the degree to which the task is structured. We need to determine whether this particular aspect of the task is the only one which would affect the favorableness of the situation. Also of importance might be the degree to which each man's task must interlock with that of others, the degree to which work must be phased properly, and the degree to which the group and the leader receive feedback on their performance.

7.   We know very little about coacting tasks. These, too, vary. The definition of the coacting task used in this book is perhaps too simple. Some coacting tasks involve the independent completion of a particular task by one man, as, for example, in drawing a house plan or in repairing a car. Other tasks involve work which subsequently must be completed by someone else. An example is found in machine shop work which may require that the lathe operator make a part which someone else must use in assembling an engine. Still another example might be in the restaurant industry in which the kitchen personnel prepares food, the waiters serve the food, and the busboys assist in serving and in cleaning the tables. The waiters have coacting tasks, as do the busboys. Yet, the income of the cooks, waiters, and busboys is dependent upon the quality of the food, on the service, and on the cleanliness and general atmosphere of the place.

8.   Still less is known about counteracting groups. Which leadership style and behavior is required by the arbitrator who has considerable power, or by the mediator who acts merely as a go-between? What leadership styles are required by the negotiators who head one of the contending parties or the man on the negotiation team whose committee prepares the position paper. And is a different leadership style required by the negotiator when the groups work with the assistance of a moderator or when there is no neutral party to mediate the dispute?

9.   We have dealt primarily with two styles of leadership, measured by high and by low LPC or ASo scores. We still know very little about individuals whose LPC falls into the middle range. It is possible that there is more than one meaning for high or middle LPC, more than one type of task and relationship orientation.

10. Chapter 14 has already indicated some of the questions which need to be answered about management at levels above that of the first-line supervisor. Other questions readily come to mind. Should staff executives be chosen on the basis of their leadership style? Should the line officer be forced to take a staff position or jobs for which he is not ideally suited in order to provide him with a broader spectrum of experience? Are communications problems more likely among individuals with different leadership styles than among those with similar styles of leadership?

11. Chapter 15 has presented a rationale and a proposed method for improving the performance of groups and organizations based on the Contingency Model. Extensive field studies are required to determine how an individual can be trained to diagnose the favorableness of his own leadership situation or that of his subordinate managers, and how he can modify the situation to adapt it to his own leadership style or that of his subordinate managers.

The list of research problems which remain in leadership theory is far from exhausted. Nor should it be necessary to point out that we are far from possessing a theory of leadership to end all leadership theories. Hopefully, however, the Contingency Model will increase our understanding of this very important and complex problem of leadership effectiveness.

Appendix A
Instructions for LPC and group atmosphere scores and sample scales

People differ in the ways they think about those with whom they work. This may be important in working with others. Please give your immediate, first reaction to the items on the following two pages.

On the following sheet are pairs of words which are opposite in meaning, such as Very Neat and Not Neat. You are asked to describe someone with whom you have worked by placing an "X" in one of the eight spaces on the line between the two words.

Each space represents how well the adjective fits the person you are describing, as if it were written:

Very Neat:____:____:____:____ | ____:____:____:____:Not Neat
         8   7   6   5   4   3   2   1
        Very Quite Some- Slightly Slightly Some- Quite Very
        Neat Neat what Neat   Untidy   what Untidy Untidy
                   Neat   Untidy

For example: If you were to describe the person with whom you are able to work least well, and you ordinarily think of him as being *quite neat,* you would put an "X" in the second space from the words Very Neat, like this:

                    X
Very Neat: ____:____:____:____ | ____:____:____:____:Not Neat
         8   7   6   5   4   3   2   1
        Very Quite Some- Slightly Slightly Some- Quite Very
        Neat Neat what Neat   Untidy   what Untidy Untidy
                   Neat   Untidy

If you ordinarily think of the person with whom you can work least well as being only *slightly neat,* you would put your "X" as follows:

                           X
Very Neat:____:____:____:____ | ____:____:____:____:Not Neat
         8   7   6   5   4   3   2   1
        Very Quite Some- Slightly Slightly Some- Quite Very
        Neat Neat what Neat   Untidy   what Untidy Untidy
                   Neat   Untidy

If you would think of him as being *very untidy*, you would use the space nearest the words Not Neat.

Very Neat:____:____:____:_____ | _____:____:____:____:____X____:Not Neat
  8   7   6   5   4   3   2   1
 Very   Quite Some- Slightly   Slightly Some-   Quite   Very
 Neat   Neat   what   Neat   Untidy   what   Untidy   Untidy
               Neat   Untidy

Look at the words at both ends of the line before you put in your "X." Please remember that there are *no right or wrong answers*. Work rapidly; your first answer is likely to be the best. Please do not omit any items, and mark each item only once.

MPC

Think of the person *with whom you can work best*. He may be someone you work with now, or he may be someone you knew in the past.

He should not necessarily be the person you like best, but should be the person with whom you have been able to work best. Describe this person as he appears to you.

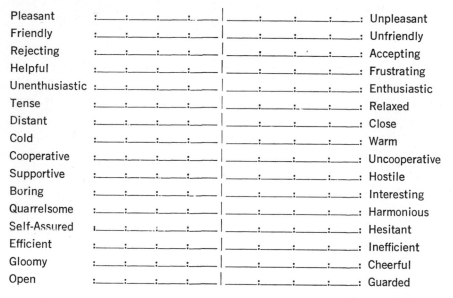

Pleasant	:____:____:____:____	____:____:____:____:	Unpleasant
Friendly	:____:____:____:____	____:____:____:____:	Unfriendly
Rejecting	:____:____:____:____	____:____:____:____:	Accepting
Helpful	:____:____:____:____	____:____:____:____:	Frustrating
Unenthusiastic	:____:____:____:____	____:____:____:____:	Enthusiastic
Tense	:____:____:____:____	____:____:____:____:	Relaxed
Distant	:____:____:____:____	____:____:____:____:	Close
Cold	:____:____:____:____	____:____:____:____:	Warm
Cooperative	:____:____:____:____	____:____:____:____:	Uncooperative
Supportive	:____:____:____:____	____:____:____:____:	Hostile
Boring	:____:____:____:____	____:____:____:____:	Interesting
Quarrelsome	:____:____:____:____	____:____:____:____:	Harmonious
Self-Assured	:____:____:____:____	____:____:____:____:	Hesitant
Efficient	:____:____:____:____	____:____:____:____:	Inefficient
Gloomy	:____:____:____:____	____:____:____:____:	Cheerful
Open	:____:____:____:____	____:____:____:____:	Guarded

LPC

Now, think of the person *with whom you can work least well*. He may be someone you work with now, or he may be someone you knew in the past.

He does not have to be the person you like least well, but should be the person with whom you had the most difficulty in getting a job done. Describe this person as he appears to you.

Pleasant   :___:___:___:___|___:___:___:___: Unpleasant
Friendly   :___:___:___:___|___:___:___:___: Unfriendly
Rejecting   :___:___:___:___|___:___:___:___: Accepting
Helpful   :___:___:___:___|___:___:___:___: Frustrating
Unenthusiastic :___:___:___:___|___:___:___:___: Enthusiastic
Tense   :___:___:___:___|___:___:___:___: Relaxed
Distant   :___:___:___:___|___:___:___:___: Close
Cold   :___:___:___:___|___:___:___:___: Warm
Cooperative   :___:___:___:___|___:___:___:___: Uncooperative
Supportive   :___:___:___:___|___:___:___:___: Hostile
Boring   :___:___:___:___|___:___:___:___: Interesting
Quarrelsome   :___:___:___:___|___:___:___:___: Harmonious
Self-Assured   :___:___:___:___|___:___:___:___: Hesitant
Efficient   :___:___:___:___|___:___:___:___: Inefficient
Gloomy   :___:___:___:___|___:___:___:___: Cheerful
Open   :___:___:___:___|___:___:___:___: Guarded

Group Atmosphere Scale

Describe the atmosphere of your group by checking the following items.

	8	7	6	5	4	3	2	1	
1. Friendly	:	:	:	:	:	:	:	:	Unfriendly
2. Accepting	:	:	:	:	:	:	:	:	Rejecting
3. Satisfying	:	:	:	:	:	:	:	:	Frustrating
4. Enthusiastic	:	:	:	:	:	:	:	:	Unenthusiastic
5. Productive	:	:	:	:	:	:	:	:	Nonproductive
6. Warm	:	:	:	:	:	:	:	:	Cold
7. Cooperative	:	:	:	:	:	:	:	:	Uncooperative
8. Supportive	:	:	:	:	:	:	:	:	Hostile
9. Interesting	:	:	:	:	:	:	:	:	Boring
10. Successful	:	:	:	:	:	:	:	:	Unsuccessful

Appendix B

AN EXPLANATORY NOTE ABOUT THE MEANING
OF CORRELATIONS

This short note is designed to assist the reader with little training in statistical methods or those who may require a brief review.

The correlation coefficient is an index of a relationship between two variables or two sets of scores. For example, it may be used to determine the relationship between intelligence scores and grades in school, or between the leader's ASo or LPC scores and group performance. In other words, each individual or each group has two scores, e.g., the leader's intelligence score and the group's performance score. We now wish to determine the degree to which high intelligence scores are associated with high group-performance scores.

Correlation coefficients range from 1.00, indicating a perfect positive relationship, to -1.00, indicating a perfect negative relationship. A perfect positive correlation would indicate that the group with the highest score on one variable, e.g., intelligence, would also have the highest score on the other variable, e.g., performance, that the group with the second highest score on intelligence would also have the second highest score on the performance variable, and so on. A perfect negative correlation would indicate that the group with the *highest* score on one variable would have the *lowest* score on the other variable, and so on. A zero correlation, .00, normally indicates that there is no relationship between the variables, that is, that scores are randomly paired. In other words, a person with a high score on one variable is just as likely to have a high score as a low score on the other variable.

A correlation of .70 between the ASo score of the leader and group performance would indicate, therefore, that the *better* performing groups tend to have leaders with *high* ASo scores and that the poorer performing groups tend to have leaders with low ASo scores. A correlation of $-.70$ indicates that the *better* performing groups tend to have leaders with *low* ASo scores.

A high positive or a high negative correlation between two variables may, then, enable us to predict the scores of one variable from the scores of the other. While the definition of "high" depends to some degree on the type of variables with which we deal, in studies of small groups, correlations between .40 and .60 (or −.40 to −.60) are considered to be moderately high, and correlations above .60 (or −.60) can be considered to be high. The larger the number of cases, the more confidence we can have that a given correlation is not due to chance. While a correlation of .50 may be due to chance when it is based on ten cases, it is highly significant ($p < .01$), and hence not likely to be due to chance, if it is based on thirty cases. In general, a correlation, or any other statistic, is said to be statistically *significant* if the results could have occurred by pure chance with a probability of less than 5 percent of the time ($p < .05$); it is said to be *highly significant* if the results could have occurred by pure chance less than 1 percent of the time ($p < .01$).

Appendix C
Correlations between LPC and ASo scores and biographical and personality variables[1]

I. Biographical data

S's completed biographical questionnaires containing information about factors such as religion, social class and family background, educational level and academic standing, high school activities, interests, hobbies, and college activities. The variables obtained from this questionnaire were as follows:

1. Age (in years).
2. Religion—This was scored according to the predominance in the United States of the religious preference. Thus, Protestant was given a score of 4, Catholic 3, Jewish 2, and other 1.
3. Religious activity—Active = 1; inactive = 2.
4. Heterogeneity index—This index was used by Hawkins (1962) and is defined here as the sum of the difference in age betwen the S and each of his brothers plus twice the sum of the difference in age between S and each of his sisters.
5. Order in family—(1 to 5).
6. Semester level—(1 to 8).
7. Grade point average—Obtained for each S from university records.
8. Campus residence—This was scored according to the number of other men living in the same house as the S. Thus, domitory = 4; fraternity = 3; independent house = 2; and other (generally private apartments) = 1.
9. High school percentile rank.
10. Socioeconomic status—Father's occupation was rated on a six-point scale of occupational status by two raters ($r = .96$, corrected for two raters). The score was the sum of the two ratings, with the higher scores indicating higher socioeconomic status.

[1] From a technical report by A. R. Bass, F. E. Fiedler, and S. Krueger entitled, *Personality Correlates of Assumed Similarity (ASo) and Related Scores* (1964).

11. Rural-urban background—S's home town was rated on a seven-point scale according to population.
12. Number of activities—This was simply a count of the total number of different interests, hobbies, and high school and college activities listed by each S.
13. Number of hours spent in activities.
14. Number of clubs in high school.
15. Number of offices held—Sum of number of offices S reported he held in high school and college activities.
16. Number of acquaintances—This measure was originally used by Steiner (1959) in his study of correlates of the ASo score, and is simply the number of personal acquaintances S reports he knows well enough to describe in a short paragraph.
17. Interests—physical versus sedentary—Two raters judged the degree to which interests reported by S were physical or sedentary (inter-rater reliability = .92, corrected for two raters). The score was the sum of the two ratings. (Six-point scales were used for ratings of this item as well as items 18, 20, 21, and 22.)
18. Interests—social versus individual—Two raters judged the degree to which S's reported interests were social as opposed to individual (interrater reliability = .89, corrected for two raters). Against the score was the sum of the two ratings.
19. Field of study—proportion of males—As an index of the relative "masculinity" or "hardheadedness" of the field of study, the proportion of males in this field of study was entered as a score for each S.
20. Field of study—difficulty—Three university deans who typically engage in student counseling were asked to rate the various fields of study listed by Ss in terms of their relative academic difficulty. Inter-rater agreement was .86 (corrected for three raters). The sum of the three difficulty ratings for each field was entered as a score for the field of study listed by each S.
21. College activities—individual prominence—Two raters rated each S's listed activities in terms of the extent to which these activities would tend to be prestigeful or would lead to S's individual prominence in the eyes of his fellow students. Interrater agreement was .83, corrected for two raters. The score for each S was the sum of the two ratings.
22. College activities—leadership—The same two raters judged the extent to which S's activities tended to exhibit or call for leadership or

managerial activity. Interrater agreement was .82, corrected for two raters. Again, the score for each S was the sum of the two ratings.

II. Response set measures

A second set of variables measured a number of individual response styles. Since the previous study indicated that the low-LPC individual appeared to give more socially acceptable responses in describing self and others, we included a number of personal response-style variables in the present study as possible correlates of the LPC measure, viz., measures of social desirability, acquiescence, and tendency to use extremes. A number of different measures of these response sets are available and the literature contains considerable controversy as to the nature and construct validity of each.[2] In a recent study Wiggins (1964) factor analyzed thirty-two different measures of social desirability and acquiescence response sets and obtained six relatively independent response-set factors. In the present study, nine different response-set measures were included so as to represent each of the six factors obtained in Wiggins' factor analysis. The measures included are listed below:

1. Wiggins' Social Desirability scale (Wiggins, 1959).
2. Edwards' Social Desirability scale (Edwards, 1957).
3. Asch's Acquiescence measure, speed of decision time (Asch, 1959).
4. Marlowe-Crowne Social Desirability scale (MC–SD) (Crowne and Marlowe, 1960).
5. Wiggins' Acquiescence scale (Wiggins, 1962).
6. F scale (Adorno et al., 1950).
7. Reversed F scale (Jackson and Messick, 1957).
8. Barron's Independence of Judgment scale (Barron, 1953).
9. Couch and Keniston's acquiescence measure, Impulsivity scale (Couch and Keniston, 1960).

The items from each of the first eight of these scales are all in the true-false format and were randomly compiled into a single inventory of 211 items. The impulsivity items required a seven-point scale of agreement and were included as Part II of the response-style questionnaire.

Several additional response set measures were included in this study.

10. Similarity test—A twenty-five-item similarity test asked Ss to indicate, on a six-point scale, the extent to which they felt pairs of relatively neutral nouns and adjectives were similar or dissimilar. The score on

[2] Christie and Lindauer, 1963; DeSoto et al., 1959; Foster, 1961; McGee, 1962.

this test was simply the sum of the item scores. A high score presumably indicates a tendency to perceive neutral pairs of stimulus objects as relatively similar, and a low score indicates a tendency to discriminate or differentiate more among relatively neutral stimulus objects.

11. Perceived similarity between most- and least-preferred coworker. One item in the similarity test, separately scored, was simply "your most- and your least-preferred coworker." Ss rated the extent to which they felt these persons were similar on a six-point scale.

12. Tendency to use extremes—Answers to the similarity test were scored for extreme responses. For this purpose, a response of 6 or 1 received a score of 3, a response of 5 or 2 was scored 2, and 4 was scored 1. Thus the higher the score on the tendency to use extreme measures, the more the individual used the extreme response positions.

13. Category width—Pettigrew's (1958) category width scale, which measures equivalence range response style or tendency to categorize broadly or narrowly, was included as an additional response-style variable, following Steiner's finding of a significant relationship between this variable and ASo.

III. Personality measures

The following personality variables were obtained for all Ss in this study:

Bass's orientation inventory (Bass, 1961)
1. Self-orientation.
2. Task orientation.
3. Interaction orientation.

Maudsley personality inventory (Eysenck, 1959)
4. Extraversion.
5. Neuroticism.

Group behavior questionnaire (*variables 6–19*)
This was a questionnaire especially designed for the present study which included fourteen items concerned with behavior in groups and leadership situations. Items were carefully selected on the basis of characteristics which would presumably differentiate between high- and low-LPC individuals in terms of hypothesized behaviors in work-group situations. Ss were asked to judge, on a seven-point scale of agreement-disagreement, the extent to which they felt the items were characteristic of themselves.

Since the format for these items was identical with that of the impulsivity-scale items previously described, the fourteen items were randomly interspersed with the impulsivity items in Part II of the response-style questionnaire.

IV. Intelligence measures

As measures of intellectual ability, scores on the SCAT (School and College Ability Test, ETS, 1955) were obtained for 114 of the 163 Ss from university counseling bureau records. Both verbal (L) and quantitative (Q) SCAT scores were obtained. No SCAT scores were available for the remaining Ss, so that the correlations involving these variables were on the reduced N of 114.

V. Interpersonal perception measures

Ss were asked to describe themselves the way they would ideally like to be (ideal self), their mother, their father, and their most-preferred and least-preferred coworkers on identical twenty-one-scale semantic differentials. From these descriptions a number of scores were obtained.

1. Self-esteem—This is defined as the sum of the twenty-one items for the self-description, with the positive or favorable end of the scale taken as the high score.
2. Ideal self-esteem.
3. Esteem for mother.
4. Esteem for father.
5. Esteem for most-preferred coworker.
6. Esteem for least-preferred coworker (LPC).
7. D score between self and ideal-self descriptions.
8. D score between self and mother descriptions.
9. D score between self and father descriptions.
10. D score between mother and father descriptions.
11. D score between most- and least-preferred coworker descriptions (ASo).
12. Variance of scales for self-description.
13. Variance of scales for ideal self.
14. Variance of scales for mother.
15. Variance of scales for father.
16. Variance of scales for most-preferred coworker.
17. Variance of scales for least-preferred coworker.

18. Interaction variance of the twenty-one scales by the six concepts. This measure was used by Hutchins (1958, 1961) as a measure of cognitive complexity and indicates the extent to which S describes different concepts differently on the several scales.

19. LPC $-\bar{x}_{LPC}$—Absolute value of the difference between S's LPC score and the mean LPC score. This was included to investigate possible curvilinear (U-shaped) relationships between LPC and the other variables. High scores on this variable indicate large distances from the mean in either direction.

20. ASo $-\bar{x}_{ASo}$—Absolute value of the difference between S's ASo and the mean ASo score. The correlations between these measures and LPC and ASo scores, as well as the deviation scores of ASo and LPC, are presented in the table below.

Examination of the table indicates that most of the correlations between LPC and ASo and the other personality, intellectual, and personal-background variables are quite low. Even the significant correlations are very low, with only 9 of the 154 correlations greater than .20. In general, it seems fairly clear that the LPC measure is relatively unique and is independent of most of the variables obtained in this study. If we examine some of the significant correlations, however, it will be noted that the low-LPC (and low-ASo) person, as compared to the high-LPC person, tends to be younger, uses more extreme responses, is a narrower categorizer, and is more interaction-oriented. The relation with category width confirms that found earlier by Steiner (1959). This suggests that the low-LPC individual has a general tendency to categorize stimulus objects more narrowly than the high-LPC person. Further, the low-LPC person is found here to be more interaction-oriented than the high-LPC person, again confirming Steiner's earlier finding, i.e., that the low-ASo person in this sense is more socially expansive than the high.

Examination of the correlations of the variables with the absolute deviations of LPC and ASo from their means again indicates a very low level of correlation. High scores on the variable LPC $-\bar{x}_{LPC}$ indicate either a high- or a low-LPC person (i.e., a person whose LPC score is considerably above or below the mean), and low scores on this variable indicate a middle-LPC person (i.e., a person whose LPC score is quite close to the mean LPC). Examination of the correlations with this variable indicates that the middle-LPC individual, as compared with high- and low-LPC individuals, is less active in his religion, more likely to come from urban areas, gives less socially desirable responses, is less authoritarian, is more critical of others in getting a job done, prefers to be a group member rather than leader, tends to esteem both himself and others less, and is somewhat more discriminating in describing others. This suggests a general tendency for the middle-LPC individual, as distinct from either the high or the low, to be somewhat more critical and discriminating in his perceptions of others, and possibly somewhat more cognitively complex.

Correlations between all variables and the LPC and ASo measures

I. Biographical and Personal Background Measures	LPC	ASo	LPC $-\bar{x}_{\text{LPC}}$	ASo $-\bar{x}_{\text{ASo}}$
1. Age	.16*	.20†	.04	.00
2. Religion	.05	.03	.04	.01
3. Religious activity	−.04	−.12	.21†	.13
4. Heterogeneity index	.08	.10	.05	.08
5. Order in family	.01	−.05	−.01	−.06
6. Semester level	.10	.13	−.09	−.09
7. Grade point average	.10	.02	.10	.13
8. Campus residence	−.10	−.12	−.09	.08
9. High school percentile rank	.05	.01	.09	.16*
10. Socioeconomic status	−.14	−.15*	.15*	.13
11. Rural-urban background	.00	.04	−.20†	−.16*
12. Number of activities	−.07	−.11	.07	.05
13. Number of hours spent in activities	−.01	−.07	−.03	−.05
14. Number of clubs in high school	−.03	−.10	.07	−.01
15. Number of offices held	−.07	−.08	.12	.08
16. Number of acquaintances	−.07	−.10	.12	.11
17. Interests—physical versus sedentary	.11	.08	−.02	−.03
18. Interests—social versus individual	.08	.02	.03	.01
19. Field of study—proportion of males	.00	.06	−.15*	.00
20. Field of study—difficulty	.05	.05	−.12	−.05
21. College activities—individual prominence	.04	−.02	.06	.00
22. College activities—leadership	.02	−.01	.04	.03

II. Response Set Measures				
1. Wiggins' Social Desirability scale	.04	−.03	.21†	.10
2. Edwards' Social Desirability scale	−.02	−.04	.00	.02
3. Speed of decision time	−.06	−.09	.04	.04

4. Marlowe-Crowne Social Desirability scale	—.04	—.11	.16*	.18*
5. Wiggins' Acquiescence scale	.00	—.02	.13	.01
6. F scale	—.08	—.12	.17*	.08
7. Reversed F scale	.03	—.01	—.03	—.05
8. Barron's Independence of Judgment scale	—.03	.02	—.03	—.04
9. Impulsivity scale	—.01	—.04	.09	.14
10. Similarity test	.06	.00	.10	.08
11. Perceived similarity between most- and least-preferred coworker	.25†	.25†	.08	—.07
12. Tendency to use extremes (2)	—.25†	—.40†	.17*	.04
13. Category width	.15*	.16*	—.11	—.08

III. Personality Measures

1. Self-orientation	.11	.11	—.05	—.04
2. Task orientation	.05	.04	.03	—.01
3. Interaction orientation	—.16*	—.14	.00	.04
4. Maudsley-extraversion	—.03	—.12	.10	.03
5. Maudsley-neuroticism	.00	.03	—.01	.00
6. Group behavior questionnaire number 1	—.06	.12	.02	.06
7. Group behavior questionnaire number 2	—.16*	—.18*	—.11	.03
8. Group behavior questionnaire number 3	.00	—.04	—.09	—.02
9. Group behavior questionnaire number 4	.04	—.00	.00	—.05
10. Group behavior questionnaire number 5	.01	.01	—.05	.10
11. Group behavior questionnaire number 6	.02	.05	.04	.04
12. Group behavior questionnaire number 7	—.03	—.00	.03	.08
13. Group behavior questionnaire number 8	.03	.06	—.08	.02
14. Group behavior questionnaire number 9	.02	—.00	.01	—.12
15. Group behavior questionnaire number 10	—.06	—.13	.07	—.02
16. Group behavior questionnaire number 11	—.04	—.10	—.17*	—.16*
17. Group behavior questionnaire number 12	.00	.08	—.17*	—.05
18. Group behavior questionnaire number 13	.00	.02	—.13	.01
19. Group behavior questionnaire number 14	.02	.05	.02	—.02

IV. Intelligence Measures	LPC	ASo	$LPC - \bar{x}_{LPC}$	$ASo - \bar{x}_{ASo}$
1. School and college ability test—verbal	.17	.12	.01	.03
2. School and college ability test—quantitative	.04	.06	.02	.10

V. Interpersonal Perception Measures

	LPC	ASo	$LPC - \bar{x}_{LPC}$	$ASo - \bar{x}_{ASo}$
1. Self-esteem	−.01	−.15*	.20†	.15*
2. Ideal self-esteem	−.15*	−.31†	.17*	.04
3. Esteem for mother	.02	−.15*	.08	.03
4. Esteem for father	−.02	−.12	.15*	.13
5. Esteem for most-preferred coworker	−.26†	−.52‡	.20†	.19†
6. Esteem for least-preferred coworker	1.00	.89‡	.14	.01
7. D score between self and ideal-self descriptions	−.05	−.04	−.09	−.14
8. D score between self and mother descriptions	.04	−.03	−.06	−.20†
9. D score between self and father descriptions	.01	−.04	.04	−.06
10. D score between mother and father descriptions	.04	−.02	−.05	−.18†
11. D score between most- and least-preferred coworker	−.89‡	1.00	−.02	.02
12. Variance of scales for self-description	.04	−.04	.05	−.07
13. Variance of scales for ideal self	.05	.04	−.06	−.05
14. Variance of scales for mother	−.05	−.14	.08	−.12
15. Variance of scales for father	−.11	−.15*	.10	−.07
16. Variance of scales for most-preferred coworker	.22†	.12	−.02	−.14
17. Variance of scales for least-preferred coworker	.35†	.10	−.20†	−.33†
18. Interaction variance	.12	−.06	−.16*	−.29†
19. $LPC - \bar{x}_{LPC}$	.14	.02	1.00	.66‡
20. $ASo - \bar{x}_{ASo}$	.01	−.02	.66‡	1.00

* $p < .05$.
† $p < .01$.
‡ Spurious correlation of a variable with its component.

Appendix D
Formal position power questions utilized by J. G. Hunt

Questions [1]

1. Can the supervisor recommend subordinate rewards and punishment to his boss?
2. Can the supervisor punish or reward subordinates on his own?
3. Can the supervisor recommend promotion or demotion of subordinates?
4. Can the supervisor promote or demote subordinates on his own?
5. Does the supervisor's special knowledge allow him to decide how subordinates are to proceed on their jobs?
6. Can the supervisor give subordinates a general idea of what they are to do?
7. Can the supervisor specifically instruct subordinates concerning what they are to do?
8. Is an important part of the supervisor's job to motivate his subordinates?
9. Is an important part of the supervisor's job to evaluate subordinate performance?
10. Does the supervisor have a great deal of knowledge about the jobs under him but require his subordinates to do them?
11. Can the supervisor supervise and evaluate subordinate jobs?
12. Does the supervisor know both his own and his subordinates' jobs so that he could finish subordinate work himself if it were necessary and he had enough time?
13. Has the supervisor been given an official title by the company which differentiates him from his subordinates?

[1] The number of "yes" answers indicates the score.

Appendix D (continued)
Rating form to determine job task structure utilized by J. G. Hunt

I.   Please rate according to the instructions in the following sections those jobs which you and the researcher have agreed are a representative cross section of jobs in your company.

II. You will note that there are four dimensions on which each job is to be rated. Each dimension is described on a separate sheet. Please rate all jobs on a given dimension before going to the next dimension. In other words, jobs are to be rated on each dimension independently of the way they are rated on other dimensions.

III. (A) In order to help you in your rating, you will note that there is a graphic scale (ranging from 1 to 11) for each dimension with job titles arranged below the horizontal line so as to cover most of the points on the scale. These are called "anchor jobs."

(B) All anchor jobs, with the exception of two, have been evaluated by a panel of judges, and general agreement has been reached that the jobs belong where they are shown on the scale. These jobs were selected from among one hundred because of the high interjudge agreement.

(C) A short description of each job on the scale is included on the same page. This is the same description that the judges used in rating the jobs.

IV. When rating the selected jobs in your company, please keep the description of the anchor jobs in mind and rate your jobs in relation to these anchor jobs.

V.   Note that in many cases there are different anchor jobs as job dimensions change.

VI. (A) In order to simplify your rating work, it is suggested that you list (on the last sheet clipped to these) your company jobs to be rated. (Note that each line on this sheet is lettered and this will be the job letter.) Then it is suggested that you familiarize yourself with the dimension you are going to rate and the anchor-job descriptions.

(B) After doing this, place the letter corresponding to the job you are rating above the anchor job which most nearly corresponds to it for the dimension you are rating.

(C) After you have done this for each job, check to see that you have placed them where you think they belong. This may mean you will rearrange some of your earlier placements. After you are satisfied that you have rated the jobs the way you want them in relation to each other and in relation to the anchor jobs, do the same thing for the next dimension. Please do not refer to job ratings on earlier dimensions when rating on later dimensions, however.

VII. Do not worry if you have not covered every number on the scale. It may be that you are dealing with a narrow range of jobs. Also, you will note that there are parts of some of the scales which have no anchor jobs, because none were found to fall consistently on those parts of the scale. If you believe some of your jobs should lie at these points, it is all right to place them there. Please make sure, however, you have placed your jobs above one of the eleven points on the scale and not in between these points.

Dimension I

Goal clarity   This is the degree to which the requirements of a job (the tasks or duties which typically make up the job) are clearly stated or known to people performing the job.

Read the job descriptions for Dimension I. Then think of yourself as the person assigned the job and ask yourself how clear *what* you are to do is to you. Do not include *how* you are to do the job. There is another dimension.

To rank this dimension, assume that the *lower* the scale number, the *lower* the goal clarity (the less clear the goals of the job).

1	I. Idle millionaire
2	II. Hobo
3	
4	
5	III. Train director
	IV. Private detective
	V. Receiving stores supervisor
6	VI. Educational director
7	VII. Notary public
8	VIII. Canvas cover repair foreman
9	IX. Bench carpenter
10	X. Chili maker
11	XI. Axle assembler

Place the letters of jobs corresponding in structure to the anchor jobs shown on the scale directly above those anchor jobs. If there is no anchor job above the number on the scale, you can still place your job there if desired.

Job descriptions for Dimension I

I. Idle millionaire.

II. Hobo. Note: Since no job evaluated by the judges was found to extend beyond 5 on this dimension, these two "jobs" have been added in an effort to broaden the scale. It may well be that some of your jobs approach these two on this dimension. You may supply your own descriptions for these two jobs.

III. Train director. Directs switching of railroad traffic entering or leaving yards to regulate movements of trains in conformity with traffic schedules and safety regulations. Signals switching directions to towerman by manipulating controls from central control room.

IV. Private detective. Performs private police work to protect property by detecting thievery, shoplifting, or dishonesty among employees or patrons of a business establishment or other private organization.

V. Receiving and stores supervisor. Supervises workers engaged in receiving and storing production materials in an industrial establishment. Note: While the above three are different jobs, they were given the same rating on this dimension.

VI. Educational director. Plans, organizes and administers training programs designed to promote efficiency through instruction of new employees in firm's policies, systems and routines. Instructs foremen in vocational training methods.

VII. Notary public. Administers oaths or affirmations where required, issues summonses for witnesses in cases before courts or other persons authorized to examine witnesses. Takes affidavits on request.

VIII. Canvas cover repair foreman. Supervises a group of workers who repair tents, awnings, and canvas covers used to protect various objects, such as motors and instruments.

IX. Bench carpenter (woodworking). Works at a bench in an industrial firm and fits and assembles prefabricated wooden sections; or cuts, shapes, fits and assembles wooden sections according to blueprints and sketches, performing general carpentry duties, such as sawing, planing, jointing, fitting, and nailing.

   X. Chili maker. Cooks specified amounts of ground meat, chili, spices, chopped onions, garlic, and beef tallow in a steam-jacketed kettle to make chili and ladles from kettle into cans. All ingredients weighed out by chili maker or according to his formula.

  XI. Axle assembler (auto manufacturing). Secures front- or rear-axle subassemblies to chassis springs on final assembly line. Bolts subassembly in place using wrenches and power-driven nut-tightening tools.

Dimension II

Goal-path multiplicity   This is the degree to which the problems encountered in the job can be solved by a variety of procedures (number of different paths to the goal—number of alternatives in performing the job—number of different ways the problems typically encountered in the job can be solved).

Read the job descriptions for Dimension II. Then think of yourself as the person assigned the job, and remembering that you have already evaluated the job in terms of *what* is expected, now shift and think of *how* you are to do the job. How many ways are there to accomplish the goal? To what extent is planning necessary to decide *how* to do the job?

To rank this dimension, assume that the *lower* the scale number, the *lower* the goal-path multiplicity (the less paths there are to the goal).

1	I. Date puller
2	II. Off-line assembler
3	III. Billing clerk
4	IV. Form builder
5	V. Drafting clerk
6	VI. Receiving and stores supervisor
7	VII. Dance hall inspector
	VIII. Chief clerk
8	IX. Buyer
9	X. Broadcast director
10	XI. Research engineer
11	

Place letters of jobs corresponding in structure to anchor jobs shown on the scale directly above anchor jobs. If there are no anchor jobs above the number on the scale, you can still place your job there if desired.

Job descriptions for Dimension II

I. Date puller. Cuts open dates, removes the stones, and cuts the dates into pieces for use in making candy.

II. Off-line assembler (auto manufacturing). Assembles units, such as windshields and lights, which are later placed on the automobile chassis as it passes over the assembly line. Uses screwdriver, power-driven nut tightener, and other hand tools.

III. Billing clerk. Prepares statements, bills, and invoices, by hand or on a typewriter, to be sent to customers, showing an itemized account of the amount they owe. Obtains information from purchase orders, sales and charge slips or other records. Addresses envelopes and inserts bills preparatory to mailing. Checks billings with accounts receivable ledger.

IV. Form builder (aircraft and auto manufacturing). Builds forms, fixtures, jigs, or templates of wood or metal for use as guides or standards by other workers in mass production of cars or planes. Studies blueprint of part for which fixture is to be built and lays out, cuts, and assembles component pieces of wood or metal. Checks and measures finished assembly against blueprint.

V. Drafting clerk. Draws and letters organization charts, schedules, and graphs. Uses simple drafting instruments such as ruling pen, lettering pen, and straightedge to produce neat, legible charts and graphs.

VI. Receiving and stores supervisor. See job description for Dimension I.

VII. Dance hall inspector. A member of the police force who inspects all dance halls for licenses and for conduct of patrons. Enforces regulations concerning such places and reports on the manner in which each is operated.

VIII. Chief clerk. Coordinates the clerical work of an establishment, directing performance of such services as the keeping of personnel and time records, standardizing operating procedures for clerical work, and purchasing and keeping inventories of clerical supplies and equipment. Directs work of several subordinate office managers. Note: While the above two jobs are different, they were given the same rating on this dimension.

IX. Buyer (retail or wholesale trade). Purchases merchandise within budgetary limitations in sufficient quantity and with sufficient appeal to sell rapidly. Assigns selling price to merchandise and initiates procedures such as price reductions to promote the sale of surplus or slow-moving items.

X. Broadcast director. Supervises broadcasting of specific radio programs. Formulates general policies to be followed in preparing and broadcasting programs. Keeps expenditures for producing programs within budgetary limits and creates and develops program ideas.

XI. Research engineer. Conducts engineering research concerned with processing a particular kind of commodity with a view to improving present products and discovering new products or to improving and discovering new machinery for production purposes. Examines literature on subject. Plans and executes experimental work to check theories advanced. Consults with other engineers to get their ideas. Prepares report of findings.

Dimension III

Decision verifiability   This is the degree to which the "correctness" of the solutions or decisions typically encountered in a job can generally be demonstrated by appeal to authority or authoritative source (e.g., the census of 1960), by logical procedures (e.g., mathematical demonstration), or by feedback (e.g., examination of consequences of decision, as in action taken).

Read the job descriptions for Dimension III. Then think of yourself as the person assigned the job and ask yourself to what extent it is possible for you or others evaluating your work to know whether the job has been done "correctly" or not. A time sequence is implied here. For some jobs it is never possible to know the correctness of the decision. For other jobs it is possible to know but only after a long period of time, say, one year or more. For others it is possible to know immediately or within a one-year period.

To rank this dimension, assume that the *lower* the scale number, the *lower* the decision verifiability (the less ways there are to verify job decisions).

1
2   I. Social welfare research worker
3
4   II. Design engineer
5   III. Service director

6	IV.	Buyer
7	V.	Cameraman
8	VI.	Account analyst
9	VII.	Cabinet assembler
	VIII.	File clerk
10	IX.	Off-line assembler
11	X.	Nut and bolt sorter

Place letters of jobs corresponding in structure to anchor jobs shown on the scale directly above anchor jobs. If there is no anchor job above the number on the scale, you can still place your job there if desired.

Job descriptions for Dimension III

I. Social welfare research worker. Performs research to facilitate investigation and alleviation of social problems. Gathers facts by reference to selected literature and by consultation. Analyzes data, employing statistical computations, and correlates information. Evaluates social projects or disposition of cases in light of findings. Estimates future needs for services and presents facts significant to formulation of future plans.

II. Design engineer. Creates designs for machinery or equipment. Draws up construction details and determines production methods and standards of performance. Investigates practicability of designs in relation to limitations of manufacturing equipment and gives advice on construction, manufacture, materials, and processes. Experiments with existing machinery to improve design.

III. Service director (retail trade). Supervises all operating and non-selling services of a large store, such as delivery, wrapping, storage, stock keeping, receiving, and alterations. Responsible for care of building and upkeep of equipment, such as elevators.

IV. Buyer (retail or wholesale trade). See job description for Dimension II.

V. Cameraman (motion picture). Photographs anybody or anything of which motion pictures may be required with a motion-picture camera. Specializes in shots from unusual angles and dangerous heights or positions.

VI. Account analyst (banking). Determines and prepares charges to be made against commercial accounts for various services performed by the bank. Prepares reports on status and value of individual accounts for bank officials.

VII.   Cabinet assembler (furniture). Assembles by hand the parts of the radio cabinet that have been cut and dressed in the machine department, fastening the joints together with glue or braces at the points of union, and holding them together with clamps.

VIII.   File clerk. Keeps correspondence, cards, invoices, receipts, and other records arranged systematically according to subject matter in file cabinets or drawers. Reads information on incoming material and sorts and places it in proper position in filing cabinet. Locates and removes material from cabinet when requested. Note: The above two jobs are different, but they were given the same rating on this dimension.

IX.   Off-line assembler (auto manufacturing). See job description for Dimension II.

X.   Nut and bolt sorter. Sorts nuts and bolts by hand according to size, length, and diameter. Discards defective pieces.

Dimension IV

Solution specificity   This is the degree to which there is generally more than one "correct solution" involved in tasks which typically make up a job. Some tasks, e.g., arithmetic problems, have only one solution that is acceptable; others have two or more, e.g., a sorting task where items to be sorted have several dimensions; and still others have an almost infinite number of possible solutions, each of which may be equally as good as others. For example, consider human relations problems or many problems managers must make decisions about.

Read the job descriptions for Dimension IV. Then think of yourself as the person who must decide whether tasks typically falling within a given job have been performed correctly or not. Ask yourself how difficult it would be to decide the relative correctness of the task solution of two people who have been assigned a given task as a part of their job and have come up with quite different answers.

Where there are a number of solutions which might be equally acceptable, you are dealing with a job low in solution specificity.

To rank this dimension, assume that the *lower* the scale number, the *lower* the solution specificity (the *more* correct solutions there are).

1	I. Social welfare research worker
2	II. Research engineer
3	III. Dancer
4	IV. Broadcast news analyst

5	V. Service manager
6	VI. Warehouse manager
7	VII. Cane cutter
8	VIII. Electrical asembler
9	IX. Candy-cutting machine girl
10	X. Dairy maid
11	XI. Barrel drainer

Place letters of jobs corresponding in structure to anchor jobs shown on the scale directly above anchor jobs.

Job descriptions for Dimension IV

I. Social welfare research worker. See job description for Dimension III.

II. Research engineer. See job description for Dimension II.

III. Dancer. Performs dances alone, with a partner, or in a group.

IV. Broadcast news analyst. Analyzes and interprets news from various sources. Prepares copy and broadcasts material over radio station or network.

V. Service manager. Supervises activities of an institution that renders service to the public, such as a business-service, repair-service or personal-service establishment.

VI. Warehouse manager. Manages one or more commercial or industrial warehouses to maintain stocks of material. Directs through intermediate supervisors checking of incoming and outgoing shipments. Keeps stock records and does other clerical tasks. Directs handling and disposition of materials through foremen and establishes and enforces operations procedures according to work requirements.

VII. Cane cutter. Cuts sugarcane in the fields during harvest season using a broad-bladed knife. Pulls off side leaves of several cane stalks with hook at end of knife and cuts the leaves from stalk with knife blade. Cuts through stalk at base of ripe section and places cut stalks in piles.

VIII. Electrical assembler (refrigeration equipment). Installs electrical equipment in refrigerator display cases working from blueprints. Cuts pockets and bores holes in wooden framing of case with electric or hand tools to install wiring and light receptacles. Attaches wires to fixtures and fixtures to receptacles, using hand tools, and tests circuits of completed case for errors in wiring or hookup.

IX. Candy-cutting machine girl. Takes cut candies from cutting machine by hand and arranges them on metal trays ready for wrappers and packers. Picks out imperfect pieces of candy and drops them into a container. When conveyors are used, arranges pieces on conveyor belt as they come from the cutting knives.

X. Dairy maid. Performs lighter types of work on a dairy farm. Milks cows. Separates cream by hand in pans or by machine with a cream separator. Churns butter with a hand churn.

XI. Barrel drainer. Empties water from barrel that has been inspected or weighed by rolling barrel onto a stand and pulling bung from hole by hand.

Bibliography

Adorno, T. W., E. Frenkel-Brunswick, D. J. Levinson, and R. N. Sanford. *The authoritarian personality.* New York: Harper & Row, 1950.

Alexander, S., and T. R. Husek. The anxiety differential: Initial steps in the development of a measure of situational anxiety. *Educational and Psychological Measurement,* 1962, *22,* 325–348.

Anderhalter, O. F., W. L. Wilkins, and Marilyn K. Rigby. Peer ratings. Technical Report No. 2, St. Louis University, St. Louis, Mo., 1952. (Mimeograph)

Anderson, L. R. Some effects of leadership training on intercultural discussion groups. Unpublished doctoral dissertation. Urbana, Ill.: University of Illinois, 1964.

Anderson, L. R., and F. E. Fiedler. The effect of participatory and supervisory leadership on group creativity. *Journal of Applied Psychology,* 1964, *48,* 227–236.

Andrews, R. E. Leadership and supervision. U.S. Civil Service Commission, Personnel Management Series No. 9, Washington, D.C., 1955.

Argyris, C. *Integrating the individual and the organization.* New York: Wiley, 1964.

Argyris, C. *Interpersonal competence and organizational effectiveness.* Homewood, Ill.: Dorsey Press, 1962.

Asch, M. J. Negative response bias and personality adjustment. *Journal of Counseling Psychology,* 1958, 5, 206–210.

Bales, R. F. A set of categories for the analysis of small group interaction. *American Sociological Review,* 1950, *15,* 257–263.

Bales, R. F., and F. L. Strodtbeck. Phases in group problem solving. *Journal of Abnormal and Social Psychology,* 1951, *46,* 485–495.

Barnard, C. I. *The functions of the executive.* Cambridge, Mass.: Harvard, 1938.

Barron, F. An ego-strength scale which predicts response to psychotherapy. *Journal of Consulting Psychology,* 1953, *17,* 327–333.

Barron, Nancy K. Unpublished M.A. thesis, University of Illinois, 1967.

Bass, A. R., F. E. Fiedler, and S. Krueger. Personality correlates of Assumed Similarity (ASo) and related scores. Urbana, Ill.: Group Effectiveness Research Laboratory, University of Illinois, March, 1964. (Mimeograph)

Bass, B. M. An analysis of the leaderless group discussion. *Journal of Applied Psychology,* 1949, *33,* 527–533.

Bass, B. M. Comparisons of the behavior in groups of self-oriented, interaction-oriented, and task-oriented members. Baton Rouge, La.: Louisiana State University, 1961. (Mimeograph)

Bass, B. M. An evaluation of the use of objective social data for training problem-solving discussants. Baton Rouge, La.: Louisiana State University, 1960. (b) (Mimeograph)

Bass, B. M. The leaderless group discussion. *Psychological Bulletin,* 1954, *51,* 465–492.

Bass, B. M. *Leadership, psychology, and organizational behavior.* New York: Harper & Row, 1960. (a)

Bavelas, A., A. H. Hastorf, A. E. Gross, and W. R. Kite. Experiments on the alteration of group structure. *Journal of Experimental and Social Psychology,* 1965, *1,* 55–70.

Bell, G. B., and R. L. French. Consistency of individual leadership position in small groups of varying membership. In A. Hare, E. Borgatta, and R. Bales (eds.), *Small groups,* New York: Knopf, 1955.

Bennis, W. G. Leadership theory and administrative behavior: The problem of authority. *Administrative Science Quarterly,* 1959.

Berkowitz, L. Sharing leadership in small, decision making groups. *Journal of Abnormal and Social Psychology,* 1953, *48,* 231–238.

Bezembinder, Th. G. G. *An experimental method to obtain pure accuracy scores in interpersonal perception.* Groningen, The Netherlands: Noordhoff, 1961.

Binet, A. *La suggestibilité.* Paris: Schleicher Bros., 1900.

Bishop, D. W. Relations between task and interpersonal success and group member adjustment. Urbana, Ill.: Group Effectiveness Research Laboratory, University of Illinois, 1964. (Mimeograph)

Blake, R. R., and Jane S. Mouton. Improving organizational problem solving through increasing the flowing and utilization of ideas. *Training Directors Journal,* 1963, *17,* 48–57.

Borg, W. R. The behavior of emergent and designated leaders in situational tests. *Sociometry,* 1957, *20,* 95–104.

Borgatta, E. F., A. S. Couch, and R. F. Bales. Some findings relevant to the great man theory of leadership. *American Sociological Review,* 1954, *19,* 755–759.

Bradford, L. P. *Group development, NTL, selected reading series no. I.* Washington, D.C.: National Education Association, 1961.

Brayfield, A. H., and W. H. Crockett. Employee attitudes and employee performance. *Psychological Bulletin,* 1955, *52,* 396–429.

Browne, C. G., and T. S. Cohen. *The study of leadership.* Danville, Ill.: Interstate Printers and Publishers, 1958.

Burke, W. Leadership behavior as a function of the leader, the follower, and the situation. *Journal of Personality,* 1965, *33,* 60–81.

Bush, G. P., and L. H. Hattery. Teamwork and creativity in research. *Administrative Science Quarterly,* 1956, *1,* 361–372.

Campbell, D. T. Common fate, similarity, and other indices of aggregates of persons as social entities. *Behavioral Science,* 1958, *3,* 14–25.

Carp, A. In S. B. Sells (ed.), *Tri-service conference on research relevant to behavior problems of small military groups under isolation and stress.* Forth Worth, Tex.: Texas Christian University, 1961. (Lithograph)

Carter, L., and Mary Nixon. Ability, perceptual, personality, and interest factors associated with different criteria of leadership. *Journal of Psychology,* 1949, *27,* 377–388.

Carter, L. F. Leadership and small group behavior. In M. Sherif and M. O.

Wilson (eds.), *Group relations at the crossroads*. New York: Harper & Row, 1953.

Carter, L. F., W. Haythorn, E. Shriver, and J. Lanzetta. The behavior of leaders and other group members. *Journal of Abnormal and Social Psychology*, 1951, *46*, 589–595.

Cattell, R. B. New concepts for measuring leadership in terms of group syntality. *Human Relations*, 1951, *4*, 161–184.

Cattell, R. B. *Personality: A systematic, theoretical, and factual study*. New York: McGraw-Hill, 1950.

Cattell, R. B., D. R. Saunders, and G. F. Stice. The dimensions of syntality in small groups. *Human Relations*, 1953, *6*, 331–356.

Caudill, W. A. Problems of leadership in the overt and covert social structure of psychiatric hospitals. In D. McK. Rioch (ed.), *Symposium on preventive and social psychiatry*. Washington, D.C.: U.S. Government Printing Office, 1958.

Chemers, M. M., F. E. Fiedler, Duangduen Lekhyananda, and L. M. Stolurow. Some effects of cultural training on leadership in heterocultural task groups. *International Journal of Psychology*, 1966, *1*, 257–270.

Christie, P., and Florence Lindauer. Personality structure. *Annual Review of Psychology*, 1963, *14*, 201–230.

Clark, R. A. Leadership in rifle squads on the Korean front line. Human Resources Research Unit No. 2, CONARC, Fort Ord, Calif., 1955.

Cleveland, S. E., and S. Fisher. Prediction of small group behavior from a body image schema. *Human Relations*, 1957, *10*, 223–233.

Cleven, W. A., and F. E. Fiedler. Interpersonal perceptions of open-hearth foremen and steel production. *Journal of Applied Psychology*, 1956, *40*, 312–314.

Couch, A., and K. Keniston. Yeasayers and naysayers: Agreeing response set as a personality variable. *Journal of Abnormal and Social Psychology*, 1960, *60*, 151–174.

Cronbach, L. J. Processes affecting scores on "understanding of others" and "assumed similarity." *Psychological Bulletin*, 1955, *52*, 177–193.

Cronbach, L. J., W. Hartmann, and Mary E. Ehart. An investigation of the character and properties of assumed similarity measures. Urbana, Ill.: Group Effectiveness Research Laboratory, University of Illinois, 1953. (Mimeograph)

Cronbach, L. J., Goldene Gleser, and Nageswari Rajaratnam. Theory of generalizeability: A liberalization of reliability theory. *The British Journal of Statistical Psychology*, 1963, *16*, 2.

Crowne, D. P., and D. Marlow. A new scale of social desirability independent of psychopathology. *Journal of Consulting Psychology*, 1960, *24*, 349–354.

DeSoto, C. B., J. L. Kuethe, and J. J. Bosley. A redefinition of social desirability. *Journal of Abnormal and Social Psychology*, 1959, *58*, 273–274.

DeZonia, R. H. The relationship between psychological distance and effective task performance. Unpublished doctoral dissertation. Urbana, Ill.: College of Education, University of Illinois, 1958.

Dubin, R. *Human relations in administration; the sociology of organization, with readings and cases.* New York: Prentice-Hall, 1951.

Dusek, E. R. Selection of personnel for arctic duty. In S. B. Sells (ed.), *Triservice conference on research relevant to behavior problems of small military groups under isolation and stress.* Fort Worth, Tex.: Texas Christian University, 1961. (Lithograph)

Edgerton, H. A. *Personnel factors in polar operations.* New York: Richardson, Bellows, Henry, 1953.

Edwards, A. L. *The social desirability variable in personality assessment and research.* New York: Dryden Press, 1957.

Eysenck, H. J. *Manual, the Maudsley personality inventory.* London: University of London Press, 1959.

Fiedler, F. E. Assumed similarity measures as predictors of team effectiveness. *Journal of Abnormal and Social Psychology,* 1954, *49,* 381–388.

Fiedler, F. E. A comparison of therapeutic relationships in psychoanalytic nondirective, and Adlerian therapy. *Journal of Consulting Psychology,* 1950, *14,* 436–445.

Fiedler, F. E. A contingency model for the prediction of leadership effectiveness. Urbana, Ill.: Group Effectiveness Research Laboratory, University of Illinois, 1963. (Mimeograph)

Fiedler, F. E. A contingency model of leadership effectiveness. In L. Berkowitz (ed.), *Advances in experimental social psychology,* vol. I. New York: Academic Press, 1964, 149–190.

Fiedler, F. E. The contingency model: A theory of leadership effectiveness. In H. Proshansky and B. Seidenberg (eds.), *Basic studies in social psychology.* New York: Holt, 1965, 538–551. (a)

Fiedler, F. E. The effect of leadership and cultural heterogeneity on group performance: A test of the contingency model. *Journal of Experimental Social Psychology,* 1966, *2,* 237–264. (a)

Fiedler, F. E. Engineer the job to fit the manager. *Harvard Business Review,* September, 1965, 115–122. (b)

Fiedler, F. E. The influence of leader-keyman relations on combat crew effectiveness. *Journal of Abnormal and Social Psychology,* 1955, *51,* 227–235.

Fiedler, F. E. Leader attitudes, group climate, and group creativity. *Journal of Abnormal and Social Psychology,* 1962, *65,* 308–318. (a)

Fiedler, F. E. *Leader attitudes and group effectiveness.* Urbana, Ill.: University of Illinois Press, 1958.

Fiedler, F. E. The leader's psychological distance and group effectiveness. Chapter in D. Cartright and A. Zander, *Group dynamics,* 2d ed. New York: Harper & Row, 1960.

Fiedler, F. E. Leadership style and the performance of co-acting groups. Urbana, Ill.: Group Effectiveness Research Laboratory, University of Illinois, 1966. (c)

Fiedler, F. E. A method of objective quantification of certain countertransference attitudes. *Journal of Clinical Psychology,* 1951, *7,* 101–107.

Fiedler, F. E. The nature of teamwork. *Discovery,* 1962, *23,* 36–41. (b)

Fiedler, F. E. A review of research on ASo and LPC scores as measures of leadership style. Urbana, Ill.: Group Effectiveness Research Laboratory, University of Illinois, 1966. (b)

Fiedler, F. E., P. London, and R. S. Nemo. Hypnotically induced leader attitudes and group creativity. Urbana, Ill.: Group Effectiveness Research Laboratory, University of Illinois, 1961. (Mimeograph)

Fiedler, F. E., and W. A. T. Meuwese. The leader's contribution to task performance in cohesive and uncohesive groups. *Journal of Abnormal and Social Psychology*, 1963, 67, 83–87.

Fiedler, F. E., A. R. Bass, and Judith M. Fiedler. The leader's perception of co-workers, group climate, and group creativity: A cross-validation. Urbana, Ill.: Group Effectiveness Research Laboratory, University of Illinois, 1961. (Mimeograph)

Fiedler, F. E., W. A. T. Meuwese, and Sophie Oonk. Performance of laboratory tasks requiring group creativity. *Acta Psychologica*, 1961, *18*, 100–119.

Fiedler, F. E., E. B. Hutchins, and Joan S. Dodge. Quasi-therapeutic relations in small college and military groups. *Psychological Monographs*, 1959, 73, no. 473.

Fiedler, F. E., and S. M. Nealey. *Second-level management: A review and analysis.* U.S. Civil Service Commission, Office of Career Development, Washington, D.C., March, 1966.

Fiedler, F. E., W. G. Warrington, and F. J. Blaisdell. Unconscious attitudes as correlates of sociometric choice in a social group. *Journal of Abnormal and Social Psychology*, 1952, *47*, 790–796.

Fishbein, M., Eva Landy, and Grace Hatch. Some determinants of an individual's esteem for his least preferred co-worker: An attitudinal analysis. Urbana, Ill.: Group Effectiveness Research Laboratory, University of Illinois, 1965. (Mimeograph)

Flanagan, J. C. Critical requirements: A new approach to employee evaluation. *Personnel Psychology*, 1949, 2, 419–425.

Fleishman, E. A. *Studies in industrial and personnel psychology.* Homewood, Ill.: Dorsey Press, 1961.

Fleishman, E. A., E. H. Harris, and H. E. Burtt. Leadership and supervision in industry. Educational Research Monograph No. 33, Ohio State University, Columbus, Ohio, 1955.

Foster, R. J. Acquiescent response set as a measure of acquiescence. *Journal of Abnormal and Social Psychology*, 1961, *63*, 155–160.

French, J. R. P., Jr., and B. H. Raven. Legitimate power, coercive power, and observability in social influence. *Sociometry*, 1958, *21*, 83–97.

French, R. L. Sociometric status and individual adjustment among naval recruits. *Journal of Abnormal and Social Psychology*, 1951, *46*, 64–72.

Freud, S. Group psychology. In J. Richman (ed.), *A general selection from the works of Sigmund Freud.* London: Hogarth Press, 1937.

Freud, S. *Group psychology and analysis of the ego.* London: International Psychoanalytic Library, 1922.

Gibb, C. A. An interactional view of the emergence of leadership. *Australian Journal of Psychology*, 1958, *10*, 101–110.

Gibb, C. A. Leadership. In G. Lindzey, *Handbook of social psychology*, vol. II. Cambridge, Mass.: Addison-Wesley, 1954.

Gibb, C. A. The principles and traits of leadership. *Journal of Abnormal and Social Psychology*, 1947, *42*, 267–284.

Gibb, C. A. The research background of an interactional theory of leadership. *Australian Journal of Psychology*, 1950, *1*, 19–41.

Godfrey, Eleanor P., F. E. Fiedler, and D. M. Hall. *Boards, managers, and company success*. Danville, Ill.: Interstate Press, 1959.

Golb, Eileen F., and F. E. Fiedler. A note on psychological attributes related to the score Assumed Similarity between Opposites (ASo). Urbana, Ill.: Group Effectiveness Research Laboratory, University of Illinois, 1955. (Mimeograph)

Gordon, M. H., E. H. Loveland, and E. E. Cureton. An extended table of chi-square for two degrees of freedom, for use in combining probabilities from independent samples. *Psychometrika*, 1952, *17*, 311–316.

Gordon, T. Group-centered leadership and administration. In C. R. Rogers, *Client-centered therapy*. Boston: Houghton-Mifflin, 1951, 320–383.

Guetzkow, H. Organizational leadership in task-oriented groups. In L. Petrullo and B. M. Bass (eds.), *Leadership and interpersonal behavior*. New York: Holt, 1961, 187–200.

Guilford, J. P., R. M. Berger, and P. R. Christensen. *A factor analytic study of planning: I. Hypothesis and description of tests*. Los Angeles, Calif.: Psychological Laboratory, University of Southern California, 1954.

Guilford, J. P., R. M. Berger, and P. R. Christensen. A factor analytic study of planning abilities. *Psychological Monographs*, 1957, *71*, no. 6.

Hackman, J. R. Effects of task characteristics on group products. Urbana, Ill.: Department of Psychology, University of Illinois, 1966. (Mimeograph)

Hall, E. T. *The silent language*. Garden City, N.Y.: Doubleday, 1959.

Harary, F., R. Z. Norman, and D. Cartwright. *Structural models: An introduction to the theory of directed graphs*. New York: Wiley, 1965.

Hare, A. P. *Handbook of small group research*. New York: Free Press, 1962.

Harris, E. F., and E. A. Fleishman. Human relations training and the stability of leadership patterns. *Journal of Applied Psychology*, 1955, *39*, 20–25.

Havron, M. D., W. A. Lybrand, E. Cohen, R. G. Kassebaum, and J. E. McGrath. *The assessment and prediction of rifle squad effectiveness*. Washington, D.C.: The Adjutant General's Office, Personnel Research Branch, 1954.

Hawkins, C. A study of factors mediating a relationship between leader rating behavior and group productivity. Doctoral dissertation. Minneapolis, Minn.: University of Minnesota, 1962.

Hemphill, J. K. A proposed theory of leadership in small groups. *Second preliminary report*. Columbus, Ohio: Personnel Research Board, Ohio State University, 1954.

Hemphill, J. K. Situational factors in leadership. Education Monograph No. 32, Ohio State University, Columbus, Ohio, 1949.

Hemphill, J. K. Why people attempt to lead. In L. Petrullo and B. M. Bass (eds.), *Leadership and interpersonal behavior*. New York: Holt, 1961, 201–215.

Hemphill, J. K., and A. E. Coons. Development of the leader behavior description questionnaire. In R. M. Stogdill and A. E. Coons (eds.), *Leader behavior: Its description and measurement*. Columbus, Ohio: Bureau of Business Research, Ohio State University, 1957.

Higgs, W. The effect of an environmental change upon behavior of schizophrenics. Unpublished M.A. thesis. Urbana, Ill.: University of Illinois, 1964.

Hoffmann, L. R. Homogeneity of member personality and its effect on group problem solving. *Journal of Abnormal and Social Psychology*, 1959, *58*, 27–32.

Hollander, E. P. Authoritarianism and leadership choice in a military setting. *Journal of Abnormal and Social Psychology*, 1954, *49*, 365–370.

Hollander, E. P. Conformity, status and idiosyncrasy credit. *Psychological Review*, 1958, *65*, 117–127.

Hollander, E. P. *Leaders, groups and influence*. New York: Oxford, 1964.

Hollander, E. P., and W. B. Webb. Leadership, followership and friendship. *Journal of Abnormal and Social Psychology*, 1955, *50*, 163–167.

Homans, G. C. Group factors in worker productivity. In E. Maccoby, T. Newcomb, and E. Hartley (eds.), *Readings in social psychology*, New York: Holt, 1958, 546–564.

Homans, G. C. *The human group*. New York: Harcourt, Brace, 1950.

Horst, P. Pattern analysis and configural scoring. *Journal of Clinical Psychology*, 1954, *10*, 3–11.

Hunt, J. G. A test of the leadership contingency model in three organizations. Urbana, Ill.: Group Effectiveness Research Laboratory, University of Illinois, 1967. (Mimeograph)

Hutchins, E. B. Effect of investigator-imposed structure on the measurement of cognitive complexity. *Psychological Reports*, 1961, *9*, 125–126.

Hutchins, E. B. Task-oriented and quasi-therapeutic role functions of the small group leader. Unpublished doctoral dissertation. Urbana, Ill.: University of Illinois, 1958.

Hutchins, E. B., and F. E. Fiedler. Task-oriented and quasi-therapeutic role functions of the leader in small military groups. *Sociometry*, 1960, *23*, 393–406.

Jackson, D. N., and S. Messick. Content and style in personality assessment. *Psychological Bulletin*, 1958, *55*, 4, 243–252.

Jackson, D. N., and S. Messick. A note on ethnocentrism and acquiescent response set. *Journal of Abnormal and Social Psychology*, 1957, *54*, 243–252.

Jaques, E. *Equitable payment*. New York: Wiley, 1961.

Jones, L. V., and D. W. Fiske. Models for testing the significance of combined results. *Psychological Bulletin*, 1953, *50*, 375–382.

Julian, J., D. W. Bishop, and F. E. Fiedler. Quasi-therapeutic effects of intergroup competition. *Journal of Personality and Social Psychology*, 1966, *3*, 321–327.

Kahn, R. L., D. M. Wolfe, R. P. Quinn, J. D. Snoek, and R. A. Rosenthal. *Organizational stress: Studies in role conflict and ambiguity.* New York: Wiley, 1964.

Kasl, S. V., and J. R. P. French, Jr. The effects of occupational status on physical and mental health. *Journal of Social Issues,* 1962, *18,* 67–89.

Katz, D., and R. L. Kahn. *The social psychology of organizations.* New York: Wiley, 1966.

Katz, I., and M. Cohen. The effects of training Negroes upon cooperative problem solving in biracial teams. *Journal of Abnormal and Social Psychology,* 1962, 319–325.

Kelly, E. L., and D. W. Fiske. *The prediction of performance in clinical psychology.* Ann Arbor, Mich.: University of Michigan Press, 1951.

Kipnis, Dorothy M. Changes in self-concepts in relation to perceptions of others. *Journal of Personality,* 1961, *29,* 449–465.

Knoell, Dorothy, and D. G. Fogays. Interrelationships of combat crew performance in the B-29. *Research Note,* CCT 52-1, USAF Human Resources Research Center, 1952.

Krech, D., and R. S. Crutchfield. *Theory and problems of social psychology.* New York: McGraw-Hill, 1948.

Lanzetta, J. An investigation of group behavior under stress. Annual status report. ONR Contract N60NR-241, Task Order V, University of Rochester, Rochester, N.Y., 1953.

Lawrence, P., and J. Lorsch. Differentiation and integration in complex organizations. *Administrative Science Quarterly,* 1967.

Lewin, K., and R. Lippitt. An experimental approach to the study of autocracy and democracy: A preliminary note. *Sociometry,* 1938, *1,* 292–300.

Likert, R. An emerging theory of organization, leadership and management. In L. Petrullo and B. Bass (eds.), *Leadership and interpersonal behavior.* New York: Holt, 1961, 290–309.

Likert, R. Patterns in management. In E. A. Fleishman (ed.), *Studies in personnel and industrial psychology.* Homewood, Ill.: Dorsey Press, 1961.

Lubin, A., and H. G. Osborn. A theory of pattern analysis for the prediction of a quantitative criterion. *Psychometrika,* 1957, *22,* 63–73.

McCurdy, H. G., and W. E. Lambert. The efficiency of small human groups in the solution of problems requiring genuine cooperation. *Journal of Personality,* 1952, *20,* 478–494.

McGrath, J. E. Assembly of quasi-therapeutic rifle teams. Urbana, Ill.: Group Effectiveness Research Laboratory, University of Illinois, 1961. (Mimeograph)

McGrath, J. E. A descriptive model for the study of interpersonal relations in small groups. *Journal of Psychological Studies,* 1963, *14,* 3, 89–116.

McGrath, J. E. Political partisanship and interpersonal perception. Urbana, Ill.: Group Effectiveness Research Laboratory, University of Illinois, 1962. (Mimeograph)

McGrath, J. E. *A summary of small group research studies.* HSR–TN–62/3–GN, Human Sciences Research, Inc., Arlington, Va., 1962.

McGrath, J. E., and J. W. Julian. Interaction process and task outcome in experimentally created negotiation groups. *Journal of Psychological Studies,* 1963, *14,* 117–138.

McGrath, J. E., and I. Altman. *Small group research: A synthesis and critique of the field.* New York: Holt, 1966.

McNemar, Q. *Psychological statistics,* 2d ed. New York: Wiley, 1955.

Mann, R. D. A review of the relationships between personality and performance in small groups. *Psychological Bulletin,* 1959, *56,* 241–270.

Marshall, S. L. A. Combat leadership. In D. McK. Rioch (ed.), *Symposium on preventive and social psychiatry.* Washington, D.C.: Walter Reed Army Institute of Research, 1958.

Martin, N. H. The levels of management and their mental demands. In W. L. Warner and N. H. Martin (eds.), *Industrial man.* New York: Harper & Row, 1959, 276–294.

Meuwese, W., and Sophie Oonk. Enkele determinanten von creativiteit, structuur en proces in kleine experimentele groepen. Unpublished *werkstuk.* Amsterdam: University of Amsterdam, 1960.

Meuwese, W., and F. E. Fiedler. Leadership and group creativity under varying conditions of stress. Urbana, Ill.: Group Effectiveness Research Laboratory, University of Illinois, 1965. (Mimeograph)

Meuwese, W. A. T. The effect of the leader's ability and interpersonal attitudes on group creativity under varying conditions of stress. Unpublished doctoral dissertation. Amsterdam: University of Amsterdam, 1964.

Meyers, H. H. Factors related to success in the human relations aspect of work group leadership. *Psychological Monographs,* 1951, *65,* 29.

Morris, C. G., and F. E. Fiedler. Application of a new system of interaction analysis to the relationships between leader attitudes and behavior in problem-solving groups. Urbana, Ill.: Group Effectiveness Research Laboratory, University of Illinois, 1964. (Mimeograph)

Myers, A. E. Team competition, success, and the adjustment of group members. *Journal of Abnormal and Social Psychology,* 1962, *65,* 325–332.

Nealey, S. M., and M. R. Blood. Leadership performance of nursing supervisors at two organizational levels. Urbana, Ill.: Group Effectiveness Research Laboratory, University of Illinois, 1967. (Mimeograph)

Neel, R. Nervous stress in the industrial situation. *Personnel Psychology,* 1955, *8,* 405–416.

Newport, M. G. Middle management development in industrial organizations. Unpublished doctoral dissertation. Urbana, Ill.: University of Illinois, 1963.

Niles, Mary C. *The essence of management.* New York: Harper & Row, 1958.

Nuttin, J. M., Jr. De ontwikkeling van de gezindheid tegenover de Walen en het persoonlijk contact. *Tijdschrift voor Opvoedkunde,* 1960, *5,* 315–333.

O'Brien, G. Methods of analyzing group tasks. Urbana, Ill.: Group Effectiveness Research Laboratory, University of Illinois, 1967. (Mimeograph)

Orne, M. T. On the social psychology of the psychological experiment: With particular reference to demand characteristics and their implications. In

C. W. Backman and P. F. Secord (eds.), *Problems in social psychology.* New York: McGraw-Hill, 1966, 14–21.

Osborn, A. F. Developments in creative education. In S. J. Parnes and H. F. Harding (eds.), *A source book for creative thinking.* New York: Scribner, 1962, 19–29.

Osgood, C. E. The nature and measurement of meaning. *Psychological Bulletin,* 1952, *49,* 251–262.

Parnes, S. J. Do you really understand brainstorming? In S. J. Parnes and H. F. Harding (eds.), *A source book for creative thinking.* New York: Scribner, 1962, 283–290.

Parnes, S. J., and A. Meadow. Effects of "brainstorming" instructions on creative problem-solving by trained and untrained subjects. *Journal of Educational Psychology,* 1959, *50,* 171–176.

Pelz, D. C. Leadership within a hierarchical organization. *Journal of Social Issues,* 1951, 7, 49–55.

Pepinsky, Pauline N. *Originality in group productivity: I. Productive independence in three natural situations.* Columbus, Ohio: Personnel Research Board, Ohio State University, 1959.

Pettigrew, T. F. The measurement and correlates of category width as a cognitive variable. *Journal of Personality,* 1958, *26,* 532–544.

Pfiffner, J. M., and F. P. Sherwood. *Administrative organization.* Englewood Cliffs, N.J.: Prentice-Hall, 1960.

Reuter, E. B. *Handbook of sociology.* New York: Dryden Press, 1941.

Roby, T., and J. Lanzetta. Consideration in the analysis of group tasks. *Psychological Bulletin,* 1958, *55,* 88–101.

Roethlisberger, F. J., and W. J. Dickson. *Management and the worker.* Cambridge, Mass.: Harvard, 1930.

Rogers, C. R. Perceptual reorganization in client centered therapy. In R. R. Blake and G. L. Ramsey (eds.), *Perception: An approach to personality.* New York: Ronald, 1951.

Rombauts, J. Gedrag en groepsbeleving in etnisch-homogene en etnischheterogene groepen. Unpublished doctoral dissertation, Louvain, Belgium: University of Louvain, 1962.

Rudin, S. A. Leadership as psychophysiological activation of group members: A case experimental study. *Psychological Reports,* 1964, *15,* 577–578.

Sample, J. A., and T. R. Wilson. Leader behavior, group productivity, and rating of least perferred coworker. *Journal of Personality and Social Psychology,* 1965, *1,* 3, 266–270.

Sanford, F. H. *ONR research on leadership.* Washington, D.C.: Office of Naval Research, 1949.

Schein, E. H., and W. G. Bennis. *Personal and organizational change through group methods: The laboratory approach.* New York: Wiley, 1965.

School and college ability test. Princeton, N.J.: Educational Testing Service, 1955.

Schutz, W. C. *FIRO: A three-dimensional theory of interpersonal behavior.* New York: Holt, 1958.

Seashore, S. E. *Group cohesiveness in the industrial work group.* Ann Arbor, Mich.: Institute for Social Research, 1955.

Sells, S. B. Military small group performance under isolation and stress—A critical review. Fort Wainwright, Alaska: Arctic Aeromedical Laboratory, June 1962. (Released by Office of Technical Services, U.S. Department of Commerce, Washington 25, D.C.)

Sells, S. B. Tri-service conference on research relevant to behavior problems of small military groups under isolation and stress. Fort Worth, Tex.: Texas Christian University, 1961. (Lithograph)

Shartle, C. L. *Executive performance and leadership.* Englewood Cliffs, N.J.: Prentice-Hall, 1956.

Shartle, C. L., and R. M. Stogdill. *Studies in naval leadership.* Columbus, Ohio: Ohio State University Research Foundation, 1952.

Shaw, M. E. Scaling group tasks: A method for dimensional analysis. Gainesville, Fla.: University of Florida, 1963. (Mimeograph)

Shaw, M. E., and J. M. Blum. Effects of leadership style upon group performance as a function of task structure. *Journal of Personality and Social Psychology,* 1966, 3, 238–242.

Smith, E. E. The effect of clear and unclear role expectations on group productivity and defensiveness. *Journal of Abnormal and Social Psychology,* 1957, 55, 213–217.

Soskin, W. F. Influence of information on bias in social perception. *Journal of Personality,* 1953, 22, 1.

Stafford, F. J., and S. W. Becker. Some determinants of organizational success. *Journal of Business,* October, 1967. (In press)

Steiner, I. D. Group dynamics. In *Annual reviews of psychology.* Stanford, Calif.: Stanford, 1964.

Steiner, I. D. Interpersonal orientation and Assumed Similarity between opposites. Urbana, Ill.: Group Effectiveness Research Laboratory, University of Illinois, 1959. (Mimeograph)

Steiner, I. D. Models for inferring relationships between group size and potential group productivity. *Behavioral Science,* 1966, 11, 4, 273–283.

Stephenson, W. *The study of behavior: Q-technique and its methodology.* Chicago: University of Chicago Press, 1953.

Stogdill, R. Leadership, membership and organization. *Psychological Bulletin,* 1950, 47, 1–14.

Stogdill, R. Personal factors associated with leadership: A survey of the literature. *Journal of Psychology,* 1948, 25, 35–71.

Stogdill, R. M., and A. E. Coons. Leader behavior: Its description and measurement. Research Monograph No. 88, Ohio State University, Columbus, Ohio, 1957.

Stouffer, S. A., E. A. Suchman, L. C. Devinney, S. A. Starr, and R. M. Williams. *The American soldier: Adjustment during army life,* vol. I. Princeton, N.J.: Princeton, 1949.

Taylor, D. W. Variables related to creativity and productivity among men in two research laboratories. In C. W. Taylor (ed.), *The second (1957)*

University of Utah research conference on the identification of creative scientific talent. Salt Lake City: University of Utah Press, 1958.

Terman, L. M. A preliminary study of the psychology and pedagogy of leadership. *Pedagogical Seminary*, 1904, *11*, 413–451.

Torrance, E. P. The behavior of small groups under the stress of conditions of "survival." *American Sociological Review*, 1954, *19*, 751–755.

Torrance, E. P. Leadership in the survival of small isolated groups. In D. McK. Rioch (ed.), *Symposium on preventive and social psychiatry*. Washington, D.C.: Walter Reed Army Institute of Research, 1958.

Traxler, A. E. *Techniques of guidance.* New York: Harper & Row, 1945.

Triandis, H. C. Cultural influences upon cognitive processes. In L. Berkowitz (ed.), *Advances in experimental social psychology*. New York: Academic Press, 1964, 1–48.

Triandis, H. C., A. R. Bass, R. B. Ewen, and E. H. Mikesell. Team creativity as a function of the creativity of the members. *Journal of Applied Psychology*, 1963, *47*, 2, 104–110.

Tyler, B. B. A study of factors contributing to employee morale. Unpublished M.A. thesis. Columbus, Ohio: Ohio State University, 1949.

United States Employment Service. *Dictionary of occupational titles.* Washington, D.C.: U.S. Government Printing Office, 1965.

Voiers, W. D. *Bombing accuracy as a function of the ground school proficiency structure of the B-29 bomb team.* San Antonio, Tex.: Lackland Air Force Base, Air Force Personnel and Training Research Center, 1956.

Voiers, W. D. A comparison of the components of simulated radar bombing error in terms of reliability and sensitivity to practice. *Research Bulletin.* San Antonio, Tex.: Lackland Air Force Base, Air Force Personnel and Training Research Center, 1954.

Warner, W. L., and J. C. Abegglen. *Big business leaders in America.* New York: Harper & Row, 1955.

Warrington, W. C. The comparative efficiency of three test designs for measuring similarity between persons. Urbana, Ill.: Group Effectiveness Research Laboratory, University of Illinois, 1953. (Mimeograph)

Way, L. *Adler's place in psychology: An exposition of individual psychology.* New York: Collier Books, 1962, 64–65.

Weitzenhoffer, A. M., and E. R. Hilgard. *Stanford Hypnotic Susceptibility Scale.* Palo Alto, Calif.: Consulting Psychologists Press, 1959.

Whyte, W. F. *Street corner society: The social structure of an Italian slum.* Chicago: University of Chicago Press, 1943.

Wiggins, J. S. Convergences among stylistic response measures from objective personality tests. *Educational and Psychological Measurement*, 1964.

Wiggins, J. S. Interrelationships among MMPI measures of dissimulation under standard and social desirability instructions. *Journal of Consulting Psychology*, 1959, *23*, 419–427.

Wiggins, J. S. Strategic method and stylistic variance in the MMPI. *Psychological Bulletin*, 1962, *59*, 224–242.

Ziller, R. C. Leader acceptance of responsibility for group action under conditions of uncertainty and risk. *American Psychology*, 1955, *10*, 475–476.

INDEX

Group Atmosphere score, and sociometric method, 32, 163
Group creativity, definition, 109–110
Group process, LPC and leader behavior, 185–196
Group tasks, Belgian navy study, 160–163
Guilford, J. P., 108, 126, 212

Hackman, R., 26
Hall, D. M., 89, 98, 135, 141, 156
Hare, P., 4, 6, 13
Harris, E. H., 252
Hartmann, W., 47
Hastorf, A. H., 11
Hatch, Grace, 51
Hattery, L. H., 107
Havron, M. D., 135
Hawkins, C., 45, 83–84, 135, 136, 183, 272
Hawthorn study, 236
Haythorn, W., 112
Headman, 8
Heat-time (see Open-hearth steel shops)
Heavy machine manufacture, 174–175
Hemphill, J. K., 7, 8, 31, 163, 201
Heterogeneity, in culture, 176–178
    and culture training, 232–233
    in interdisciplinary groups, 172
    in language and culture, 154–173
    and negotiation, 232–233
    and organizational engineering, 250
    in religion, 111–115
    and situational difficulty, 171
Higgs, W., 59
High school basketball teams, 66–69, 136
Higher management, 198, 235–246
Hilgard, E. R., 115
Hoffman, L. R., 109
Hollander, E. P., 249
Homans, G. C., 8
Horst, P., 152
"How Supervise" test, 136
Hunt, J. G., 28, 173–176, 224, 225, 241, 244, 254
Husek, T. R., 214
Hutchins, E. B., 134, 202, 225, 277
Hypnosis study, 54–55, 115–116, 139

Ideal self-esteem, 276
Independence of judgment scale, 274
Indian study, 176–178
Industrial work situations, 173–176, 223–225
Industrial workshops, 223–225
Infantry squads, 83, 135
Initiation of structure, in Belgian navy study, 192–195
    and group performance, 195
    and LPC, 45
    and quasi-therapeutic attitudes, 201
    and situational favorableness, 192–195
    training in, 178
Intelligence, and group performance, 5, 85, 210–219

Intelligence, and situational favorableness, 263
Intelligence measures, 276, 280
Interacting groups, classification of, 22–35
    definition, 18–19
Internal stress (see Counteracting groups; ROTC creativity study)
International Harvester Company, 252
Interpersonal perception scores, 38–39
    and accuracy, 39
    and LPC, 276
    ASo, 280
    (See also Least preferred coworker scores)
Intragroup stress, 199–210
    (See also Counteracting groups; ROTC creativity study)

Jackson, D. N., 36, 274
Jacques, E., 251
Janssen-Beckers, Annie, 155
Jones, L. V., 176
Julian, J., 58, 59, 222, 231
Junior melter (see Open-hearth steel shops)

Kahn, R. L., 236, 250
Kasl, S. V., 239
Kassebaum, R. G., 135
Katz, D., 236, 250
Katz, I., 156
Kelly, E. L., 39
Keniston, K., 274
Kipnis, Dorothy, 222
Kite, W. R., 11
Knoell, Dorothy, 16, 249
Krech, D., 7
Krueger, S., 49, 272
Kuethe, J. L., 274

Laboratory training, 252, 253
Lambert, W. E., 110
Landy, Eva, 51
Lanzetta, J., 18, 26, 111
Lawrence, P. R., 243, 244
Leader, ability and performance under stress, 199–219
    anxiety and performance, 214–219
    definitions, 7–8
    effectiveness of, defined, 9–10
    functions of, 20
    influence of, 142–148
    (See also Situational favorableness)
    intelligence of, 199–219
    therapeutic role of, 200–204
    use of consultants, 96
Leader Behavior Description Questionnaire, 192
    (See also Consideration; Initiation of structure)
Leader consideration (see Consideration)
Leader-member relations, 29–32
    moderating effect of, 93–95
    and Octant VIII–A, 150
    relative importance of, 144
    research problems in, 262–263